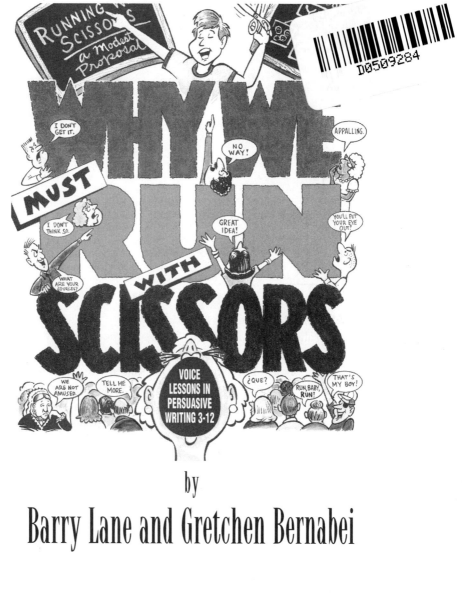

WHY WE MUST RUN WITH SCISSORS

VOICE LESSONS IN PERSUASIVE WRITING 3-12

by

Barry Lane and Gretchen Bernabei

DISCOVER WRITING PRESS

Discover Writing Press
PO Box 264
Shoreham, VT 05770
1-800-613-8055
fax # 802-897-2084
www.discoverwriting.com

Copyright © 2001 by Gretchen Bernabei and Barry Lane.
ISBN # 0-9656574-7-7
Library of Congress control number 00 092519

Cover art by Robert Rehm
Book design by Jim Burns
Illustrations by Matilde Bernabei, Grace Lane and Barry Lane
Back cover photo by Matilde Bernabei

For information about the seminar which goes along with this book or other seminars call Discover Writing Company 1-800-613-8055 or visit our Web site: www.discoverwriting.com

06 05 04   10 9 8 7 6 5 4 3

For Matilde, Bert and Dixie, with all my love
G.B.

To the memory of Amy Biehl and Zunade Dharsey
and to the children of the New South Africa whose
voice lessons continue to teach the world to hope.
B.L.

Table of Contents

Traits Key

I = Idea Development
O = Organization
V = Voice
W = Word Choice
S = Sentence Fluency

CHAPTER 4
MEN WHO RUN WITH SCISSORS: USING PARODY AND HUMOR TO TEACH PERSUASIVE VOICES

CHAPTER 5
VOICE PLAY: SNAPPING THE GAP BETWEEN THE VOICE AND THE PAGE

CHAPTER 6
KNOWING THE RHETORICAL MOVES

CHAPTER 7
BEGINNINGS AND ENDINGS—THICKENING THE STEW

CHAPTER 8
ELABORATION: THE FIRE, NOT THE FOG

CHAPTER 9
TIPS FOR STANDARDIZED TESTS: WRITING A LETTER ABOUT AN ISSUE

CHAPTER 10
PERSUASIVE TEST TRIAGE: MEDICINE BAG OF DEVOLVED ESSAYS, RUBRICS, AND OTHER TOOLS AND TIPS

APPENDICES

Acknowledgments

With special thanks from Gretchen to the following:
Sue Shoopman, my constant imaginary-pajama-breakfast-table audience and staunch teacher of reading, mudpies, and all other things.
Patricia S. Gray, Anita Arnold, and Mary Howard, my own personal triumvirate of unflagging generosity, encouragement, and right-headedness.
Dottie Hall, my leader and actual friend, who daily helps me to understand my students' mothers and my daughter's teachers.
Scott Brady, weaver of stories, who is really related to Mathew and not Diamond Jim.
Alicia Narvaez, formatter extraordinaire, and brewer of mighty mean coffee.
Dan Kirby, who has shown me how students do feel their teacher's close attention to the writing, even long after the lessons are over.
Joyce Armstrong Carroll and Edward Wilson for demonstrating that teaching is not just about our interactions with students, but with each other too.

And the following, who have in their own elegant ways, shown me that you don't have to spend much time with someone in order to shape their thinking:
James Moffett, Gabrielle Lusser Rico, Pat Porter, Onalee Seamans, Giacomo Leone, Caroyl Green.

With special thanks to these teachers, whose play with their own students continues, and who have generously shared their work and their students' writing with us:
Belinda Licea, from San Antonio; Maureen Flores, Barrington Elementary in Austin; Jeff Anderson, Rogers Middle School, in San Antonio; Kim Grauer, sounding board and reality-checker, from Jefferson High School; P. Tim Martindell, my teaching playmate and ESP mysterioso from Houston.

And my dear, enthusiastic Sandra Day O'Connor High School colleagues, many of whose students are represented here: Geri Berger, Laura Lott, Scott Stone, Julie Schweers, Barbara Edens, Grant Pruin, Donna Guerrero, Suzy Groff, Cyndi Pina, Jana Laven, Debbie Sonnen, Steve Roediger, Cathy McFeaters, Marcus Goodyear, Jann Fractor, Annie Smith, Kristi Shaner, and Lisa Fernandi.
GB

Barry thanks his mother for all the persuasive practice as a teenager and his own daughters Jessie Lynn and Grace Shoshana for keeping him up to date on the latest methodology. Thanks to principal Gail Ryan and Karen Master's third graders, Abby Sessions and her Shoreham fifth graders; Louise Van Schaack and her fourth grade, middle and high school students of Flint, Michigan, who all helped by letting me experiment in their classes. Thanks to Barbara Reed Nelson who continues to inspire and Gloria Tibbetts who put the persuasive writing bug in my ear..

I owe lessons in chapter 2 in part to Judy Kendall and the entire Amy Biehl Foundation. Our trip to South Africa has awakened voices in me that refuse to shut up even years later.
More special thanks to the amazing Vicki Spandel who shared her splendid 6-trait rubric, and Tiffany who makes it all worthwhile. Walt says hi.
BL

Why Voice Lessons in Persuasion?

Fisher Price toy company was making a new model pre-school and they wanted to get it right so they interviewed 3-year-olds in all 50 states. They asked these children what they wanted to know most about the pre-school they would be attending in a year. What do you think the most-asked question in all 50 states was? Not, "Is the teacher nice?", not "Do they have toys?", not even, "Will I have my own desk?" The most-asked question in all 50 states was, "Is there a toilet?"

From the very start children see school as a sterile place that may not meet their most intimate needs. A seventh grader sits at his desk on the first day of school. He's trying to write about what he did on his summer vacation. In his mind he thinks, "I went to the beach. There I met a girl named Jennifer. Her long hair was the color of the sand. Her eyes were like jewels. We almost kissed. How I wish we'd kissed." Then this same student writes, "My Summer Vacation. I went to the beach. I played in the water. It was a lot of fun."

Though we could say that a prompt like "What I did on my Summer Vacation" is probably the worst writing assignment known to man, the real problem of such an assignment is that it's given on the first day of school, when students know little of their teacher, classmates or expectations. Their assumption of an uncaring neutral audience shuts down a real voice and the young writer starts pretending to play a role. The student voice emerges: calm, monotone, invisible, afraid to reveal anything remotely personal. Like the character of Eddie Haskell on the old show Leave it to Beaver, it says exactly what it thinks Mrs. Cleaver wants to hear and reserves its real feelings and thoughts for more intimate settings like Wally's bedroom.

In the area of persuasive writing this becomes painfully obvious. We want students to have opinions, to be passionate about these opinions and to defend them with strong, well thought out and elaborated arguments. Yet more often than not they end up listing three supporting details for each bland topic sentence. And sometimes the more we encourage them to get passionate about a topic, the more they cling to the old formulas of success, all the time protecting the more authentic voices which lie within them. Once in a while a teacher will come along who recognizes this gold mine and finds ways to get students digging at the ore. Years later when sitting at their thirtieth-year class reunion, the students will remember this teacher and say things like, "She treated us like grownups." Or "He really listened to what I had to say, no matter how silly it seemed to me." Or "You looked forward to going to school because you didn't know what to expect." Or "He made learning fun."

The mini-lessons in *Why We Must Run With Scissors* are aimed at creating more teachers who inspire and delight their students. Our goal is to create classes where students are free to explore the multiplicity of voices that swarm within them and craft those voices into passionate, funny, scathing, heartwarming, ridiculous, sad, cogent, critical, ribald, eloquent pieces of writing: writing that jumps off the page, stomps on your chest, tickles your chin, rubs your belly, fills your heart with meaning and purpose; writing that pushes its way out of the box and into the real world.

How To Use This Book

The first five chapters of the book contain exploratory lessons that dig at the voices inside your students and develop a sense of where opinions lie. Lessons include: developing a sense of audience; learning how to find subjects we are really passionate about; seeing the value of dissent; and exploring persuasion in literature, drama, parody and song. Our goal in these early chapters is to create a smorgasbord of lessons that will help you see the joy that happens when we transform the monologue of one voice talking to a teacher into a sea of voices persuading, everything from your baby brother to Odysseus's Cyclops to the President of the United States. Some lessons in this section challenge students to get passionate about something in the big world; others encourage them to get deeply silly in their opinions; others help them to see persuasion in their lives and in literature. There are many students in your class. Some will be inspired by laws to change the world, others by laws that say they shouldn't change their underwear. And though the subjects may change, the methods of persuasion remain strikingly similar. We hope that you do the work right along with your students so that your students can learn from you and vice versa.

Chapters 6-10 tune students in to the many possibilities of craft in persuasive writing. Writing a persuasive essay is not about filling out a form but rather finding a form that best fits the message you want to get across. Lessons in this section include: rhetorical devices such as fallacies, organizational strategies, beginnings and endings, transitions, and meaningful elaboration. These lessons will provide a palate of possibility for students wrestling thoughts and opinions into essays.

A Word About State Writing Tests

Ideas presented in this book have been very successful at helping students succeed with flying colors on the state writing test in Texas, yet there are many people prescribing more formulaic answers to succeeding on the same test. Certainly formulas and graphic organizers can help students to shape their thoughts into paragraphs and essays, but what they can't do is reach inside a student's heart and pull out a bouquet of roses. In other words, a formula may help a student achieve a score of 2 on a writing test, but (if it's a good test) the 4 is reserved for the writer with a bit more spark.

In Chapters 9 and 10 we show how the ideas in this book help students succeed with confidence even in an artificial writing situation like the prompted state test. Many of the voice lessons in this book can help us nurture that seed of originality that leads students' writing to the front of the pack. These chapters will show you practical ways to assess their progress.

Assessment Driving Instruction: The Six Traits

It's one thing to write persuasively and another to be able to assess your own successes and failures so that you can evaluate what's going wrong and what's going right. Because we believe that assessment should drive teaching, we have indexed this book around the 6 traits, the assessment guide that makes the most sense to us and is now in wide use across the US. For those unfamiliar the six traits they are:

Idea Development	(Are the ideas elaborated?)
Organization	(Is it put together in a logical way?)
Voice	(Is there personal expression ? [This is our personal favorite])
Sentence Fluency	(Does the piece have a rhythm or is it a dull monotone?)
Word Choice	(Is there unique or surprising language that shows the writer stretching the language? Do the words make the meaning clearer or do they confuse?)
Conventions	(Would an editor cringe or smile calmly?)

On the inside front cover you will find a brief description of the traits and an index to lessons.. We apologize that none of the lessons deal directly with grammar and conventions. This is a subject that so much has been written about, and there is only so much you can do in one book.

A Word About Grade Level and Learning Styles

We have experimented at grade levels 3-12 with the lessons in this book. Though in general less persuasive writing is done at the elementary level, we have found younger writers to be masterful persuasive writers. We hope the lessons in this book will help inspire elementary teachers to teach persuasion as part of their curriculum. To that end in most chapters we have added a "For Younger Writers" section at the end of the spin-offs for each lesson. These activities have worked well with younger writers though they should not be seen as only for younger students. We all know that age is relative when it comes to any given class, and we hope your students daily inspire you in turn with their maturity and childlike wonder. To encourage more teaching diversity, we have also included activities to engage different learning styles throughout the book.

Using the Appendices

Each lesson in this book is on two pages beginning on the left-hand side. The lesson number is in the mouth of the Voice Lady in the upper left-hand corner. The Resource Man at the end of the lesson will show you supplementary resources and note appendices when present. Since these appendices are numbered the same as the lesson, just note the lesson number and turn to the appendix. This way you can find the appendix without page references. Use the 6-trait reference on the inside front cover of the book to locate lessons in a snap and create your own index to favorite lessons in the grid on the inside back cover.

If you have further questions about how to use this book or suggestions for improving it, consult the Question and Answer section after chapter 10 or the advice column at www.discoverwriting.com .

Where to Start

Though the book is presented in a consecutive way, we encourage teachers to experiment with lessons in whatever order works for you. These lessons are meant to supplement work in your writing classroom. They are not ends in themselves, but catalysts that attach themselves to the writing classroom you are creating. Students who write regularly on topics of their own choice such as "Why We Must Run with Scissors" will always get further than those who respond simply to a teacher's weekly assignments.

Finally, we recognize that these days there is a lot of pressure in education making students and teachers think smaller. The national push for higher educational standards and a rabid obsession with testing has created an atmosphere in schools that focuses more on test scores and test prep and less on real thinking and real learning. Though we have included many very practical lessons to deal with these concerns, our greatest hope is that lessons in this book will help both teachers and students to expand beyond the little walls of their classroom and become citizens of the new millennium, citizens who know what's truly important and express it with their hearts, their minds and their pens. (see chapter 2). This is a big job, and it requires a big spirit that won't be squished into a little box in the name of education. So take one deep breath, set your eyes on the stars and let's get to work!

Gretchen S. Bernabei   *Barry Lane*

Surfing the Tide of Persuasion

The foolish and the dead alone never change their opinions.

James Russell Lowell

Think back to your first year of teaching, your first day of school. Did your students file in quietly, take their seats and gaze up at you in silence and innocent wonder? Did you scan the classroom and note thirty trusting and simple faces? Lives ready to begin, under your tutelage?

Or, as your classroom filled, did you note that the students strode in chock-full of experiences and opinions, attempts, failures, and triumphs? Lives already fully underway? The cup was already full and you perhaps wondered where to even begin adding your two cents.

By the time they get to our classrooms, students are at best masters, or at the very least constant practitioners in the arts and crafts of persuasion. They have convinced their weary mothers to stay up late to watch that special show, they have talked their fathers into lending them the car, and have found ways to convince their grandmother that they really need that latest toy. With a little tickling, students can articulate the truth about what persuasive techniques work for them and on them, in different situations. They can invent their own set of rules and methods based on what they notice. Our teaching art lies in showing them how they have outlined a form also invented by a Roman named Nestor, or how very similar their ideas are to Aristotle's, who we all know was a master at getting his mother to let him stay up late so he could contemplate the metaphysical nature of the universe and drink cocoa.

We learn from Lev Vygotsky that there is a difference between spontaneous and scientific knowledge: spontaneous concepts are those that students pick up from their experience, like finding the way home, or getting along with peers. Scientific concepts are new ideas given to them in school, to be learned and potentially applied to life, like verb tenses or mathematical formulas. Teaching masters like Janet Emig, Donald Graves and Jerome Bruner tell us students learn best when they mine their spontaneous knowledge for skills they already use. Simply put, we learn by doing; then we go on to do more through learning.

The activities in this first chapter will have students reflecting on persuasion: what it is, how it works, and how it has sounded in conversations they already know. They will dig through their own experiences as both persuaders and persuadees, uncovering the diverse and dynamic ranges of methods which have worked and those which have backfired. Teachers can refer back to these techniques while students build their own personal banks of persuasive methods. In other words, if persuasive writing is surfing, step one is to locate the waves in all of us. Only then can we start to figure out how to ride them.

Are You Good at Persuasion?

There is no conversation more boring than the one where everyone agrees.
Michel de Montaigne

The Point: We are all skilled at persuasion, but we don't always stop to reflect on our skill. This ten-minute lesson is about mining our memory for experiences as persuaders and sharing them with each other. Activities like this build confidence in our innate persuasive abilities.

Teaching it:

How good are you at persuading others? Have you ever talked someone into doing something they never would have done without you?

When I was 14 years old I talked my parents into getting a Greyhound bus pass and traveling from Boston to San Francisco. They made it to California exhausted and flew back home, and even today my mother says she can't understand why they ever agreed to do such a crazy thing. I don't really remember what I said to them, but it must have worked.

When did you persuade someone to do something they wouldn't normally do?

Let's freewrite for nine minutes about a time we persuaded somebody. If you run out of ideas, try writing your thoughts or just list moments.

(Set timer for nine minutes and everybody writes. An alternative would be to have students talk in small groups.)

Let's look at what we have written. Can we draw any generalizations?

(Make a list, drawing from student volunteers.)

Debriefing:

What methods were most helpful to you in persuading others?
Is annoying someone till they give in a method that might work when you are writing a persuasive essay?
How can you persuade those who think differently from you?

Student Responses:

I'm good because if it doesn't work, then I'll bother them and be annoying until they give in. -Jeffrey

I'm not good at persuasion, because once I notice that they will say no, I leave them alone. -Edgar

I know I'm good at it. I got credit at the store down the street, and they don't give credit. -Jerome

Yes. I've persuaded friends, school administrators, students, girlfriends, and other people to do things. -Ernest

No, because I can't make or even try to tell people what they should do. In some cases, yes, because they'll be my friends and they'll look at it as advice. -Adriana

I think I'm good at persuading people when I really want to, depending on what it is. I usually get my way, but not for anything bad or against their will. -Melody

No, because when I try, it never works. -Albert

Yes, because I will not stop on doing something or saying something until I get what I want. Me, I will just keep picking at it. -Eulalia

Some generalizations we drew about ourselves as a group:
- We generally don't give up if it's something we really want.
- We don't like to try to persuade people to do things against their will.
- We can judge whether we're effective by watching the person's actions.
- Nagging works on family and friends.

Spin-offs:
- Write a very short list of rules for persuasion based on the findings of the above activity.
  Examples:
  Rules for Persuading
     Don't give up
     Don't persuade people against their will
     Nagging works with family

- Draw a line down the center of a page. On one side write "Times I Persuaded" on the other "Times I Was Persuaded"

For Younger Writers:
In your journal make a timeline of your life. As you run your hand along the years, thinking of yourself at that age, persuasive moments will no doubt follow. Write them in and share them with the class.

Resources:

Slobodkina, Esphyr. *Caps for Sale.* New York: Harper Collins, 1968. This classic story models a man who not only uses persuasion in his attempts to sell hats, but even more so in his attempts to get monkeys to return the hats they have swiped from him.

Funny Persuasion

Cats are smarter than dogs. You can't get eight cats to pull a sled through snow.

Jeff Valdez

The Point: Persuasion pervades our lives. You might even say, as infants we were the most persuasive. Why else would our parents spend so much of their time catering to our needs? Yet as time went on our powers of persuasion diminished and we had to learn new strategies and search for new targets. This activity teaches us to see that we are already master persuaders and our best efforts often tickle the funny bone of memory.

Teaching it:

Did you ever persuade someone to do something strange or funny?

When I was in college, my friend Renate told us about how she lived in Germany when she was a child. When it was freezing cold outside, she used to talk her younger sister into touching her tongue to the outside door-knob of the house. It would stick. Renate got into bad trouble with her parents doing that.

(Note: This will work better if you tell your own story.)

Can you remember a strange or funny thing that you ever persuaded someone to do? Write it down, in the next few minutes. Begin with the words "one time." If you think of more than one, make a list.

(Everyone writes for 5-10 minutes.)

Now ask yourself what methods you used to achieve your goal and list them.

For example: I told my brother that mud was good for him. That didn't work, but when I told him it tasted like chocolate, that did the trick.

Debriefing:

How does your audience reflect the argument you construct?
What points make a strong argument?

Student Responses:

One time I tried to get my cousin to drink mud. He almost did. -Raymond

One time I tried to make someone try to dress as a girl.-Julio

One time I tried to make my cousin shave his head. -Andres

One time I tried to make my little brothers run around my house three times naked. -Denise

One time I tried to make my friend buy a country music CD by telling him it was heavy metal. -Ernestallen

One time I tried to make my homeboy eat a taco of jalapenos and toothpaste.-Gilbert

Spin-offs:

- Take one of the student responses above, or one from your own class. Choose two students as actors role-playing the persuasive situation. As teacher/director you can freeze the action at any moment and ask the audience for suggestions on how to make it more persuasive.

- Interview a family member and ask them who they persuaded in their family. Record their stories and collect them to make a class family memoir of persuasion.

- Turn your family interviews into a family tree poster where each ancestor is annotated with who they persuaded and the methods used.

  For example:
  Dad persuades Mom to marry him even though she is making double his salary at her job.
  Method: He lies, tells her he is foreman when he is really a factory worker.

- Write how-to or top ten poems based on memories. A how-to or a top-ten poem tells the reader how to accomplish the persuasive task at hand.

  Top Ten Ways to Get Your Brother to Drink Mud
  10. Tell him you eat it all the time.
  9. Tell him that mud has a sweet nutty flavor.
  8. Tell him it's not mud, it's chocolate.
  7. Hold his arms and stuff it in his mouth.
  6. Spread the mud inside a peanut butter sandwich.
  5. Offer him ice cream if he eats the mud first.
  4. Attach the mud to a booger.
  3. Put the mud inside a cupcake.
  2. Hand him the mud and say, "Eat it now or I'll give you a bath."
  And the number one method to get your brother to eat mud is: **Eat it yourself first.**

Resources:

Shannon, David. *No David.* New York: Scholastic, Inc., 1998. In this picture book a parental voice vainly tries to get David to behave by saying "No, David" to everything he does. The author claims to have written it when he was five, and it is a great example of ineffective persuasion until the end when Mom tries a new approach: "Yes, David." Use this book to illustrate that No is weaker than Yes.

Brown, Marcia. *Stone Soup.* New York: Scribners, 1975. In this classic story, first published in 1947, three soldiers use personality and wiles to trick villagers into contributing ingredients for soup. What often works in persuasion is not reasoning, but other, more human characteristics.

What Can Change Your Mind?

The man who never alters his opinion is like standing water, and breeds reptiles of the mind.
William Blake

The Point: Persuasive tactics don't always come from books or from outside experts. We have been persuaded frequently throughout our lives. Examining what changes our minds is the first step in examining which methods work and which do not.

Teaching it:

Have you ever bought something you didn't intend to or agreed to do something you couldn't even imagine ever agreeing to?

What makes persuasion work? What makes you agree to do something that you didn't want to do before? What makes you believe something that you didn't believe before?

Think of advertisements or nagging brothers and sisters. What got to you?

Now make a list of these persuasive moments and ask yourself what made you finally cave in.
(This can work well with students working in pairs.)

Debriefing:

What methods would work well in our essays?
Which would be less effective on paper?

Student Responses:

My beliefs:
Asking myself, "Would I get into trouble?"
Asking myself, "Would I do this on my own?"
Money, or if they give me something.
When people tell me the good things about something. If I like the idea and the good things outweigh the bad, I'll go for it.
If they do it first.
Daring me.
A lot of people cheering for me to do it.
It depends on who it is and how they tell me.
If they can make me curious.
I believe I get persuaded when I begin to feel good.
If they blackmail me with something very dear to me.
When they find your weakness and attack it.
Money could make me do something, if it's enough.

When my job is on the line, I don't have a choice.
If they told me that if I didn't, my grandma would get mad.
Bribery.
Threatening.
Temptation.
Proof.
If I hear things like, "Come on, Roxanne, you promised!" or "Pleeeeease, please, please."
The promise of the way things may turn out afterwards.
The possibility of winning something.
Embarrassing me in front of people.
If they make it sound fun and exciting.
If it all seems worth it.

Debriefing:

Is there a difference in the methods used to persuade you?
If so, which methods leave you feeling genuinely persuaded and which are more temporary?
Have you used these methods on others?
What are your weak spots? How do they get to you?

Spin-offs:

- Reprint student answers on slips of paper and have students group them into categories. When you look at the categories we have created, do you see any patterns developing? Try writing one true statement about each category.

- Write a true statement about persuasion for each category we have invented.

For Younger Writers:

What are your personal weak spots? Make lists and we will collect them as a class book called something like "Our Achilles Heels." Knowing the commonality of our own weaknesses helps us to think about the weak spots of our readers.

Resources:

Gallo, Donald R., ed. *No Easy Answers: Short Stories About Teenagers Making Tough Choices.* New York: Delacorte Press, 1997. This amazing collection of short stories presents relevant and engaging situations in which young people face consequences of having been persuaded.

Three Things You've Really Tried to Persuade Other People to Do for You: A Brainstorming Activity

There is no human problem which could not be solved if people would simply do as I advise.

Gore Vidal

The Point: Persuasion is part of our everyday life, and the more students realize they are already competent persuaders, the more confidence they will bring to their writing. This short activity again dredges up real life examples of persuasion for them to reflect about. It works best as a class warm-up or as an afterthought, when the atmosphere is casual and students seem to have greater access to their subconscious levels. Have them do the lists of three, then share. You'll end up with a surprisingly wide range of real-life needs for persuasion.

Teaching it:

You try to get your friends to do things with you and for you all the time. Everybody does. Think of the time you talked your big sister into doing the dishes when it was your turn or how you talked your parents into letting you go to the dance even when they knew your homework wasn't done.

(Teachers, find your own personal examples to share.)

Think now of OTHER people, not your friends or peers. List three things that you've tried lately to persuade other people to do for you.

(Take 5-10 minutes to write)

Now stop. Look at your list and reflect about how you managed to persuade these people. Which methods had the most effect, which the least.

(Note: often the three B's work— Bullying , Bribing and Badgering— but are they true civilized persuasion that would work in an essay? Probably not. Blackmail is not a fine art. Point this out, the difference between threat and reason . It's an important distinction we will explore throughout this book.)

Debriefing:

What patterns do we see?
Which seem positive?
Which negative?
Which will work on paper in a persuasive essay?
Which will not work? Why?

Student Responses:

To leave me alone	I told him there was a good show on TV.
To let me stay out longer	I did my homework.

To do me a favor	She owed me one!
To help me clean my room	He made it messy too.
To give me a day off	I told them I'd come in early tomorrow.
To take my shift at work	We agreed to switch shifts.
To buy Avon stuff	It smelled better than they thought.
To allow me to leave work early	I'll told them I'd come in early tomorrow.
To dress like I do	I told her I was cool.

Spin-offs:

• Start a persuasive list in your journal or writer's notebook. Record all the little daily persuasions. Include the times you were persuaded or when you persuaded others. Make note of the methods used.

• Write a how-to picture book for young children based on one of things off your list. For Example: How to Get Your Sister to Help You Clean Your Room Each illustrated page of the book can be another method. (This can also be done as a class.)

• Write a how-to poem where you are an expert telling the audience how to do something. Each method is a new line in the poem. *For example:*
"How to Get Your Little Brother to Leave You Alone"
>   Tell him his favorite show is on TV.
>   Give him a book to read.
>   Give him the keys to mom's car.

Resource: Appendix 4

Twain, Mark. *Tom Sawyer.* New York: Penguin, 1986. Probably the most famous example of positive persuasion is the white- washing scene, excerpted in Appendix 4.

Coxe, Molly. *Cat Traps.* New York: Random House, 1996. This book for beginning readers demonstrates (with very few words) a succession of persuasive attempts as a cat tries to find something to eat. Use it to demonstrate patterns.

When Does Persuasion Backfire?

Good advice is one of those insults that ought to be forgiven.
Unknown

The Point: Persuasion can backfire for a number of reasons, but the most common one involves a failure to acknowledge the personal limits of the person being persuaded. Getting students in touch with their own personal limits helps them to imagine the limits of their reader. The following quick activity will improve their awareness of audience.

Teaching it:

Think of a time when someone was trying to get you to do something or to buy something, and you heard yourself think, "NO WAY." Maybe it happened right at the first. Maybe it was something that happened just before your decision, and it changed your mind. In the next few minutes, jot down what you think about this question: when does persuasion NOT work?
(Talk and write for 5-10 minutes)

Debriefing:
What makes persuasion fail?
Why is it different at different times? And for different situations?

Student Responses:
When they show you the side effects, or what happens afterwards
When they try to rush me
When death is involved
When the person talks more about their own experiences than mine
When you know the consequences, and they're bad
When they say I HAVE to do it
When you know someone has gotten hurt from it
When you've already heard bad things about it
When embarrassment is involved
When it would make me uncomfortable in any way
When they're too pushy, rude, snotty or beautiful (When they push on you, you rebel. When they are rude, you don't care. When they're snotty, you laugh. And when they're beautiful, you know it's probably fake.)
When you know you can't trust them. (My brother wanted to borrow my car. I would have loaned it to him, but I knew he'd wrecked his last two cars.)
When you know they're lying
When they keep insisting and nagging even after I say no
Their tone of voice
When I'm feeling hardheaded or just not listening, when I don't feel like taking in information
When there's a "BUT" in their talk, like "It's so easy, but if we get caught…"

When I think they're just using me

When they insult me

When the little voice in my head says no, not to do that, or it says, "How could you believe THAT?"

Spin-offs:

- Find a partner to work with and pick one of the situations. Create a short skit where you act out the moment where persuasion failed.

- Create a character called Bob or Judy —-the world's least persuasive person. Combine as many of the attributes described above as you can to create a scene where he or she try to sell a particular product to some stranger. This writing will get funnier the more insensitive the salesman becomes. Try acting this one out as a skit, too.

- Create a script for a television commercial or poster that tells the absolute truth about the product you are selling.

Resources:

Wood, Audrey. *Elbert's Bad Word.* New York: Voyager Books, 1988. Elbert, the main character of this light-hearted picture book, has a brush with bad language. The consequences show the kind of "back-firing" that produce almost instantaneous learning.

Martin, Jane Read and Patricia Marx. *Now Everybody Really Hates Me.* New York: Harper Collins, 1993. This picture book demonstrates the problems with "because I'm right and you're wrong" attitudes. The protagonist is a little girl spending a time-out in her room for misbehavior.

nine out of ten dentists agree.
ALL TOOTHPASTES ARE THE SAME!

6 I'll Never Buy...

Every generation laughs at the old fashions but religiously follows the new.
Henry David Thoreau

The Point: Thinking about stuff you'll never buy helps you examine your own personal limits and prejudices. This lesson asks students to make a list of things they can't imagine ever being persuaded to buy and then try to sell them to each other.

Teaching it:

You can compile student contributions and post the group list to use as a resource.

Look at the sample list below.

In your lifetime, you have bought some things. In the future, you'll buy many others. You can predict what some of them will be.

Can you think of some things you would never buy no matter how hard someone tries to sell you? In the next three minutes, see if you can list three things that you will NEVER in a million years be persuaded to buy.

Share your list with a partner .

Now pick one thing off the list and try to sell it to the person who won't buy it. List on paper some of the key selling points of the thing.

(Tip: Ads create images to flesh out the lies. Have students come to class with ads clipped from magazines.)

Debriefing:
Did you create a convincing argument for the product you were selling?
How did you do it?

Spin-offs:
- Make a collage or catalog of all the things you won't buy.

- Make an ad designed to get someone not to buy a product off your list. Include all the truthful details you can think of.

- Draw a picture of your limits. What do they look like?

- Make a poster with the title "Know Your Limits." Put an image that relates to your limits.

Student Responses:

Fourth grade:	King	Drugs	Menudo
Drugs	A lion	A Volkswagen beetle	A girdle
Spiders	**Seventh grade:**	Lip enhancement	A silver station wagon
Rusty cars	Hair dye	A wig	Jock itch medication
Cats	Stuffed animals	**Ninth grade:**	Spinach
A hamburger from Burger	Speedos	Hemorrhoid medication	Spandex

Selling Girl's Underwear to Boys

Are there any guys out there who are tired of their moms yelling, "Why the heck is this A.C. bill so high!" Well if you are one, boy do I got the product for you-- Victoria Secret underwear. These underwear are loose so that air can flow cleanly through leaving you cool and fresh. I know what you're saying-you're saying that Victoria Secret is for girls. Wrong! If you wear these great undergarments it will really bring out your feminine side. Now, your saying why would I want that? Well, this is why. If you're more feminine, girls will start to like you more. And if girls like you, then guys will want to be your friends. And pretty soon you'll be really popular. Now your saying those little things must be pretty uncomfortable. Well, sorry but you're wrong again! These undergarments have been clinically proven to be more comfortable than your average tighty-whiteys or Joe-boxers, but you have to be 11 or older for them to fit just right. Now you're thinking they're cool, but what about sports? Well, son we've got that covered too. We have regular, classy, and sporty. The sporty kind have tight, yet comfortable legs which hold your legs tight and firm so you can run, jump and tackle with ease. Wow! Now that you've heard about these great undergarments why don't you do yourself a favor and call this toll free number and order your pair of Victoria Secret underwear for $7.25 today! But wait, there's more! If you call in the next five minutes we will knock the price down to $7.00. Call now, 1-800-U-DAH-MAN.

Nathan Uland , seventh grade

For Younger Writers:

Write a menu for a restaurant where you would never eat. Make sure you list all your least favorite foods.

Resources:

Adbusters Culture Jammers Headquarters. 3 May 2001. <http://www.adbusters.org>. Ads for things you won't buy. This web site is devoted beating image-making advertisers at their own game. They conduct ongoing spoof ad contests your students will want to enter.

Seuss, Dr. *Green Eggs and Ham*. New York: Random House, 1960. This well-known, well-loved classic models the dialogue of persuasion, focusing on food that could have come from the "I'll never buy" list.

Today's All-You-Can-Eat Special

Liver & Spinach Souffle with Beet Sauce

"Oh well ... okay ... grrrrr": The Sound Of Persuasion

All right, I will learn to read, but when I have learned, I never, never shall.
British novelist David Garnett at age 4, to his mother

The Point: Some aspects of persuasion become visible when we look at what works on us. Having students think or talk about what makes someone agree, even reluctantly, to do something helps them to understand the power of persuasion. When the roles are reversed, these patterns can become tools for them as persuaders themselves. These next two lessons help students explore the often subtle feel and sound of persuasion.

Teaching it:

Can you think of a time when you were persuaded to do something you didn't want to do? I can.

Roller coasters have always scared me. Terribly. Once when I was about 20, I was on a trip to a theme park with a group of teenagers I used to work with. This one kid named Don convinced me that the roller coaster wasn't really very scary at all; in fact, he had been disappointed that it was so tame. And even though I had been sure I wouldn't ride a roller coaster, Don convinced me to take a ride on it.

Name a time when you did something that you didn't want to do, something that you were FINALLY persuaded to do. And you may have heard yourself say something like "Oh well…okay…grrrr." Take just a couple of minutes to think one up and jot it down.

After you have jotted it down, see if you can remember what they did or said that persuaded you.

Debriefing:

What was the deciding factor in your changing your mind?
How did the persuaders manage to appeal to your interests while at the same time meeting their own?
Would you fall for the same argument a second time?

Student Examples:

To wear an ugly dress. They told me lime green was my color and I would be unique.
To go home. (I don't like going home.) They said mom made lasagna.
To go to church with my aunt and uncle. They told me the preacher was sick: no sermon.
To work when I was off. They said it wouldn't be busy and I could do homework on the job.
To babysit little brats. They told me they were going to play outside.
To go late to work. The worst that could happen was you get fired.
To walk in to a class late. We had a substitute that day.
To jump out of a car. They do it in movies.

Spin-offs:

- Look at the list above and the one you made with your class and group them into categories. List these on a big sheet of paper and hang them in the classroom as a reference.

- Invite students to create a new dance called the sweet persuasion. It begins with persons firm in their beliefs, but their firm beliefs eventually crumble and they submit. In other words, it moves from a march to a dying swan. Their dance can be balletic or simply a modern popular dance like the twist or the jerk.

- Pick something you would never do and write a top ten reason poem about why you won't do it.

For Younger Writers:

- Draw a poster ad to get someone in your family to do something for you.

- Draw a picture of a person's face the moment he or she is being persuaded to do something. What expression do you see?

Resources:

Mazer, Ann. *The Salamander Room*. New York: Dragonfly Books, 1991. The child in this picture book tries to convince the parent to get him a pet salamander. It's written in dialogue: the parent poses a problem question, and the child answers with a solution. The book is a wonderful model for problem-solution structures.

THE FACTS ARE IN!
Cleaning Your Sister's Room
· Improves manual dexterity
· Hones organizational skills
· and enhances self-esteem

"Oh Well...Okay...Grrrrr"
The Sound Of Surrender

Do whatever he says; he's crazy.

A cop in a bad movie

If people don't want to come out to the ball park, nobody's going to stop them.

Yogi Berra

The Point: Human voices have a particular sound when they are being persuaded. If you listen carefully you can hear it. This fun activity can help a class to realize that their spoken and written words have a distinct power on an audience. Bring a telephone into your classroom and extend the "Oh well...okay...grrrr..." activity. The audience can analyze the speaker they don't hear perform and can predict patterns about what makes someone finally agree to do something. They can also have fun guessing the content.

Teaching it:

Pick one of the topics from the "Oh well...okay...grrrr..." list (in the last lesson). Imagine the conversation between the persuader and the persuadee that happened before the persuadee said, "Oh well..okay..." Then pretend you're the one being persuaded. Imagine what you'd say. Here's a telephone. In the next five minutes, write whatever notes you need to use in order to take this telephone and show us how your end of the conversation might have sounded. Remember: the persuader didn't get you to agree at first.

(This can work well in pairs. One student does the persuader and the other student writes down only the responses and pauses, etc. Then they switch.)

Example:

Grades 3-6:

Situation: A friend wants you to go see a movie you have already seen.

Hi? What's up..........I saw it last week with my brother. It was great.....well, not really... I got a lot of stuff to do......y'know, clean my room......you're right....sure...I'd rather go but how can I talk Mom into letting me........she won't buy that, believe me......No,...I could never lie..........that was a long time ago.......if you tell her I'll never speak to you again.

Grades 7-12:

Situation: Mom wants you to babysit the kids.

Hello? (pause) Oh, hello, Mom. (pause) Okay, sure. What is it? (pause...grimace) Saturday? This Saturday? (pause) Uh...I was thinking about going to the mall with Maria...(pause) Yes... (pause) Uh huh... (pause) Right... (pause, grimace even worse) All three of them? (pause) Mom... (pause, tap foot) They're horrible! They're brats! (pause, pace) All day? But... (pause, pace more) No, I don't, but... (pause, stop pacing) She will? (pause) Uh huh...how much? (pause, grimace) Well... (pause) Okay, Mom.. (sigh) tell her I will. (hang up, stare, and freeze.)

Debriefing:

What do you notice about the person being persuaded?

What did the face look like?

How does the body posture change?

Spin-offs:

• One fun variation is to have students perform the part of the persuader, and have the audience figure out whether the listener on the other end of the telephone agreed or didn't.

• Write a free verse poem titled something like "The Persuaded."
Include just one half of the telephone conversation.

• Write a radio play called "How _____ talked me into _____." Use some of the ideas from the activity above. Have students tape their plays and share them with the class.

• Write the other side of the telephone conversation, as the persuader, leaving out the side of the persuaded.

• Write both sides of the dialogue, in script format.

Manager:	Can you come in today?
Me:	Today's my only day off this week!
Manager:	Come on…we're short of people.
Me:	So?
Manager:	You owe me!
Me:	For what?
Manager:	What do you mean for what? Remember? I let you go home early Saturday.
Me:	What…that makes no difference. I always stay late for you.
Manager:	Don't forget you're getting a raise. I always help you out. Come on…return the favor.
Me:	Dang! I had plans for tonight.
Manager:	I'll give you this coming Friday off if you come in tonight.
Me:	Dang…Okay, but I'd better have Friday off.

(April Herrera, 11th grade)

Resources:

Raschka, Chris. *Ring! Yo?* New York: Dorling Kindersley Publishing, 2000. This picture book models the one-sided phone conversation. At the end of the book you have a script of the other side.

Wood, Audrey. *The Red Racer.* New York: Aladdin Paperbacks, 1996. This picture book deals with a child's Christmas wish.

Viorst, Judith. *Alexander, Who's Not (Do You Hear Me? I Mean It!) Going To Move.* New York: Scholastic, Inc., 1995. This delightful picture book is most useful for the resistant voice of the child who does not want to move.

"No way. Can't be done." What's Your Limit?

There is only one thing about which I am certain, and that is that there is very little about which one can be certain.

W. Somerset Maugham

The Point: No matter how open-minded and reasonable people might be, they can still probably imagine one or two things that they consider themselves absolutely incapable of doing. It's revealing to explore these inner limits with your class, because it tunes them in to the barriers they will face in the audience they are trying to persuade.

Teaching it:

There are some things we cannot be persuaded to do. For example, no one has ever persuaded me to buy a pet poodle because I hate yippy dogs. Understanding what we can't be persuaded to do can help us understand barriers in our readers that our writing will try to overcome. Take a couple of minutes and answer this: what is one thing that NOBODY would ever be able to persuade you to do? Explain why it's a closed issue to you.

Student Responses:

Grades 7-12:

To disown or ruin the friendship I have with my parents.

To drop out of school, because I've been in school too long to let all these years go to waste.

To go river rafting or in a canoe.

To get on a plane. Me? Hell no, never.

To ruin my friendship and love that I have for my grandma and cousin.

To sleep in a bed with a snake right beside me or to jump off Hemisfair Tower.

To get a sex change.

To join the KKK, do drugs, or go on Ricki Lake.

To jump off a cliff, shoot up, or be a stunt man.

To steal.

To kill, murder.

To have an abortion.

To marry someone I don't want to marry.

To be a mob or Mafia member.

To give up my kids.

To be a prostitute.

Patterns we notice (or...what do these have in common?):

We consider the following to be non-negotiable:

    *Hurting ourselves

Chapter One

*Hurting other people
*Endangering our closest relationships
*Acting outside our values

Debriefing:

Why do we have limits?
How do persuaders overcome limits in their audience?

Spin-offs:

• How could you persuade someone to do something he or she was dead set against? Make a list of all the things you could say and try to find the negotiating points or some common ground.

• In some literature you're reading, name a character and list several things that character would never do.

• Has anyone ever surprised you by going beyond what you thought were their limits? Write about this.

• Draw or create a picture, poster or collage, representing your personal limits.

For Younger Writers:

• Make a collage of things you will never buy.

• Interview your parents and find out about their limits. Ask them about times they were persuaded to do something they didn't want to. Write about their answers to your questions.

Resources:

Ads for things you would never buy. Bring in mail order catalogs.

Johnson, Angela. *When I Am Old With You.* New York: Orchard Books, 1990. This picture book shows a touching speech written by a child to a grandfather, showing all the things they'll do together when the child gets as old as the grandfather. It would be an interesting model for showing what would happen if any laws of nature (or man) were rewritten, to make them more like what we wish.

I Cannot Tell a Lie
Pinocchio's Personal Limit

Real Persuasion
in the Real World:
Educating Hearts and Minds

It is only with the heart that one can see rightly; what is essential is invisible to the eye.
Antoine de Saint-Exupery

When two of Ann Barnett's sixth grade classes at Truitt Middle School in Houston Texas found out about the millions of children who were child bonded laborers or child slaves, they decided to do something about it. After convincing Ann they really wanted to make a difference, her classes, with the help of a Web site called www.freethechildren.org, spent their time writing persuasive speeches and advertisements for the sixth Grade homerooms and organized a readathon fundraiser for *Free the Children*. Four thousand dollars and a new Ecuadorian school later, Ann's students are creating their own Web site and, though now in seventh grade, some are still involved in this project. And by the way, their seventh grade language arts teacher reports they still speak out passionately about the issues in persuasive writing, as well as other forms of writing.

Ann attributes this to the real life purpose for writing, and a very real motivation they developed working on the project. They wanted to be successful because they were working towards a real goal. Their passion came through in speeches, advertisements, and follow up letters. And all of Ann's classes the subsequent year have eagerly tackled the same issue and project - and are hoping to be even more successful.

Real writing grows when teachers risk teaching bigger than the walls of the classroom, even in times when state watchdogs seem to be conspiring to make teaching smaller with lists of hoops and tests to jump through. Ann Barnett's motto for teaching is not that every child can learn, but that every child will learn, and she insures this by creating a classroom where kids voices count and real things matter. Learning in such a class is not something students endure, but rather something that's hard to resist.

How do we create classes where students don't complain about homework? How do we unlock the passionate voices of students whose minds and imaginations often seem numbed by consumerism? How do we move beyond self-centered wants to Real opinions about the Real world.

Lessons in Chapter 2 are aimed at coaxing out passionate ideas, opinions and voices from the busy and confusing lives of students. The first lessons help students reflect about responsibilities and concerns in their personal life, and later chapters move toward lessons on finding passions in the world at large. As you experiment with your class, be patient with them. Deeply felt opinions don't always lie on the surface. They grow with time and reflection.   At worst, lessons in this chapter can help build a bank of possible persuasion topics to draw on in their writing. At best, one of your students might become an Amy Biehl whose passion for abolishing Apartheid in South Africa began in 6th grade and lives on today, years after her tragic death in 1994. (www.amybiehl.org)

Real Responsibilities, Real Concerns

Baby: An alimentary canal with a loud voice at one end and no responsibility at the other.
Elizabeth Adamson

The Point: Opinions don't grow on trees; they grow in the soil of lives filled with responsibilities and concerns. This brainstorming exercise will generate a list of non-school responsibilities students actually hold, as well as real concerns they have. It will create a shared awareness of what student realities can be and will be a springboard for student action papers and movements.

Teaching it:

Life is not simple for people your age in this day and time. Sometimes we teachers forget and think that students only have our classes to worry about.

But that's not true, is it?

What is responsibility? Let me read the definition. Let's break the word into two parts: Respond and Ability. Responsibility: the ability to respond. As a baby we have no ability to respond. Others respond to and for us, but as we grow up we assume more and more responsibilities. Some are forced on us and others we volunteer for.

Think about the responsibilities you have. Which are voluntary? Which seem involuntary?

One huge responsibility is going to school and carrying your weight there, passing your classes and succeeding. But ASIDE from this one, what other responsibilities do you have anywhere else in your life?

List as many as you can in five minutes.

(Hand out 3 X 5 index cards; then write and share.)

Debriefing:
Have your responsibilities increased over the years?
Do you see them increasing in years to come? If so, how?
What concerns do you have about your responsibilities?
What are the consequences if you don't fulfill them?
Why do we have responsibilities? How does it affect us?

Student Responses:
3rd-6th grade
I have to make my bed and feed my bunnies. If I don't lock them up well, an owl could get them.

I have to put away the clean dishes from the dishwasher. If I don't I can lose my allowance and my mom will get mad at me.

I have to feed the sheep and give them water or they will get sick and die.

I have to sweep the kitchen floor once a night. If I don't your feet might stick to it in the morning,

6th-12th grade

Besides my first responsibility, school, I have other important ones. Like: going home after school and making sure it looks clean, so that when my parents get home they have a nice looking house. One other one is to cook. I cook two or three times a week, because my mother is too tired from work. I would have a job, but my parents said that I only need to concentrate on school. And I thank them when they tell me that. -Jeffrey

In addition to going to school, one of the concerns I have right now is getting a job. -Ernestallen

Sometimes I have to rush home and change from school clothes into regular clothes to go to driving school. -Raymond

In addition to school, my other concern is my family and friends. But mainly my family because you never know if your friends are really truly your friends. -Olivia

Working 40 hours/week at Wendy's. Paying a car payment. Paying for car insurance. Looking for another job. Chores at home that need to be taken care of. Responsibilities at work that need to be taken care of. Saving money for important things. -Lala

An additional responsibility I have is to help my mom around the house. She takes care of my grandma during the day, so at night I help her with my grandma and my brother. -Josie S.

Spin-offs:

- Now that you have identified your responsibilities, reflect about the nature of responsibility. How do you feel about it? What would life be like without it? How does it change your sense of identity? What responsibilities do you feel to the world at large? This journal writing may dredge up important positions.

- Make a list of responsibilities you may have ten years from now. List concerns which might grow from these responsibilities.

- Create a dance entitled, "The Birth of Responsibility." It chronicles the movement from child to adult. Movements should show a gradual assuming of more responsibility as time goes on.

- Write and illustrate a picture book that traces the responsibilities of one character through time.

For Younger Writers:

- Draw a self-portrait in the center of a piece of white paper. Leave space all around the drawing. Now draw your responsibilities.

- Make a responsibility time line of your life from birth to present and on into the future. Write in key dates and which responsibilities kicked in.

Resources:

Browne, Anthony. *Piggybook*. New York: Alfred A. Knopf, Inc., 1986. Reference Materials: In this picture book, a mother rebels because of the "piggish" ways of her family, none of whom share in any of the family responsibilities around the house.

Real Student Concerns – Building A Source List

You must learn day by day, year by year, to broaden your horizon. The more things you love, the more you are interested in, the more you enjoy, the more you are indignant about, the more you have left when anything happens.

Ethel Barrymore

The Point: If students are going to speak as citizens who want to see change, then they must write about issues which concern them. If teachers hand issues to the students and say, "Write about these," the results will be teacher-owned. This exercise produces a bank of student-owned, student-generated issues of concern.

Teaching it:

Today we are going to talk about concerns. What does it mean?
(Cite definition)
What concerns you? What does it mean to be concerned?

You're aware of things going on in our class, in our school, in our neighborhood, in our town, in our state, in our country, in our world. I want you to think about all the things that go on in the world RIGHT NOW. Think about one thing that really bothers you, that nags at the back of your mind sometimes; something that you think just ISN'T RIGHT. Write that one thing down.

(Hand out slips of paper)

If you can think of more than one, of course you may write down more.

Debriefing:

Was it hard to think of concerns or did they come flooding through your pen?
Can you classify your concerns into personal vs. global?
If so how many fall into each area?
If you have few concerns, is that a concern to you?

Student Responses:

What bothers me is...

3rd-5th

People having wars.	Kids in other parts of the world starving.
People hitting other people.	Drinking and driving.
Swearing at each other.	Scary ugly things of TV that give me nightmares.
Killing.	Factories poisoning the air.
Boys kissing girls.	People who like to hate.
	Mean people.

6th-12th

Kids shooting other kids because they were teased, or because they don't fit in. They should find another decent way to cope,
    and deal with it.

Racial slurs that still go on in the South.

All the haters just won't leave me or all the true non-haters alone. Why can't they just stay out of our business? Too many haters.

Abortion. I think it's wrong to murder unborn babies.

How people can't get along with each other. They almost always start wars with each other.

How we as the U.S. help other countries, yet we have problems of our own that we haven't taken care of yet.

That we get involved in problems like Kosovo, but not in China, where things are a lot worse.

Racism. I don't understand how in the world people can judge other people by the color of their skin, their religion, their
    ethnicity, their background. When you cut us open, no matter how different we seem, we all bleed the same color.

Spin-offs:

* Extend this lesson over several weeks. Make a concerns box in the front of the room. Students can add new concerns whenever they want.

* Read the front page of the newspaper each day. Identify more common concerns.

* Research the next steps: What would be a suggestion that would help with any of these issues? To whom would you address your concern and/or suggestion? Where can you find the address for that person or how could you reach them? What other forms of action could students realistically take?

* Post opinions on current issues in online magazines for teenagers, like "Hot Topics" in the Get Personal section of www.teenpeople.com.

* Categorize the issues. Look for trends. Have students summarize these issues into one or two words each. Then invite students to group the issues into like groups, and name the categories they come up with. These would make a wonderful report about "what we (or our students) are most concerned about."

For Younger Writers:

* Launch a letter-writing campaign. See "Dear Mrs. Ryan," appendix 11.

* Make an ad poster for the area of concern you are most interested in.

* Write a list poem that begins with the words: "Things That Bug Me."

* Find e-mail addresses of powerful people and build a class address book.

Resources: Appendix 11

Lewis, Barbara A. *What Do You Stand For? A Kid's Guide to Building Character.* Minneapolis: Free Spirit Publications, Inc., 1988. This book is full of activities for values clarification and personal-strength finding.

Markle, Sandra and William. *Gone Forever! An Alphabet of Extinct Animals.* New York: Scholastic, Inc., 1998. In alphabet-book format, this book advocates preservation of species that still exist today. It's a useful model for adapting any social need into an alphabet book.

Get Curious; Get Questions

When you don't ask the right questions you get stuck.
Dion

The cure for boredom is curiosity. There is no cure for curiosity.
Ellen Parr

The Point: Curious questions open new doors in persuasive writing. The following lesson, which can be used to explore any subject, teaches students to ask questions that go beyond concerns to find the positions and interests that lie beneath them.

Teaching it:

Questions are fuel to ideas. Ask one question and you find several more. Thoughts sprout branches when we ask questions. If you don't believe me try this.

1. Write down one concern from your list. For example, "People having wars."

2. Now ask as many questions as you can in five minutes. For example, why do people have wars? When was the first war? Are there more wars today than there were years ago? What is war? Will wars last forever? How does war affect countries?
(Set timer) Begin.

(Share)
3. Now look at your questions and try sorting them by types. Here are some suggestions.

Factual questions: When was the first war?
Wonder questions: Why do we have wars?
Silly questions: What if people made guns that shot candy?

Look at all the questions we generated in such a short time. Whenever you get stuck in your writing, try asking questions.

Debriefing:
Which questions interest you? Which bore you?
Is there a particular type of question that intrigues you more than another?

Spin-offs:
- Make a poster called "Types of Questions" and hang it in class.

- Go to the library or the Internet and try researching just one of your more interesting questions.

- Practice writing down questions whenever you have a spare moment. Keep a small notebook and see how long it takes you to fill it with questions. Go back over your questions and circle the ones which spark your curiosity. Try answering these.

For Younger Writers:

- Write an illustrate a picture book with a title like "A Book of Questions."

- Brainstorm a list of unanswerable questions, then try to answer them in a poem.

"Where do poems hide?"

Poems hide in your eyes
    when you look at me.
Poems hide in your heart
    at every beat.
Poems hide in your face
    because it's so beautiful.
Poems hide in your
    blushing red cheeks.
Poems hide in your
    elegant hands every time
    you stroke my face.

Madeline Jurish, age 7

Resources:

Fox, Mem. *Wilfrid Gordon McDonald Partridge*. Brooklyn: Kane/Miller Publishing, 1985. In this picture book a young boy helps an old lady regain her past by asking everyone in the nursing home, "What is a memory?"

Nicholaus, Bret and Paul Lowrie. *The Mom and Dad Conversation Piece: Creative Questions to Honor the Family*. New York: Ballantine Books, 1997. This wonderful, small collection contains 256 thought-provoking questions which uncover family values, choices and culture.

Neruda, Pablo. *The Book of Questions*. Port Townsend, Washington: Copper Canyon Press, 1991. This entire book is comprised of poetry, all in question form. "Do we learn kindness, or the mask of kindness?"

Decisions Being Made Right Now: A Newspaper Hunt

Living in a vacuum sucks.
Adrienne Gusoff

The Point: To be empowered citizens, students need to see the immediate need for their clear voices. The first step is to become conscious of the thousands of adult decisions that are made daily right under their noses. The following lesson helps students to see this world of decisions and start forming their own opinions.

Teaching it:

Decisions are being made all the time. Some affect us directly, some indirectly. Here is today's newspaper. Think about the world news. Think about the local news.

What changes do you think are being made right now, here in town? (Brainstorm for a few minutes.)

Take a piece of paper and fold it down the middle vertically. On the left-hand side, title the column "About Me." On the right-hand side, title the column "Not Affecting Me." (Demonstrate.)

For the next 20 minutes, scan a newspaper with your group. Look for anything you can find that looks like a decision is being considered somewhere. Jot it down on the side of your paper where you think it belongs.

Debriefing:

How easy was it to find change?
When you look at your two lists, which is longer?
What other issues could you stick on the left or right side?
Why do most of us limit our concerns to the local?

Student responses, from reading a March, 1999 copy of the *San Antonio Express:*

About Me:
Should students be able to buy soda during the school day?
When students get in trouble with the law off school grounds, should schools have the right to expel them?
Should gym classes be co-ed?
Should students pressure other students to drink?
Should people listen to horoscopes?
What's the best way to clear up a complexion?
Is it better to go to the prom with a date or with a friend?
Should we continue the practice of electing a prom queen and king?

Not Affecting Me:
Should people give their time to help other people?

Should we keep bombing Kosovo?
Should we recognize/reward basketball stars?
Who should win best daytime soap actor?

Spin-offs:

- Choose one of the issues from the bank your class makes. Research an address of someone in authority, someone who has the power to vote on a policy, rule, or law from the list above. Write a letter to that person, expressing your view.

- What are some issues not on the list which you think do affect you more? Make your own list.

- Identify the issues present in a novel your class reads. As a character from the novel, identify your position about one or more issues, and address it to another character, or to a person in authority in the novel.

For Younger Writers:

- Parent issues: imagine rules you will be making for your children when you are a parent. Write what you will tell them about your feelings about one of the rules.

- Controversy Cards: Jeff Anderson, a teacher at Rogers Middle School in San Antonio, keeps a file of perfect, short, colorful articles laminated onto 5 x 8 cards, which he uses to have students debate and formulate persuasion. Where does he get the articles? Old issues of *Scholastic Magazine*. Create your own controversy cards.

- Make a collage of photos from magazines or newspapers that show people making decisions. Add thought bubbles above the heads of the people that describe their decision-making process.

Resources:

The local newspaper

Galvan, Peggy, ed. *365 Ways You Can Make the World a Better Place in the New Millennium*. New York: Troll, 1999. This little paperback is packed with ideas written by students, useful either as a bank of ideas, or as a model for publishing.

Scholes, Katherine. *Peace Begins With You*. New York: Little, Brown & Co, 1989. This book is non-fiction and good for an activism resource.

Lionni, Leo. *Six Crows*. New York: Scholastic, Inc., 1988. This fable demonstrates the need for dialogue for solving group survival problems.

> **Person 1:** What do you think about apathy?
> **Person 2:** I don't know and I don't care.

Dear Class

What you teach your own children is what you really believe in.
Cathy Warner Weatherford

The Point: When teachers get passionate about something, it gives students permission to get passionate too. Displaying your curiosity on a regular basis is probably the best way to charge up the batteries of your students' opinions.

Teaching it:

(Gretchen Bernabei wrote a letter to her sixth grade class. To see how they reacted, turn to the appendix and read the article, "Baby Steps: Story of a Peace Movement." Write your own letter to your students about a problem you have struggled with. Raise questions like the ones Gretchen did, suggest solutions, and most important of all, ask your students to respond.)

Lately I've been thinking a lot about something and have decided to write you a letter about it. I made a copy of my letter for each of you and would like you to take a few minutes to write back to me.

(Read, respond, and share responses.)

Debriefing:

What was it like to answer my letter?
Did you say what you wanted to or did you hold back because I am your teacher?
What should we do from this point?
Is just expressing it enough?

Example:

Dear Students,
Today in class when I looked at your faces, I could picture you as young children. I imagined what you might have looked like when you were three years old. And when I tried to tell you about something that happened over the week-end, I couldn't finish. So I hope you will read this and know it comes from somewhere deep in my heart, to each one of you.

It started Sunday, when Matilde was in her crib, taking a nap. I opened up the newspaper and saw the front page. There was a story about the little boy who was watching TV at home one night a couple of weeks ago. Both of his parents were there. There was a drive-by shooting, and a bullet went through the wall and shattered his arm.

Do you know what he said? When he realized that something was very, very wrong? He said, "Oh, Daddy."

Imagine. A shot had ripped apart his arm, and he took a breath and said, "Oh, Daddy."
Take a little breath and say those words to yourself. "Oh, Daddy."

Now imagine being a daddy. Imagine hearing shots outside and trying to tell your family to get down. And then you hear your little three-year-old son take a breath and say, "Oh, Daddy." Imagine doing all you can to protect your family and hearing one of your precious children say those words.

Now imagine your own mother or father. Can you picture how they used to look at you, full of love, when you were three? Now can you imagine your mother's face when the doctors take you away from her?

Whose family deserves that? Nobody's. Nobody's.

Well, my heart ached for that little boy, for his daddy, for his mama, and for his three little sisters. I read that they had no home now. The mother and father had been sharing a little bed in the hospital. I stared at the newspaper, thinking about the extra room we have in our house. We don't have money, but I felt that we had so much, a safe house and a big yard. I felt like it might be crazy, and maybe they might not need it or want it, but I just felt like I had to offer to share what we have with them. Where would they go?

So after talking it over with my husband David, a little later in the afternoon, I went to the only place I knew to find them. Matilde sat in her carseat, and I drove to the Santa Rosa Children's Hospital. I wasn't sure what to say to Leticia and Edward, but I had to go see them. Room 608, the information lady told me.

I watched Matilde's face on the elevator. She was jabbering baby-talk as it went up, and we soon found room 608. I knocked on the door and heard, "Come in."

Leticia, the mother, turned and looked at me when I walked in. I could see that she was tired but beautiful. I glanced over at the patient with his arm up in the air, in traction. I really wasn't prepared for how he looked, even though I had seen his picture in the newspaper. In real life, he looked so tiny. Little Edward. His eyes were tired-sparkly, beautiful brown. His head turned to look at his mom, and his neck was so little on the pillow.

His mother and I talked to each other for a few minutes, and she told me that they had found an apartment which they would be moving into soon. I told her that she and her family were welcome at our house if they needed it for a day, an afternoon, a week, whatever. We only talked for a few minutes about what it had been like that night. I gave her our phone number.

As I left, I turned at the door. I wanted to say, "God bless you." My voice just wouldn't come out. So with Matilde in my arms, I closed the door.

Do you know any three-year-olds? Do you know how it feels to put your arms around a little puppy-warm doll-body and hoist him or her up on your hip? How you run around acting insane to get them to laugh? Words are still new to a three-year-old mouth. You want to watch them living in a world of play, and laughing with the world from waking-up time until tucking-in time. That's cool.

So now I think about gangs. Groups of friends? Friends who look out for you? That's not too bad. But people who pick up weapons and say that the law is bad? People who write F.T.P.? F.T.L.? Who hired these police? Who made these laws? We people did. You did. Your parents did. Their parents did.

Who shot that three-year-old? All gang members did. Anyone who ever touches a gun and thinks it would be fun did. Anyone who ever stops thinking about other people's rights did. Every fifteen-year-old who mouths off at a teacher so he won't look like a wimp did. Every person who scribbles a gang name on a book-cover did. Every person who passes gang graffiti and doesn't stop to erase it did. We all had a part in pulling the trigger when Edward was shot.

Who can stop gang violence? We all can. But students, you more than anyone can. How? By knowing how uncool gangs are. Selfishness is not cool. It's not cool to hurt others. It's not cool to destroy. It's not cool to take. It's not cool to kill. Picture your mama's face. Picture your family members. Listen to the little voice taking a breath and saying, "Oh, Daddy." Listen to that voice, students. It's the voice of your own children. Let's join together to give, to make the world a better place, everywhere we go. No one is alone when we love each other. God bless you.

Love,
Gretchen Bernabei

Spin-offs:
- Have your students write back to you and you write one letter back to them. Create a year-long correspondence. Create a book with highlights of the correspondence.

- Write to an expert in a field that concerns you.

- In 1987 a sixth grader named Samantha Smith wrote a letter to Soviet leader Mikhail Gorbachev. The letter made world news when Gorbachev read it at a press conference. Write your own letter to a world leader. Raise questions in your letter and demand answers. Get passionate. Find the address of the political leader and mail your letter.

For Younger Writers:
- Read the picture book *Dear Mr. Blueberry* to your class. Mr. Blueberry is an expert on whales and Emily writes him to tell him about the whale in her backyard pond.

- Pick an endangered species and write a letter to a wildlife expert. Pretend you are the expert and write back.

Resources:

Appendix 14, Bernabei, Gretchen. "Babysteps: Story of a Peace Movement," *Voices from the Middle* 3, 2 (April, 1996): 19-24. Urbana, IL: 1995. This article tells the story of how one letter, expressed to students, turned into action all over the neighborhood.

James, Simon. *Dear Mr. Blueberry.* New York: Simon and Schuster, 1996.
This sweet picture book traces the correspondence between a little girl name Emily and an expert on whales. Emily thinks there is a whale in her pond, and Mr. Blueberry must convince her otherwise.

Students painting hearts over gang graffiti.

The Power of One: Action and Forgiveness

You will find as you look back upon your life that the moments when you have truly lived are the moments when you have done things in the spirit of love.
Henry Drummond

Do not wait for leaders; do it alone, person to person.
Mother Teresa

The Point: When we ask students to write about what affects them, they often ignore the larger world in favor of the smaller one. In other words, they may be more concerned about the politics of a new vending machine in the school and less about the AIDS crisis in Africa. This blind spot comes partly from living in a consumer culture which has learned to successfully cut itself off from the world of humanity and dwell in the world of material things. It also comes from the egocentrism of youth, but we all know that our students will surprise us when we give them cause to, especially when we show them role models their own age who have made a difference in the world. The following lesson will help open the discussion of what it means to put your personal grievances behind you and become a citizen of a larger world.

Teaching it:

Take out a piece of paper and number it to nine. I'll ask questions, and you write a short answer for each one. The first five questions are about action. The next five are about forgiveness.

1. What does it mean to take action?
2. What stops people from taking action?
3. Have you ever felt like there was something going on that you really wished you could change? What was it?
4. Can you think of one way to make the world a better place?
5. Can you think of times in your life when you have had to forgive someone?
6. When should we forgive?
7. When should we not forgive?
8. What is the effect of forgiving and not forgiving?
9. What, in your opinion, are the world's top three problems? List them.

(Share and discuss)

Here is a story about one girl who decided to make a difference. Listen to her story as you think about which problem you'd like to work on:

When Anisa Kintz was eight, she was bothered by racial divisions everywhere, including her Conway, S.C., school playground. So Anisa founded an organization to promote unity and named it "Calling All Colors." Today, Calling All Colors has grown to include 26,000 students from places as far away as New Zealand.

Teaching it:

When Anisa held her first Calling All Colors conference five years ago, she decided she didn't want members to just listen to a lot of adult speakers. "We decided to create [opportunities] for kids to talk about their experiences with racism," Anisa says. Most important, participants are taught how to fight racism in their own communities.

Choose one problem of your own now. Explain why it's a problem and what you think should be done about it.

(Share and publish)

Debriefing:

What stops us right now from taking action?   How many people share the same feelings we have?

What do we want to do about it?   Did anyone think you were the only one who felt as you do? What changed?

Spin-offs:

* Do one thing good for someone else just for the sake of it. Report to the class about it.

* Write a skit that defines a problem you would like to do something about. Include the solution to your problem in your skit.

* Read the story of Amy Biehl, keeping an eye on the work of her parents. Write about times in your life when you had to forgive someone who had wronged you. How did it affect you? How does not forgiving help or hurt us?

* Create an action plan for yourself.

For Younger Writers:

* Make a poster to promote one of the causes from your list.

* Write a top ten poem about the cause of your choice. Example: "Top Ten Ways to Save the Rain Forest."

* Write a poem called, "Top Ten Reasons to Forgive _____."

Resources: Appendix 15

Appendix 15, Stories of Young People Who Made a Difference.

Free the Children, International. 7 May 2001. http://freethechildren.org. Twelve-year-old Craig Kielburger started this web site to help children combat child slavery worldwide.

Amy Biehl Foundation, Perpetuating Amy's Work in South Africa. 5 May 2001. http://amybiehl.org. Read the inspiring story of Amy Biehl, whose parents forgave her murderers and continue her work to help continue the freedom struggle in the new South Africa.

Write Around

Never doubt that a small group of thoughtful, committed citizens can change the world. Indeed, it is the only thing that ever has.
Margaret Mead

The Point: Ideas and opinions thrive through interaction. The write around allows students to pass notes in order to dig up authentic issues and questions through thinking on the paper. Try this lesson with your students, then take it to a faculty meeting to tackle the latest issues.

Teaching it:

(Students will do a short freewrite, focusing on an opinion they have of some rule or policy they think needs changing. Then they will pass their writing to another student, who will read the writing and then add his or her own "take" about that issue.)

Do you love getting notes? Have you ever noticed that sometimes you start by trying to say something to someone else about what you think and you end up finding out what you think? Today we're going to write notes.

Get into a group of three or four people. Bring paper and a writing instrument.

Now think about an issue to write about, something going on in the world or in our community that bothers you, that you'd like to sound off about. Once you have an issue, write a note for five minutes about your issue. Raise questions in your writing, tell your opinion or simply describe the matter in detail.

(After five minutes, say "pass." Students will pass their paper to the next student.)

Read the paper you were just passed. Pretend you overheard that person saying what you're reading, and then chime in on the conversation.

(Teacher keeps time, saying "pass" every five minutes, until three or four people have responded.)

When you get your note back, read it over.

(Share.)

Debriefing:

When you got your note back and read what others wrote, did anything surprise you? What?
What interesting questions arose in your notes?
Did you have enough time to write or were you longing to write more?
What were the key points of agreement in your write around?
What were the key points of disagreement?

Spin-offs:

- Extract a few central ideas gathered in your write around and write an exploratory draft of a position paper.

- Pick a crisis in the world or in a story. Identify the conflict from each point of view and do a write around where each person's job is to take the opposite point of view of the person who writes to him or her. When you get your paper back, pretend you are a mediator. Find the common interests of the two parties and draft a compromise that might serve both parties.

- Try a "talk around" where one person talks for five minutes and everyone in the group of three listens. Then the next person talks for four minutes. Everyone listens. Then the next person talks for three minutes and everybody listens. Write down key points in the conversation where people agree or disagree. Use these as a jumping off point for exploratory writing.

- This is a fun way to talk without paper. Get a small pillow or cushiony ball to pass around. Students get into groups of five. Decide on an issue to work with. When you throw the ball you say a word that symbolizes the problem. When the person catches it they must have a word that stands for the solution.

Example:

Thrower:	Fear
Catcher:	Hope
Thrower:	Hate
Catcher:	Love

Resources:

Appendix 16 a b

Appendix 16a, Essay by Andrew Green, about note-passing in class.

Appendix 16b, Student samples of write arounds.

Weisenthal, Simon. *The Sunflower: On the Possibilities and Limits of Forgiveness.* New York: Schocken Books, 1997. Weisenthal writes a letter to the world about his experience as a concentration camp prisoner, when a dying German soldier asks him for forgiveness for atrocities against Jews. Weisenthal refuses to grant it but years later sends his story to famous people all over the world and asks what they would have done. This book contains their responses. Your students can write their own.

We Have a Dream

I have a dream that my four little children will one day live in a nation where they will not be judged by the color of their skin but by the content of their character. I have a dream…

Martin Luther King, Jr.

The Point: Racism is still America's most challenging issue, but if it weren't for activist citizens like Rosa Parks and Martin Luther King, where would we be today? However, each generation has the power to find its own cure for the cancer of racism, and it begins by having students reexamine history and look forward. The following lesson helps students get inside the past and dream of a better future.

Teaching it:

(Tell the story of Rosa Parks or Martin Luther King, Jr. Below are two ways to do the same lesson. One uses Rosa Parks, the other Martin Luther King Jr.)

At the Lorraine Hotel in Memphis, Tennessee there is a plaster cast of Rosa Parks. She sits on the original bus behind the plaster cast of the driver who yelled at her to sit in the back and slammed his wooden stick. It's not unusual to see young children sitting beside Rosa Parks and whispering in her ear. What would you whisper to her? What are your dreams for the future? Can you persuade the world to know they are true?

Pretend for a minute you are sitting beside Rosa Parks. What would you say to her about the world you live in? What could you tell her about the future? What would you say to her?

In 1963, before 250,000 people, Martin Luther King, Jr. gave his famous "I Have a Dream" speech. Let's read it together.

(Read the speech aloud with your class.)

Let's think about Dr. King's dream. Has it come true yet? If not, why not? If you could talk to Dr. King, what would you say to him? Write a letter to Dr. King or create your own "I have a dream" speech.

Debriefing:

What issues did you raise in your letters or speeches?
What is the biggest obstacle to the elimination of racism?
Have you been a victim of racism? How?
Have you been a perpetrator of racism? How?
Why do we care about race?

Spin-offs:

• Write and deliver your own "I have a dream" speech to your class. Make a personal action plan to make your dream a reality.

- Read Alis Headlam's editorial, "Confronting Racism," Appendix 17. Do you agree or disagree with her? Write your own plan for eliminating racism.

- Underline the most striking lines in Martin Luther King's speech. Copy them on paper and arrange them into a poem adding your own words to bind them together.

- Imagine a racist, a person who believes in the importance of hating people not like himself or herself. Write a letter to this person trying to persuade him or her to reexamine racist opinions. Remember to use real examples to back up your position. You must convince the person, not simply yell at him or her.

- Make up a story about overcoming racism.

For Younger Writers:

- With several partners, create a dance that describes the journey from slavery to freedom. Use the work of the Bahai Youth Workshop (see Resources) as a model.

- Make a list of words that have to do with racism, slavery and hate. Next, make a list that has to do with love, tolerance, freedom. Build a poem, alternating these words for effect.

- Pretend you are person living hundreds of years in the future when racism is a thing of the distant and uncivilized past. Write a description of the period of Rosa Parks and Martin Luther King. Describe your understanding of what racism was and why it existed.

Resources: Appendix 17

Appendix 17, "Confronting Racism," by Alis Headlam.

Bahai Youth Workshop. 11 May 2001. <http://www.geocities.com/Athens/9144/>. The Bahai Youth Workshop is a non-profit organization that sponsors a traveling troupe of teenagers who perform dances which express unity in diversity and healing the racial divide. For information on the group nearest you.

Colbert, Jan, Ann McMillan Harm, and Roy Cajero. *Dear Dr. King: Letters from Today's Children to Dr. Martin Luther King, Jr.* New York: Hyperion Books for Children, 2000. This small paperback contains letters from today's children to Dr. King.

Martin Luther King, Jr. 8 May 2001. http://www.stanford.edu/group/King/ You can find the "I have a dream" speech and all his collected work on this web site.

Ringgold, Faith. *My Dream of Martin Luther King.* New York: Dragonfly Books, 1998. The story of Martin Luther King told through a child's fictional dream.

Ringgold, Faith. *If a Bus Could Talk: The Story of Rosa Parks.* New York: Simon & Schuster, 1999. The story of Rosa Parks told through a fictional all-knowing bus. This book tells a painful story through the safety of an historical frame.

Mankind Was My Business: Lessons from Marley's Ghost

"It is required of every man," the Ghost returned, *"that the spirit within him should walk abroad among his fellowmen, and travel far and wide; and if that spirit goes not forth in life, it is condemned to do so after death. It is doomed to wander through the world.*
Jacob Marley's ghost, from *A Christmas Carol* by Charles Dickens

The Point: Life is precious. Each moment counts. Yet many strive only for their own little piece of the pie and neglect any larger responsibilities. We literally mind our own business and forget our larger purpose. Like Scrooge in the beginning of Dickens's famous *A Christmas Carol,* we forget that mankind is our business. In some ways the whole story of *A Christmas Carol* is a persuasive essay aimed at Scrooge and the miserly part of him that lives in all of us. Jacob Marley's ghost frames the argument, and the three spirits provide the convincing elaboration to transform the old curmudgeon. Examining Marley's speeches in the first section of Dickens's classic can help students of any age reflect on the urgent need to act in ways that enhance all humanity.

Teaching it:

(Read A Christmas Carol to students, or play tape.)

If we look at *A Christmas Carol* as a persuasive essay, whom is it persuading? Obviously, Ebenezer Scrooge starts out as a mean spirited old geezer and ends up a loving and giving human being. The question I have is, "What does he realize at the end that he doesn't know at the beginning?"

In this excerpt, the ghost of Jacob Marley speaks with Ebenezer Scrooge. Scrooge tries to console Marley by telling him he was always a good man of business.

"Business!" cried the Ghost, wringing its hands again. "Mankind was my business. The common welfare was my business; charity, mercy, forbearance, and benevolence were, all, my business. The dealings of my trade were but a drop of water in the comprehensive ocean of my business!"

It held up its chain at arm's length, as if that were the cause of all its unavailing grief, and flung it heavily upon the ground again.

"At this time of the rolling year," the spectre said, "I suffer most. Why did I walk through crowds of fellow-beings with my eyes turned down, and never raise them to that blessed Star which led the Wise Men to a poor abode? Were there no poor homes to which its light would have conducted me?"

Scrooge was very much dismayed to hear the spectre going on at this rate, and began to quake exceedingly.

"Hear me!" cried the Ghost. "My time is nearly gone."

(Later Jacob Marley's ghost walks to the window and pulls back the sash.)

Teaching it:

The apparition walked backward from him; and at every step it took, the window raised itself a little, so that when the spectre reached it, it was wide open. It beckoned Scrooge to approach, which he did. When they were within two paces of each other, Marley's Ghost held up its hand, warning him to come no nearer. Scrooge stopped.

Not so much in obedience, as in surprise and fear: for on the raising of the hand, he became sensible of confused noises in the air; incoherent sounds of lamentation and regret; wailings inexpressibly sorrowful and self-accusatory. The spectre, after listening for a moment, joined in the mournful dirge; and floated out upon the bleak, dark night.

Scrooge followed to the window: desperate in his curiosity. He looked out.

The air was filled with phantoms, wandering hither and thither in restless haste, and moaning as they went. Every one of them wore chains like Marley's Ghost; some few (they might be guilty governments) were linked together; none were free. Many had been personally known to Scrooge in their lives. He had been quite familiar with one old ghost, in a white waistcoat, with a monstrous iron safe attached to its ankle, who cried piteously at being unable to assist a wretched woman with an infant, whom it saw below, upon a door-step. The misery with them all was, clearly, that they sought to interfere, for good, in human matters, and had lost the power forever.

What does this scene mean to you? What is Marley's ghost telling Scrooge? Why is he telling it?

Try writing Marley's message as an essay or a poem.

Debriefing:

What things in your life are like Scrooge at the beginning of *A Christmas Carol?*
Which things in your life reflect Scrooge at the end of *A Christmas Carol?*

Resources:

Dickens, Charles. *A Christmas Carol.* http://www.dickens.com.

Patrick Stewart Audio tape. Stewart's one-man audio play brings the heart of *A Christmas Carol* alive.

Spin-offs:

* Draw a picture or make an abstract painting or a sculpture to represent what Marley's Ghost is telling us about life on Earth

* Design a dance called the Marley Scrooge that illustrates Marley's message to Scrooge. (Note: Tire chains might prove a great accessory.)

- Write a play of your own and make your own updated version of *A Christmas Carol*.

For Younger Writers:

- Draw a picture of Jacob Marley's ghost and then one of Scrooge at the end of the story. Write about your drawings.

- "I bear the chains I forged in life," Marley's ghost says. What does he mean by this? What are the things that chain us in life? What are the things that free us? Make a construction paper chain, writing one thing from your list on each link.

- Pretend you are Ebenezer Scrooge at the end of *A Christmas Carol*. In your journal write three things you might do today to show your transformation.

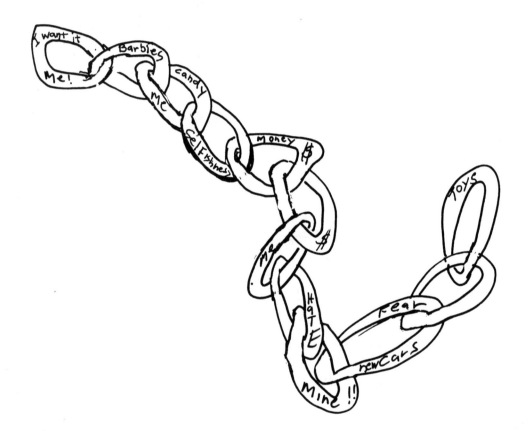

Persuasion in Literature

Literature was not born the day when a boy crying "wolf, wolf" came running out of the Neanderthal valley with a big gray wolf at his heels: literature was born on the day when a boy came crying "wolf, wolf" and there was no wolf behind him.

Vladamir Nabokov

"To be or not to be."

Hamlet (stating his position)

For English teachers, literature provides a treasure trove of persuasive rhetoric. How do fictional characters conduct themselves and use persuasion? How do the characters get themselves out of scrapes? How do they fashion their own destinies? How do they change their worlds? Imagine the mental processes students use when scanning through a plot, looking for moments when "plain old information" becomes a struggle between wills, a challenge, a fight of some kind. These are the moments that adult readers notice easily, but sometimes these conflicts pass right over younger readers who read more for plot than for character. The result? "This is boring."

On the other hand, when students take on the role of the character and speak in the character's voice, they engage in an amazingly complex combination of skills. At the very least, they are matching word choice to fit setting, character, and dialectical requirements; they are adapting the forms and conventions of language to suit the genre of writing they have chosen. But on a larger scale, the very act of pretending or role-playing means that they operate within a system of rules and symbols, systems that Lev Vygotsky describes as important for several reasons: it provides them with practice in developing appropriate voice for an audience and is also a precursor to civilized behavior.

Simply put, language play makes us better people, and the fun and creativity make it painless too!

This chapter begins with a lesson to help refresh students' working definitions of persuasion with detailed lists of how persuasion functions. Next is a lesson to guide students as they scan a piece of literature with a persuasive search-lens, seeking and listing moments in which any character tries to persuade anyone else to do something. Then with a list of characters' persuasion goals, students can do so much more than just write an advertisement or an essay. They can reenter the literature and speak as the character, using the persuasive rhetorical devices appropriate to setting, purpose, and audience.

What is the end result in their writing? You'll see a wider array of well-toned writing muscles and more willingness to pick and choose from among their rhetorical tricks.

Persuasion in Literature: Preparation – Step 1

A man never tells you anything until you contradict him.
George Bernard Shaw

The Point: Students can find dozens of instances of persuasion in any story. Before they can begin the hunt, though, a little readiness will help them start off on the same foot, with the same idea of what exactly it is that they are hunting for. The first step in analyzing stories for instances of persuasion is to make a concrete list of what persuasion is, what it does, and what it looks like. You may want to refer back to similar lessons in chapter one. This list will be useful as a reference tool when students address pieces of literature.

Teaching it:

What is persuasion? Not in school, but in the real world, what is persuasive talking and writing? Why do people do it?

(Have students answer aloud, or on paper if they are a quiet group, and then amass their answers into a list.)

Debriefing:
What do these things have in common?
What does persuasion NOT do?

Student responses:
Fourth grade
To convince someone to give you something
To convince someone to buy you something
To goad someone into doing something else
To goad someone into doing you a favor
To convince someone to agree with you

Ninth grade
To get something for themselves
To gain something
To get revenge
To get people on their side
To get someone to see something their way
To get followers
To make people change their minds
To manipulate in some way
To sell something

Eleventh grade

To remove obstacles

To ask for something

To control someone

To bring in customers

To get someone to think like we do

To get someone to look at it my way

To instigate, i.e. confrontation

To cause someone to change their thoughts

To keep others from reaching their goals

Spin-off:

• Choose any one of the goals. Create a scene, either as yourself or as a character from a book.

• Here's a fun one. There is a new game show on TV. It's called "Persuasion." Decide what the show is about, how the contestants compete, how it is scored, etc.

• Bring in persuasive ads that you think are aimed at people your age. Explain to the class exactly how each ad works. What do you have to believe in order to believe the ad?

For Younger Writers:

• Think of a time when you got what you wanted. What method of persuasion did you use? What works best with Mom? What works best with Dad? What works best with everybody?

• Make up an ad for the best method of persuasion.

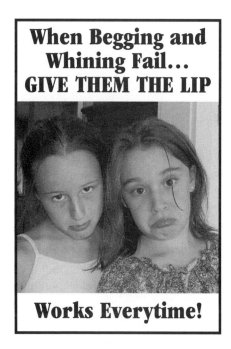

Treasure Hunt for Moments of Persuasion in Literature – Step 2

"Little pig, little pig, let me in!"
        B.B. Wolf (stating his position)
"Not by the hair of my chinny chin chin."
        Little pig (stating his position)

The Point: Two forms of persuasion are prevalent in classrooms: advertisements and persuasive essays. In real life, however, persuasion is pervasive and takes many forms, and this is mirrored in literature. Knowing how to create persuasion is not the only useful set of skills for creative, problem-solving students; recognizing persuasion in motion is also valuable.

    First, the teacher will direct the students to focus on a story that they all know. Together, they'll look at the list they created in the preparation exercise and find moments in the story where any of those goals are being tried. This exercise will simply compile a list of moments in a work which can be used further in subsequent exercises.

Teaching it:

Let's think about what we just read together.

Now let's look at the list we compiled, "What persuasion does."

Can you think of any moments in the story where someone is trying to do any of these things?

(Use some examples as models.)

Take several minutes and list as many moments like this as you can.

(Compile their responses into a larger list.)

Debriefing:
What patterns do you see in the lists we've compiled?
Why is there so much persuasion in literature?

Student responses:
Younger Writers:
Moments of persuasion in "The Three Little Pigs"
The wolf tries to convince the first pig to let him in.
The first pig tries to convince the wolf that he can't come in.
The wolf tries to convince the second pig to let him in.
The second pig tries to convince the wolf that he can't come in.

Moments of persuasion in *The Odyssey*
Telemachus tries to persuade the nurse not to tell his mother he is leaving.
Athena begs Zeus to let Odysseus return home safely.
Athena persuades Zeus to send Hermes to order Calypso's release of Odysseus.
Hermes persuades Calypso that she must give up Odysseus forever.
Calypso tries to persuade Odysseus to stay and be immortal with her.
Calypso tries to convince Odysseus that she is better than Penelope.
Nestor persuades Telemachus to search for his father in Sparta.
Athena persuades Telemachus to become "his father's son".

Moments of persuasion in *Romeo and Juliet*
Paris convinces the Capulets that he should marry their daughter.
Romeo persuades Juliet that his affection isn't fake.
Friar Laurence tries to convince Romeo that he's in too big a rush.
Tybalt persuades Romeo to fight.
The Nurse tries to convince Juliet to forget Romeo and marry Paris.
Juliet tries to persuade the Nurse to take her to the church.
Juliet tries to persuade Friar Laurence to give her sleeping drugs.
Capulet tries to convince Juliet to marry Paris.
Capulet convinces Tybalt to leave Romeo alone at the feast.
The Prince tries to convince the two families not to fight any more.
Romeo's friends convince him to go to the Capulets' party.
Romeo persuades the apothecary to sell him poison.

Moments of Persuasion in *To Kill A Mockingbird*
Scout tries to convince Jem not to go after his pants.
Atticus tries to persuade the jury of Tom Robinson's innocence.
Calpurnia persuades Atticus that Tim Johnson has rabies.
Atticus tries to convince Scout not to beat people up.
Scout tries to convince the teacher about the Cunninghams' ways.
Mayella tries to convince the town that Tom Robinson tried to rape her.
Mr. Ewell tries to convince the jury that he saw a rape.
Sheriff Heck Tate tries to convince Atticus that Mr. Ewell's death wasn't the children's fault.

Spin-offs:

• Write about the trends you notice in the work. (See sample, Appendix 20.)

• Choose a character and a moment, and practice the character's rhetorical persuasive skills in essay form, developing classical reasoning and using one of several structural forms.

• Write about the relationship between persuasion and plot. (Can there be a plot without moments of persuasion? Does conflict always result in persuasion? Does all problem-solving require characters to take positions and defend them?)

For Younger Writers:

- Write the character's words (real, imagined, or both) in a word bubble, and draw the speaker. At the bottom, write, "My name is (character's name) and I want _____." And at the top, "A persuasive moment from (name of work_)." For example, Austin fourth-grader Tanya Arana writes, "My name is Charlotte and I want to tell people not to eat Wilbur," and "A Moment of Convincing from Charlotte's Web."

- Take any single moment and rewrite the speech or conversation, using your own imagined words.

- Rewrite the moment in a modern setting.

- For a major project or a group project, make a character journal similar to The Jolly Postman, embedding a number of pieces described above.

- Act out a persuasive scene from a story, but do so in your own words.

Tanya Arana

Resources:

Ahlberg, Janet and Allan Ahlbert. *The Jolly Postman*. Boston: Little, Brown and Company, 1986. Many different genres of writing are incorporated into this clever book. It's a perfect model for unifying different pieces into one thematic thread.

Moss, Marissa. *Amelia's Notebook*. Berkeley: Tricycle Press, 1995. This delightful journal demonstrates a hybrid between journaling and scrapbooking and can serve as a perfect model for turning an assignment like "Ten persuasive moments in Huck Finn" into "Huck Finn's journal."

Romano, Tom. *Blending Genre, Altering Style*. Portsmouth: Boynton/Cook Publishers, 2000. Tom Romano has pioneered the "multi-genre" style of writing research reports, and this use of multiple genres is easily adapted to a study of persuasion in literature.

Jacqueline Peréz

Stepping into a Character's Shoes – Step 3

A detective digs around in the garbage of people's lives. A novelist invents people and then digs around in their garbage.

Joe Gores

Hamlet as performed at the Brooklyn Shakespeare Festival: "To be, or what?"

Steven Pearl

The Point: Now that students have thought about persuasion and located persuasive moments in literature, they are all set to create original persuasion from within the piece of literature. If they choose one moment from the list of persuasive moments, and one form of writing from the genre list, they are ready to start playing with a point of view, and through this play they begin unraveling and analyzing the literature you study.

As a teacher, you can use this in many ways, from comprehension quizzes to final projects. Along with knowledge of persuasion, activities like this promote knowledge of character, plot, dialect, style and acting. They also help engage and motivate students.

Teaching it:

Choose one of the moments of persuasion from your list. Now look at the genre list. Adopt the voice of the speaker and write the moment in another form or genre: poem, children's book, want-ads, scripted telephone conversation, letter from one character to another, diary entry, legal document, prayer, song, whatever fits best, in your opinion.

Debriefing:

Does your writing mirror the point of view of the character you chose? If so, how?

Student Responses:

Write a real estate ad to sell Wuthering Heights to a prospective buyer. Be sure to include details about the structure.

> For sale: Wuthering Heights. A delightful manor in the English moor. Quietly removed from society, this Gothic style house is perfect for any misanthropist. Strong foundation and deeply set windows protect the house from England's stormy weather. The plethora of grotesque carvings around the door give this house its own uniqueness. You'll forget the gloomy exterior when you step inside. The house has plenty of room and dark corners. The chimney will warm you on those cold English nights. Very historical. Come by and see for yourself! - Lauren Sewell, 10th grade

Write an ad for *Animal Farm,* the movie.

> Tired of going out and watching the same human heroes beat overrated animal antagonists? Then "herd" on over to your nearest theater and go see *Animal Farm*. These overworked and underfed "Beasts of England" have had enough of Mr. Jones and they want the farm…for themselves!

Ladies, lonely on Sunday nights as your boyfriends watch "pig-skin"? Then join the "flock" and watch as our four-legged and feathered friends fight for their rights!

"Two legs bad and four thumbs up!" say Siskil and Ebert. So rebel against the old TV reruns and movies, and join Old Major, Snowball, Boxer, Moses, Napoleon, Squealer and the other animals on Manor Farm as they change it to Animal Farm! Remember, to them, man is the other white meat. - Gwen Adams, 9th grade

Resources:

Appendix 21abc

Appendix 21a, Student Multigenre Samples from *The Odyssey*. From Calypso's plea to Odysseus to stay, to a recipe for a hero, students demonstrate what happens when they match up a moment of persuasion with a choice from the genre list.

Appendix 21b, Genre List. This list is a bare-bones but exhaustive list of many forms of writing as they exist in the real world. Students can match up persuasive moments to the types of writing here and produce wonderful surprises.

Appendix 21c, Treasury of Projects. On this list, students find instructions for many writing projects in many different forms, complete with instructions for converting moments from literature into the various forms.

Appendix 21d, Student Sample: Cyclops, Redrawn by Brendan Keifer. The Cyclops never looked so good.

Lane, Barry. *51 Wacky We-search Reports* Shoreham, VT: Discover Writing Press, 2001. This book, written for students grades 3 –8 and beyond, models funny research papers and illustrates time-proven techniques for facing the facts with fun.

Maguire, Gregory. *Wicked: The Life and Times of the Wicked Witch of the West*. New York: Harper Collins Publishers, 1995. This wonderful novel is told by Dorothy's wicked witch. It's a perfect example of speaking as a character.

Scieszka, Jon. *The True Story of the Three Little Pigs*. New York: Viking Penguin, 1989. This picture book has quickly become a classic for switching points of view or narrator voice. Rhetorical choices have never been so fun.

Romano, Tom. *Blending Genre, Altering Style*. Portsmouth: Boynton/Cook Publishers, 2000. The pioneer in multi-genre work, Tom Romano offers many samples and suggestions to turn this act of play into serious, formal inquiry.

Writing Persuasive Essays in Response to Literature

Fiction is obliged to stick to possibilities. Truth isn't.
Mark Twain

Hope is a thing with feathers / That perches in the soul, / And sings the tune without words / And never stops at all.
Emily Dickinson (stating her position)

The Point: When students use literary characters or literary works to back up their points in essays, they're fulfilling the dreams of English teachers the world over: they are leaning on literature to make meaning in their lives, to make sense of the world.

Teaching it:

Choose a human dilemma in any piece of literature, and ask students to discuss their points of view about that dilemma. Have them jot down anything quotable that their classmates say about people or human nature. Then ask the students to choose one of those, whichever statement they consider most true, to use as a thesis statement for an essay. Instruct them to use actions of the characters in the literature to illustrate their theses.

We have read *To Kill A Mockingbird,* and now you have thought about how people face forks in the road. Write an answer to this question in the next couple of minutes. Let's share answers and discuss them. Here's the question: What is the difficult truth about people, when faced with those choices? (Or rephrased, why don't people all make the same choices? What makes us decide when to step off the more traveled path?)

Sample student responses:

Ninth graders' comments, on the subject of human choices when faced with forks in the road:

Mike : The path which you take should be based on what you need at that time.

Michelle P: Sometimes the two paths actually represent an easier and harder way of life.

Carina: Sometimes it's clear when someone has made the wrong decision.

Michelle K.: Going where you haven't been means learning.

Justin: Choosing the path less taken means that you get to lay down your own gravel.

Craig: It's human nature to blame others for being on the wrong road.

Kara: Destinations vary, depending on your route.

Kendall: Sometimes the choice is dictated by a person's will to be "cool."

Justin: The freeway was once a country road, too. The road more traveled is more carved and paved, and you know the way. You know what's ahead. On the road less traveled, you have to find your own way.

Mike: You take more of a chance, more risk, on the untraveled road.

Melissa: Choices like these are all a matter of what you want out of your life.

Scott: Kindness is the only way out of the worst choices.

Debriefing:

Was it surprising to hear how much wisdom came from the class?
Did anyone hear an opinion worth pondering? Worth proving?

Spin-offs:

- Choose a statement and prove that it is not true, using examples from the literature to back yourself up.

- Get a copy of today's newspaper and create statements from the articles on the front page. Decide whether you agree with these statements or disagree and write about this.

- Try writing statements that grow from the messages of advertisements. Make lists of the messages of ads and share them with each other.

- Write scenes in which characters from the literature act out their own debates about the truth of these statements.

For Younger Writers:

- Make a greeting card or poster of a statement of truth.

- A popular, entertaining debate game show at Oxford University in England involves taking a famous quote and either arguing against it or defending it. For example, British playwright Tom Stoppard successfully defended the quote, "Wagner's music sounds better than it is." Standing behind a quote helps us to search for textual or anecdotal evidence to back up opinion. Judging such a contest gives students invaluable practice assessing the strength and weaknesses of arguments.

- Begin by picking the quotes. Each contestant gets three minutes to defend a quote. Judges score on "real reasons." Three real reasons means they win.

Resources:

Appendix **22**

Appendix 22, Student Sample Essay: "A Pit of Ignorance," by James Higdon.

Rosenblatt, Louise M. *Literature as Exploration.* New York: Modern Language Association, 1995. This classic book began the reader-response movement in literature, changing forever the perception that literature has finite themes and uses.

Gonzalez, Ralfka and Ana Ruiz. *My First Book of Proverbs: Mi Primer Libro de Dichos.* San Francisco: Children's Book Press, 1995. This beautiful book has a proverb on each page, accompanied by gorgeous artwork. The proverbs could be used as starters for persuasion or opinion statements.

The Insight Garden: Growing Opinions from Art, Literature, and Life Seeds

Everything has been figured out except how to live.

Jean-Paul Sartre

The Point: Art is a way of making sense of the world. Great paintings, like great novels or great music, connect us and invigorate our own sense of who we are. Connecting between the visual and literal arts helps us and our students to develop opinions and create bridges between our lives and the work of artists. In this short guided writing exercise, students expand on an opinion and a piece of artwork. This synthesizes their experience from literature and life.

Teaching it:

(On an overhead projector, place a piece of artwork and an opinion or theme statement which correlates with a piece of literature you are reading in class. This guided writing will take ten minutes.)

Look at the artwork.
In the next minute, copy the opinion statement.

For the next three minutes, explain the statement and its validity. (What does it mean? What is your interpretation of it?)

Take a breath and indent. For the next three minutes, tell how it connects to the literature we're reading in class.

Take a breath and indent. For the next three minutes, tell how it connects to your life, our world.

Take a breath and indent one more time. In the next minute, finish with something this discussion leaves you wondering about the statement.

Note: *This is only one way to present this material. The shortness of the writing time often helps students to focus and find their opinions, almost like the word association technique used by psychiatrists. Try a more leisurely approach and see what results you get.*

Debriefing:
Did looking at the artwork change the way you started writing?
How difficult was it to connect the idea to your life?

Chapter Three

Student Samples

Charlotte's Web,
written by NJWPT workshop participants, 2/8/0
We are all searching for a path, or a place to belong.
Special friends sometimes have to stand by and watch.
Sometimes it feels like the only person you can count on is yourself.
How hard is it to be part of this world?
Together we can light the way.
The best ideas are often generated in isolation.

Romeo and Juliet
Loyalty between family members is one of the greatest passions in life.
Nothing soothes a wounded heart like a little time and space.
Some kinds of beauty last forever.
Poor communication can cause serious problems.
Human beings work harder to achieve the impossible.
Love is springtime of the soul.
Peace and hate co-exist everywhere.
Romance doesn't change, no matter what culture, no matter what century.

Spin-offs:

• Complete the exercise, using only these directions:
   Explain the opinion statement with the artwork. Can you connect it to the literature you're reading? To your life? To the world? You have ten minutes.

• Flesh the essay out with "thick description" (sassy leads, dialogue, snapshots, examples, elaborata) for a full essay.

• Incorporate vocabulary words into these pieces.

• Copy occasional anonymous short essays onto transparencies for group proofreading.

Resources: Appendix 23

Appendix 23, Student Sample: Connecting *The Odyssey* and "St. George and The Dragon," Man's Fascination with Monsters, by Adrian Ramos. A ninth grader shares his ten-minute writing.

Kellaher, Karen. *Picture Prompts to Spark Super Writing*. New York: Scholastic, Inc., 1999. This activity book presents art pieces on reproducible pages.

Cowan, Elizabeth and Gregory Cowan. *Writing*. New York: John Wiley, 1980. In this book, the authors introduce the "cubing" exercise, which is a short method for guided writing. The cubing exercise has been adapted for this lesson.

Men Who Run with Scissors: Using Parody and Humor to Guide Persuasive Voices

Comedy is the last refuge of the non-conformist mind.
Gilbert Seldes

The gods too are fond of a joke.
Aristotle

A few years ago, OprahWinfrey interviewed Jim Carrey. She asked him who was his greatest comic influence. He didn't bat an eye and said the name of his seventh grade teacher. Can you imagine having Jim Carrey in your seventh grade class? Would that constitute grounds for early retirement? Here was a kid who would spend hours making faces in the mirror and then bring those faces to school to try out on his friends. How did she manage to not only control him, but inspire him for years?

This is how Jim Carrey described it. "She realized early in the semester that there was nothing she could give to me that I couldn't get from the kid sitting next to me, so she said, "Jim, I'll make a deal with you. You give me the 45 minute period and I'll give you the entire class for five minutes once a week." That was all it took to turn a goof off into a serious comedian. The young Jim Carrey would spend hours working on his five minute routines, and was so afraid of losing his stage time that he did all the class work his teacher told him to do and even worked some of his comedy into those assignments.

The lessons in this chapter are given in the same spirit as Jim Carrey's teacher. They aim to liberate the funny voices of your students but at the same time get the serious lesson on persuasive writing across. Laughter can help us teach because it opens our eyes to gut-wrenching irony, liberates the voice of young writers, exaggerates and amplifies our best lessons, and last but not least, it's fun. Writing successful parody, like writing a powerful serious persuasive essay, demands a deep understanding of the topic; an ability to reframe, rethink and reevaluate; and a passion for synthesizing unlike ideas to create something wild, wacky and wonderful.

So why is humor often ignored in curricula and state mandates? Answer: It can lead to inappropriate and downright silly behavior. How do we avoid this? Just as we can teach students to work together in groups effectively, we can set a few simple guidelines to help regulate the flow of humor in the class. Here they are.

Humor Guidelines

1. Bathroom and bodily fluid jokes are very funny but not appropriate for school. You are allowed to laugh at them, even fall on the floor, foaming at the mouth. But please don't repeat them in class. You can simply say, " We did a bathroom joke," and we will all know why your face is beet-red and your eyes are spinning back into their sockets.

2. No jokes about other students in the class or school without their permission. The last thing we want to do with a joke is hurt someone's feelings.

3. There are two types of humor: good humor and bad humor. Good humor makes us laugh, and afterwards it lifts our spirits almost like a great song will. Bad humor makes us laugh, and afterwards we feel a little sad and dumb and even a little mean, usually because the joke is at someone's expense.

You can make a simple test to see if a joke is good or bad humor: When you tell a joke or write some humor, ask yourself, "What am I laughing at?" If the joke is about a person, ask yourself, "If this person were in the room how would he or she feel?" If the answer is terrible, then you know you have some bad humor happening. Much of political humor is bad humor because it is at the expense of some public figure, but the best political jokes and cartoons are making fun of a situation or process. This is humor both sides can laugh at and be united. For example, during missile treaty negotiations between the Soviets and Americans the two groups reached an impasse. They took a break and one of the Soviets began with a joke: "What is the difference between capitalism and communism? In capitalism Man exploits Man; in communism it is the other way around." This one simple joke allowed BOTH sides to laugh and the negotiations continued.

4. Try to write good humor and the world will grow bigger and brighter. You are allowed to write and laugh at bad humor, but you are also required to identify it. In other words, "This is a funny joke but it's bad humor, because it is at the expense of the President."

5. Some humor is beyond analysis. Just laugh.

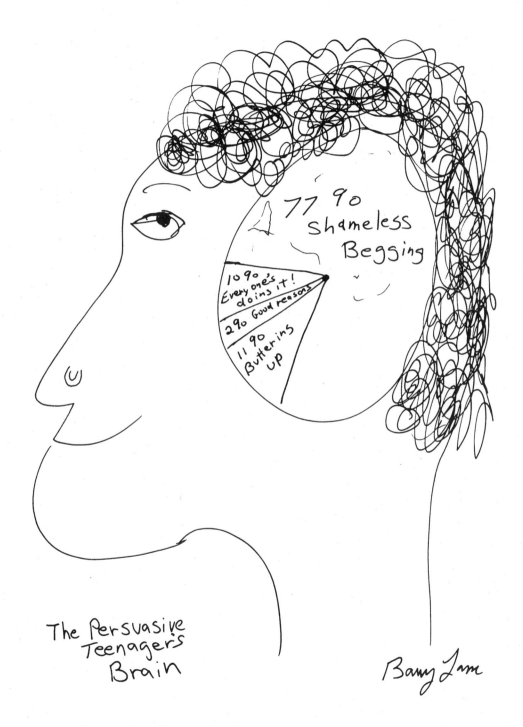

The Persuasive
Teenager's
Brain

Barry Lane

Outrageous Opinions

To lose one parent is a tragedy. To lose both parents is just plain carelessness.
Oscar Wilde

The Point: Real opinions live deep within all of us, but gaining access to them can sometimes be a complex and harrowing process. Outrageous opinions, however, grow on the surface like fungus and daytime TV talk shows. It has been said that America is held together by a loose tapestry of outrageous opinions. Actually, it hasn't been said till now, and that's how you feel when you have strong opinions: like your view of the world is unique and important. Mining this opinion field rich in gems can be a great way to get your students motivated later to dig deeper for their own real opinions. This makes the first lesson a great group brainstorming activity as well as an individual activity.

Teaching it:

Did you ever hear someone say, "Well everybody KNOWS that…" and then say something really bone-headed? Like this: "Everybody KNOWS that reading damages your brain." In the next five minutes, see if you can come up with five or more of these outrageous opinions, opinions that can be completely disproven.

Note: One trick to finding outrageous opinions is to flip-flop normal ones.
Example: Instead of Never read in the dark.
Always read in the dark.

Debriefing:
Was it fun thinking up outrageous opinions?
Which opinions are the most outrageous?
Which seem almost true?

Student Responses:
Kids who play with matches never get burned.
Cafeteria food should be much more expensive.
Dogs should run for president.
Glue is delicious.
The buses here always run on time.
Every cigarette you smoke adds 10 seconds to your life.
Drinking is good for your general health.
It's okay to steal, as long as you don't get caught.
Kids should always pick their own bedtimes.

Spin-offs:
• Make a large poster of your outrageous opinion. Hang them in the halls to confuse other classes.

• Make a T-shirt or bumper sticker to show off your outrageous opinion.

- Create a skit to act out your outrageous opinion. This could also evolve into a 30 second TV commercial that you put on videotape.

- Watch TV commercials for an hour and write down the opinions of each commercial.

  Examples: Toothpaste makes your teeth brighter.
  Mountain Dew gives you energy.
  Are any of these opinions outrageous?

For Younger Writers:

- Collect all the classes' outrageous opinions and make a children's book with each opinion in a sheet protector in a third ring binder.

- Get out a soap box (milk crate or chair) and practice standing on it and proclaiming your opinion. To do this well you must stand on the box, raise one hand in the air, and speak loudly with great conviction.

- Draw a picture that gets across your opinion without using any word.

Resources:

Beard, Henry. *The Way Things Really Work.* New York: Viking Penguin, 1998. This spoof of *The Way Things Work* shows graphic cartoons for outrageous opinions.

Defending An Outrageous Opinion

Why does man kill? He kills for food and frequently there must be a beverage.
Woody Allen

Progress might have been all right once but it has gone on too long.
Ogden Nash

The Point: Defending a ridiculous idea is a good rehearsal for defending a position that's not authentic (for example, the state writing test). Drama can bring delight and joy to a not-so-joyful assignment. This lesson will help your students learn the joy of faking it.

Teaching it:

(Begin by building a list of outrageous opinions, from previous lesson.)

See that list of Outrageous Opinions on the wall?

Pick out one that you'd NEVER in a million years actually argue for. Imagine that somehow, you now want to advocate it. Write a letter to someone in authority and tell them why you think it's a seriously good idea. For this letter, don't write the whole letter. Only write the beginning, and one reason you "believe" the way you do. Explain that one reason fully. You don't need to develop it further than just one reason, just to see how you sound.

Make your voice sound as believable as you can by coming up with facts, stories or images to back up your outrageous idea.

(Write for ten minutes.)

Debriefing:
Was it hard to defend your opinion?
What is your favorite back up detail?

Student Responses:
Dear City Councilman,
    The rule, the wearing of shoes indoors will be prohibited, that you would like to enforce is an extravagant idea. I support it all the way. I have often wanted to take my shoes off indoors, but have not because of embarrassment. Many problems can be prevented with this rule.
    I know 93.7% of people in the U.S. have carpet in their houses. How many times have you heard your mother yell, "You just tracked mud all over the floor. Now you need to clean it up." Well, I have heard it often. And let me tell you something, mud is not easy to get out of carpeting. If we had that rule, carpet in homes, schools, office buildings and stores will last a lot longer and will not have as much dirt.

Imagine that you are in a hurry and you're shopping for clothes in a mall. You go into Dillard's and try an outfit on. Now, you have to put your shoes back on, run to another store, take off your shoes to change, put them back on when you're done, then go to another store and so on and so on. Shoes take me the longest to put back on, because I have to sit on the floor (not all stores have seats in the changing rooms) and lace up my shoes and stand back up. If we were not allowed to wear shoes in stores, then that would be one less thing to slow us down and worry about. It would also be more comfortable to walk around the mall, especially if you are wearing high-heeled shoes that day.

Since you wouldn't wear your shoes as often, they would be able to last a lot longer. This means, those leather boots you have in your closet that are all scuffed up and look old could have had a much longer life span. You could have used the money you would have saved, instead of buying another pair, and spent it on a CD, makeup, or on gifts for your teacher! You could save a lot of money that way.

So you see, passing and enforcing this rule would save you time and money, and you would be able to be comfortable. Working mothers and fathers would love you for helping them have a few less things to think about. If the rule is passed, life will be a lot easier to live.

Sincerely,
Suzanne Koenig

Spin-offs:

- Try delivering your opinion as a speech without cracking a smile.

- Write an outrageous editorial or op ed piece. See if you can give some rationality to your outrageous opinion. *For example,* see Appendix 25b, "Brian for President."

- Read a selection from *Letters from a Nut* by Ted Nancy. Ted writes outrageous request letters to unsuspecting institutions. *For example:* " I wanted to know if you possibly found a Prussian military sword that I think I may have left in your hotel restaurant the night of Saturday, July 7th." Ted Nancy

For Younger Writers:

- Make ad posters to support your outrageous opinion.

- Write and shoot a 30-second commercial for your outrageous opinion. Target a disbelieving audience. See appendix 25c, "TV Commercial Tips."

Resources: Appendix 25

Anger, Ed. *Let's Pave the Stupid Rainforests and Give School Teachers Stun Guns and Ways to Save America.* New York: Broadway Books, 1996. Ed Anger lives up to his name. He is a perfect example of over-the-top opinion, and his writing may offend some. (Appendix 25a.)

Nancy, Ted L. *Letters from a Nut. New York:* Avon Books, 1997. These silly letters written to serious corporations model how even the most outrageous requests are taken seriously by those paid to do so.

Elvis Was Abducted by Aliens and Other Conspiracy Theories

You'd be paranoid too if everyone were after you.

Anonymous conspiracy theorist

The Point: Conspiracy theories are a strange phenomenon in America and a great way to teach about wacky persuasion, because no matter how bizarre your idea, you still need even wilder facts to back it up. Here is a way to have fun with the paranoid gene that lies in blood of Americans.

Teaching it:

What is a conspiracy? It's when one person believes he is being fooled by an organization or a country or a group of people.

Did you know there are people in the world who still believe no one ever walked on the moon, and even more who believe that President John F. Kennedy was not assassinated by Lee Harvey Oswald, but by a group of Martians posing as secret service agents? Perhaps even you have caught Elvis out the corner of your eye at the supermarket.

It's fun to make our own conspiracy theories. Here's a step-by-step process.

1. Make a list of commonly known facts about the world.
   We breathe air.
   HIV causes AIDS.
   Gravity keeps us on earth.
   The pyramids were built by the ancient Egyptians.
   Water turns to ice when it goes below freezing.
   Babies wear diapers because they don't know how to go potty.

2. For each fact try coming up with a conspiracy theory. You can use a sentence to help. Most people think_____ but the real reason is _____.

3. Come up with facts to prove your theory. See how many facts you can come up with.

Examples: People think that babies wear diapers because they don't know about toilets; the real reason is they're just lazy.

Debriefing:

Have you ever thought about the idea that maybe everyone else (besides you) is in on something?
Is your theory funny? Why? Why not? What's your favorite detail?
Did you hit a blank wall? If so, how did you get past it?

Spin-offs:

- Research American conspiracy theories on the Internet or at the library. Pay particular attention to the facts and evidence. List at least ten facts or evidence about one theory. Ask your students to prepare a presentation where they analyze the facts and tell students what their most compelling and least compelling facts are.

- Look up the UFO crash in Roswell, New Mexico in 1948. Here it is suggested that a small group of uninsured aliens crashed and were recovered by the US government in the famous Area 51. There is a whole museum devoted to this conspiracy theory. Ask your students to take one side or the other and present a short speech reviewing the most compelling evidence.

For Younger Writers:

- Write your own Top Secret file book about the world as we know it. Each student does his or her own illustrated page which you can put into a class binder.

- Pretend you have a secret that nobody else knows. Fold a piece of large blank construction paper the fat way and write the secret inside. Now fold it three more times. Go back and design your paper so that when a person unfolds the paper he or she finds a new hint with each unraveling. The final fold reveals the secret.

Example: You think that clouds are water vapor floating in the sky.
Next: But one day you look closer and think you see something behind them.
Next: At first you think it's the sun.
Next: But then you see it glistens.
Next: Like a butter knife.
Last fold: The clouds are God's frosting.

Resources:

Wisneiwski, David. *The Secret Knowledge of Grown-ups*. New York: Scholastic, Inc., 1998. In this book the author presents himself as a grown-up who has defected with secret files to tell you the real story about important misconceptions and untruths like: "You should eat your vegetables because they are good for you." He tells us the real story.

Conspiracy Theory. Dir. Richard Donner. Perf. Mel Gibson. Warner Videos, 1997. Conspiracy theory continues to be a part of our culture, as this film demonstrates.

JFK. Dir. Oliver Stone. Perf. Kevin Costner. Warner Brothers, 1991. This movie is probably the most flagrant example of a conspiracy theory that many believe.

Dressing as the Enemy

I argue very well. Ask any of my remaining friends. I can win an argument on any topic, against any opponent. People know this, and steer clear of me at parties. Often, as a sign of their great respect, they don't even invite me.

Dave Barry

The Point: Jonathan Swift was a famous eighteenth century satirist. He wrote an infamous essay called "A Modest Proposal" in which he pretended to be an Englishman with a great plan to solve what at the time was called "The Irish Problem." Swift mimicked the voices of English planners of his day who had very rational and well thought out plans for helping to feed and clothe Ireland, a country which England had brutally invaded and occupied for many years. About two thirds of the way through Swift's essay the reader finds out that his plan is to eat Irish babies.

Swift reeled in his audience by dressing as the enemy. Then he amplified the voice of that enemy by exaggerating his point of view to the point of absurdity. This sophisticated technique can be taught to your students to help them see that one funny way to persuade your audience is to mimic the serious voice of the opposing side so that you can expose their flaws.

Teaching it:

Talk to your students about the two or three sides of many arguments. Your audience is used to hearing one person argue one side and the other argue the other side. You can throw your reader a curve ball by pretending to take the other side in order to expose what's wrong with it.

In other words, I believe in capital punishment because it's important for civilized people to have the right to brutally murder those who choose to brutally murder us. Killing is an important part of civilized society.

After you have chosen an opinion, take the opposite point of view of the one you have chosen.

Example: Recess should be longer.
Opposite: We should eliminate recess, today!

We should wear school uniforms.
Opposite: We should all go to school naked.

Read examples below.
Try to write in such a way that the reader thinks you are on the level. (Don't tip your hand in the first paragraph, anyway.) Like a good virus which adapts to the DNA of its host, take apart the argument from the inside out. In other words, school uniforms are good because they promote order. Some of the most important societies of the 20th century stressed the importance of uniforms. In Nazi Germany where uniforms were worn by many, there was very little crime.

Debriefing:

What happened when you dressed as the enemy?
Did you learn anything new about your subject?
Can you use this strategy in your writing?

Spin-offs:

- Look at enemies in nature and make a list like the one below. Argue from one point of view of one side taking the other side's point of view.

  lions zebras
  cats   mice
  cats   dogs
  deer   hunters

  Example: Dogs are much better than cats because they always bring fleas into the house. It's very hard on fleas to live in the cold winter, and they do much better inside where they can feed on the blood of humans. Cats are much cleaner, so fleas don't find them as attractive; so if you are a flea lover, make sure you get a dog.

- Read "A Modest Proposal" by Jonathan Swift. Notice how cleverly Swift masks his point of view in the beginning. Try writing a similar essay on a current topic. Make sure to disguise your bias until very close to the end. The key to dressing as the enemy is the ability to sound like your opponent.

For Younger Writers:

- Make an ad poster that dresses as the enemy. Make sure you slip in your point of view into the ad so that a viewer may not see it at first.

- Write a speech that begins in the point of view of your opponent and ends up spoofing that point of view. Deliver the speech to a group of people and see how long it takes them to get it. (Note: if you do this well, sometimes nobody will get it.)

Resources:

Swift, Jonathan. *A Modest Proposal and Other Satirical Works.* New York: Dover Publications, Inc., 1995. In this classic satire Jonathan Swift pretends to be an English planner who has the perfect solution to the Irish problem. Only near the end do you find out his solution involves eating the babies.

"Brian for President" sample, Appendix 25b. A man receives complaints about e-mail. He reacts with a rousing call for all email readers to always "reply to all." Listen to what happens when you combine a stirring and reverent tone with a silly and frivolous point.

Lane, Barry. *The Backwards World.* Shoreham, VT: Discover Writing Press, 2002. This picture book models the joy of flip-flopping an essential skill for taking the other side. In the backwards world the books read you.

Dumb Laws

One must never look a dog in the eye.
Actual law on the books in Illinois

The Point: Laws do not appear on their own but are a product of the society that created them. Some, like "Thou shalt not kill," are easy to understand. Other more obscure laws, like "A woman must never kiss a man with a mustache," (still on the law books in Illinois) are more puzzling. This funny lesson shows your students that even the wackiest rules get more meaningful if you back them up with real reasons.

Teaching it:

Go to the Web site www.dumblaws.com and find hundreds of ridiculous laws which are still on the books today. Find the laws for your state.

Can you think of any ridiculous laws? Can you make some up?

Think of these rules. On the index card, list five or so, in the next few minutes.

Now that we have our list we are going to have some fun. Get into groups of four. One person is the judge, one the defendant, one the prosecuting attorney, and one the defense attorney. The situation is that the defendant has broken one of the laws on our list. Choose one. Now let's write a play of the trial. The defendant is on the stand being examined by the prosecutor, who must make a convincing argument about the defendant's offense. Next the defense attorney cross-examines the defendant.

Write up your trial as a little sketch.

Debriefing:
What were the strongest reasons in each lawyer's case?
Which were the weakest, the silliest, the funniest?

Spin-offs:
• Go to www.dumblaws.com and find lists of blue laws for the states you live in. Pretend you are a lawyer in court arguing the importance of this law to a skeptical jury.

• Try writing a letter to the police or to a judge in a town. Ask them if they know the origin of some of these peculiar laws.

For Younger Writers:
• Pick a few dumb laws and make a wanted poster for someone who broke one.

• Write top ten poem listing reasons for a dumb law (For example, "Top Ten Reasons Why You Shouldn't Tie a

Giraffe to a Telephone Pole").

• Create dumb laws to add to your class rules. Make a list and come up with some reasons why they are important.

Resources:

Dumb Laws. http://www.dumblaws.com Look up your state and find the dumb laws.

It is against the law to make faces at dogs.

Actual law in Normal, Illinois

All residents shall bathe every Saturday night.

Actual law in Barre, Vermont

No children may attend school with their breath smelling of "wild onions."

Actual law in West Virginia

Citizens may not greet each other by "putting one's thumb to the nose and wiggling the fingers".

Actual law in New York City

It is illegal to sell Limburger cheese on Sunday.

Actual law in Houston, Texas

Appreciation Week

The Point: Here is a screwball assignment that helps students learn to use their funny bone and imagination. Students can have some fun mimicking appreciation weeks, finding funny things to appreciate and resulting actions that would demonstrate appreciation. The act of creating such a parody mirrors the abstract process which often occurs on prompted tests, where you must write a persuasive essay on a topic in which you have little interest. Here is a fun way to prepare for a less fun assignment.

Teaching it:

Did you ever hear of "Secretary Appreciation Day?" What kinds of things might people do for their secretaries to show that they appreciate them?

What if there were "Pet Appreciation Week"? Can you imagine some funny things that people might do for their pet to show their appreciation?
*Eat dinner on the floor with him.
*Bury a steak in the yard with him.
*Jump all over him when you see him.
*Roll around in something dead with him.

Now I want you to think of one idea for a new national appreciation day or week, for something we see in our lives. List an idea or two about what we would do to show appreciation for that.

Debriefing:

Did the ideas come easily or was it hard to think up silly things to appreciate?
Of your list which appreciation weeks are the funniest? Why?

Student responses:

Nagging Appreciation Week:
   Nag at five different people every hour.
   Volunteer to spend eight hours at a preschool so you can experience nagging.

Dog Appreciation Day:
   Buy your dog an artificial leg.
   Bring the neighbor dog over.
   Rent a mailman.

Dog Appreciation Week

* Bake a bone cake.
* Terrorize the cat.
* Sing dog songs.
* Switch!! You sleep outside and your dog (or dogs) sleep on your bed.

Hattie Bernie

Dedicated to the dog you love!!

The Impossible Job

The thought of being President frightens me and I do not think I want the job.
Ronald Reagan in 1973

I would have made a good Pope.
Richard M. Nixon

The Point: One of the most persuasive pieces of writing a person has to do is a job application letter. In a brief amount of time you have to express your desire for a job and also tell your qualifications for that job. Why should they hire you when they could hire someone else with more experience who is better qualified? You have to build up your positive qualities and downplay the negative. This funny exercise teaches how to be persuasive even when you have little in your favor.

Teaching it:

Below are some impossible job scenarios. Pick one or make up your own. See how many positive points you can make in your letter. Use your imagination and past experience. Remember to locate the one most positive piece and put it up front. Ignore or simply mention a few drawbacks.

You	Job
have no experience are afraid of kids	teacher
are blind	air traffic controller
have never cooked before	chef
are in a wheelchair from a ski accident	ski patrol director

Debriefing:
Were you able to make a convincing argument?
Do you think you'll get an interview?

Student Responses:
Impossible Job Letter

I really think I would be a great neurosurgeon because I am very social and I listen very well. I am patient and I never become frustrated. Here are some qualities I believe I have:

loyal	social
attentive	patient
persistent	

I believe I would be a great surgeon. I am very prepared for this job because I recently went through a two week first aid course instead of medical school. I have been diagnosed with Parkinson's and I have an extreme shake in my right hand, but I am positive that this won't get in the way. I hope that you will present me with a doctor's license because I won't let my patients down.

Sincerely,
Georgy Tremble
(Ken Marshall)

Spin-offs:

- Think of a job you are really unqualified for, like say, the President of the United States. Write a letter proving why you should have the job. Begin by listing. Remember the more seriously you take this assignment, the funnier your letter may be. Remember to downplay your weaknesses and play up your strengths.

- Create a skit of an impossible job interview where the applicant must convince the interviewer to hire him or her despite formidable odds. Begin by breaking into pairs and start writing, and acting.

- Write a resume that is guaranteed not to get you the job.

For Younger Writers:

- What is your dream job? Pretend that if you write a good enough letter someone who is doing that job might let you try it for a day. Include information in your letter that will show them that you know a lot about the job they do.

Resources: Appendix 30

Krensky, Stephen. *How Santa Got His Job*. New York: Simon and Schuster, 1998.
This cute children's picture book traces Santa's resume through several failed jobs which lead to his dream job at the North Pole.

Bolles, Richard N. *What Color is Your Parachute 2000: Practical Manual for Job-Hunters and Career-Changers*. New York: Ten Speed Press, 1999. This ultimate job hunters' manual is filled with wonderful advice aimed at helping job hunters connect with their ultimate job.

HELP WANTED one plump man, postal experience and good rapport with deer and elves a must.
Call 1-800-North Pole

Ruffling an Audience

31

If any cleric or monk speaks jocular words, such as provoke laughter, let him be anathema.
Ordinance, Second council of Constance, 1418

The Point: If students are to become savvy, culturally aware speakers, they must be sensitized to audience values or biases. In real life, when groups gather together, they have common purposes. Have you ever heard a speaker say something to which the audience reacted with grumbled comments to each other? Students have little experience with group agendas and reactions. Having them purposely create statements which would cause a small group uproar is a fun way to acquaint them with the dynamics of audience values.

This exercise gives students practice at cracking the group codes.

Teaching it:

All groups have an agenda. And while we respect all people, it's interesting to see how groups act as a common being when they share values. Think of audiences seated together, listening to a speaker, all cheering or booing simultaneously. Who are they? They might all belong to the same club or interest group. List as many different kinds of sub-groups as you can in the next five minutes. (See list below.)

Now, think about what an opinion is. Some people may agree with it; others will disagree. Opinions often have the word "should" in them.

Pick an audience sub-group from the list we made. Pretend you are in the middle of a speech to that audience. Imagine giving them an opinion that makes the whole audience physically react, moving around in their chairs, looking at each other, or making angry grumbling sounds of disagreement.

For example, I've just told a group of meat packers that everyone should be vegetarians. It's the only healthy choice.

Now write your opinion down on a strip of paper, WITHOUT identifying the audience.

Now we'll share them with each other and figure out what group they offend.

Tip: It will work best if the opinion you write MIGHT actually be reasonable to some people.

Debriefing:
What makes an opinion offensive to a group?
If you change the group is the opinion still offensive?

Student samples:
List of groups

Artists	Musicians	Mothers of kindergartners
Skaters	Girl Scouts	Graffiti artists

Convicts in a prison	Survivors of a concentration camp	Cross dressers
Flood victims	Escapees from foreign oppression	Hair dressers
Actors at an Academy Awards night	Newly sworn-in police officers	Dog owners
Wrestling fan club members	Army enlistees	Church congregations
Shoe salesmen	Gang members	Travelers at an airport
Smokers	Women in the restroom line at a	Hungry restaurant customers
Ex-smokers	concert	Campers
Doctors	Football players	Spring breakers at the beach

Offending Statements

Prisons should be made less pleasant in order for people to dread going there more. (Convicts in prison)

Children should never be expected to sell items for an organization; this practice exploits children, using them for fundraising. (Girl Scouts)

Schools should not promote sports that have high risks of injury to students. (Football players)

People should not place so much importance on physical appearance. (Hairdressers)

Spray paint will never be considered an art form. (Graffiti artists)

Wrestling is fake. (Steve Austin fan club members)

Sex offenders should be able to have the chance to rehabilitate and be able to live in any community they choose. (Rape victims support group)

Spin-offs:

- Write multiple opinions targeting the same sub-group. Make a poster, for example, "Top Ten Things NOT To Say at A Hairdressers' Convention"

- Win over a ruffled audience: Choose an opinion and sub-group, then develop an argument which might serve to win them over. Question: what skills did you have to use in order to get this imaginary audience to listen at all in the first place, and change their minds, in the second place?

- Make a TV commercial aimed at offending its target audience.

Resources:

Film: *The Producers,* 1968. In this classic film (now a popular Broadway musical) Gene Wilder and Zero Mostel play theatrical producers who strive to create a play that will offend its audience so that they can pocket the production money. Of course, their plan backfires when the musical *Springtime for Hitler* becomes a hit.

Why We Must Run with Scissors

In the backwards world the Wampanoag discover London.
Barry Lane

Propaganda is the art of persuading others of what you don't believe yourself.
Abba Eban

The Point: As we have seen throughout this chapter, students can have some fun using a serious tone to defend something absurd. Nowhere is this more apparent than when we flip-flop rules for safety. In the following lesson, the group focuses together on one crazy rule and individually comes up with one way each that the rule would benefit society. This will demonstrate structure and elaboration for one well-developed essay.

Teaching it:

(Give everyone an index card. Choose a rule from the list of ridiculous rules.)

Let's choose a rule from the list of Ridiculous Rules of Safety. Pretend that you are serious about this new rule. Think of ONE way that this new rule would help everyone; one reason it would actually be a great idea. Explain your point.
(Write for five minutes. Pick up the cards and read them aloud.)

Debriefing:
Which of these reasons are most interesting?
Which are funniest?
Which are the most truthful?

Student responses:
People should only run with scissors in their hands. Here is a list of reasons why:

People need scissors more often than any other tool. One time I was running around, and I knew I had to cut something and I was in a hurry. All of a sudden, I couldn't find any scissors. If only that great rule had been passed, I could've had the scissors right there! (Lisa Moorad)

The crime rate would drastically decrease. When you're running down a dark alley, muggers wouldn't think of mugging you. (Robert Paiz)

If you were to fall down and get hurt, when the ambulance arrives, the paramedics need to get your shirt off without moving you. They would already have a pair of scissors to cut off your shirt. (Craig Mitchell)

If you run with scissors, you can get some momentum going when you decide you want to cut something. For instance, when you want to cut something that's on the other end of a football field, you just run like crazy and get momentum going, so it will be a nice, pretty cut. (Justin Saavedra)

This would help lower population density. Only very careful people would survive. (Taeylor Barcellona)

You need protection when you are running in the neighborhood. Once I was running in my neighborhood, and a dog attacked. If it weren't for the scissors, I'd be dead. (Kendall Hall)

How often do you find yourself running past someone holding a permission slip? The bottom needs to be cut. You would have the scissors to cut it off for them. This would be needed, because sometimes students are in a hurry to get to school, and they tell parents, "Sign this!" and they're like "Give me a pen!" So you do, but you can't cut it off. (Carina Jones)

If you're running, that usually means you're in a hurry. And if a person sees you running with scissors in your hand, they'll move out of your way. And if their back is turned, you start screaming "I have scissors in my hand!" And they'll turn around, see you coming, and move. Running with scissors is so important when you have to get somewhere in a hurry. (Kara Kiehne)

Running with scissors is a great idea, because if you fall down and stab yourself, you will know you were running too fast. It's like a speedometer. Depending on the depth of the cut, you will know exactly how fast you were going when you fell. (Michelle Paquette)

Spin-offs:
- Compile the notecards from the exercise and create a book. Illustrate it.

Resource: **Appendix 32**

Appendix 32, "Devil's Advocate" List of Ridiculous Rules.

Blasting the Beauty Myth: Truth in Advertising

Advertisements contain the only truths to be relied on in a newspaper.
Thomas Jefferson

The Point: Without a doubt, the most common form of persuasive writing in society is advertising. From the moment we are born we are fed images that tell us who we are, what to think and how to look in the interest of selling us things. Nowhere is this more apparent than in what society tells young girls and woman about themselves. This lesson shows students how to talk back to advertisements and create both humor and persuasive truth.

Teaching it:

(Have students search for ads depicting women and men and have them bring them into the classroom.)

There are two questions to ask when you look at an ad: who specifically is the audience, and what is the message? Look the ad on the opposite page beneath and give the people words to describe what they are telling you about yourself.

Ask yourselves this one question: what truth did they leave out of the ad?

Next imagine ways you can put the truth back into your ad.

For example: Put a drunk in a beer commercial. Put cancer in a cigarette commercial.
See appendix 33a, "Don't fall for the beauty myth."

Debriefing:
Does your truth blast apart the message of the original?
Is it funny? If so, why?
Why is truth funny?

Spin-offs:
- Find an image of a man from a magazine and try to blast apart that image with some truth about the man.

- Create a collection of ads and paste them in your journal with space beneath. For each one write one sentence that tells us exactly what the advertiser wants us to think based on the image. For example, "The Marlboro man: If you smoke cigarettes you will be macho."

- Take an ad for a harmful product and create the most outrageous lying image that you can think of. Give it to the product. For example, "Fresh Air Cigarettes. The athlete's choice."

For Younger Writers:

• Get up early one Saturday morning and tape several advertisements for toys in between Saturday morning cartoons. There is usually a huge difference between commercials aimed at girls and boys. Bring them into class and show them. What's the difference between ads for girls and those for boys? Write a sentence that says what the ad is telling you. Do you believe it? Write about it.

Resources:
Appendix 33

"Don't fall for the beauty myth," appendix 33.

Adbusters. 3 May 2001. <http.//www.adbusters.org> This Web site is dedicated to the fine art of culture jamming, using ads to battle against advertising.

Used with permission of the Media Foundation. www.addbusters.com

Voice Play:
Snapping the Gap Between
the Voice and the Page

Writers aren't exactly people…they're a whole lot of people trying to be one person.
F. Scott Fitzgerald

Justin sat staring at his paper. He wrote maybe ten words and then stopped. Around him, his classmates were busily filling up their papers. Justin was doing math, figuring how many more words he'd have to creak out until it would be enough. Without some kind of change, Justin's "voice" on paper would never be fluent. And, as a persuasive writer, Justin's future would be doomed.

Do you have any Justins? Do you have any students who dread hearing the sound of their own writing aloud, whose formal voices on paper are so distant from themselves that they cannot bear to pretend that the voices are "theirs"?

This chapter contains exercises especially for those most reluctant writers. They are designed to change writing into talking, so that students learn to anticipate a vocal audience when they sit down to write. Students learn to hear writing not as an end, but as a vehicle for communication between people. This helps them eventually to bring these voices to the page with renewed confidence. The monologue of a writer who hears only his or her own voice is transformed into what Gabrielle Rico calls the multilogue, many voices that we can bounce off and react to.

And just how does this work?

Through dialogue. "Dialogue," Rico says, "is the bridge between monologue and multilogue."

Tinkering with the way we read a piece of writing can be a form of composing that mirrors the mental process of a fluent writer. The playful reading exercises in this chapter can help students like Justin hear more voices in their head when they write.

At a writing assessment workshop, a parent once asked the teacher, "What is voice?" The teacher turned to the third graders, and a little girl in the back raised her hand. "That's my tongue on the page. That's voice," she said. The lessons in this chapter will help get the tongues on the pages.

Protocol: There are two items of protocol for all of the following voiceplay exercises.

First, teach students how to be an audience. The role of audience member is difficult work, even though it seems passive. Audience members might make reactive non-verbal noises (intakes of breath, chuckles, etc.) but they do not utter words of any kind. They make their words wait until the performance is finished. They keep their bodies still and their eyes fixed on the faces of the performers. When the performers freeze at the end to signal that they have finished, the audience signal back their recognition of the ending by giving applause.

Second, teach students who are performing how to signal that they are finished. They do not say their last line of text and follow it with "and that's it…" or "ta-da!" or "The end!" Instead, they say their last line of text and freeze their faces and bodies in stillness for about five seconds. (Five seconds is a long time!) They stay frozen that way until the audience releases them with applause.

These two customs feel a little strange to students at the very first, but they add polish and quickly become an accepted part of the play.

What you will need:

The following voice exercises do not generate writing. They are to be used on pieces of writing which have already been written. Personal narratives work well. So would any essays that are not formal in diction. Ask your students to look through their journal and find a piece of writing that they wouldn't mind sharing, or look through their writing folder and find a piece of writing that they wouldn't mind reading aloud. You can also experiment with published writing. Once everyone has selected a piece, you are ready to begin.

Besides the students and their drafts, you will need highlighters and a prop telephone.

How long does each exercise take? In a one-hour class period, you will have enough time to have students select a piece (five minutes), prepare it for the exercise (about seven minutes), and present it. Arranging students in a circle makes the performing quick and informal. A short discussion at the end will give students a chance to make their observations about the effects of the play on the writing. And you will see changes in the writing, even among students like Justin.

Grace L.

Freeze To Frame

The opposite of talking isn't listening. The opposite of talking is waiting.
Fran Lebowitz

The Point: Pauses create power in both writing and speech. Pablo Casals said that music was the spaces between the notes. This voice lesson helps students see the power of the pause, especially at the end of a persuasive speech.

Teaching it:

To be performed individually.
Each student selects ONE SENTENCE from any piece.
Perform in read-around style, with students in a circle.

Instructions to the writer/performer:
  Freeze for five seconds.
  Say your sentence.
  Freeze at the end. Stay frozen until the audience applause releases you.

Debriefing:
As reader, was freezing difficult?
As audience, did you know when to applaud?
What would be the value in framing a piece with freezing?

Spin-offs:
• Use facial expressions with the freezes.

• Practice taking on the frozen poses of people in ads, paintings or photographs.

• Pay attention to Dan Rather or other news anchors. Notice how just before the camera cuts away from them to the news story, they sit frozen and stare at the camera. This is particularly noticeable when there is a mix-up and the story never comes on the screen. One way to learn about freezing is to practice the news anchor screw-up freeze. Pretend you are a news anchor introducing a story. Example: And now we go to Buenos Aires where Angela Howk has the full story on the revolution there. (Anchor freezes for five seconds, then realizes the tape isn't running, breaks the freeze, and makes awkward comments like: "I guess we'll hear from Angela later in the broadcast.")

For Younger Writers:
• Pretend you have just done a performance. Take your bow and stand there for five seconds as the audience claps.

Chapter Five

Resources:

Paintings or photos with people in them, like the one below of people at Disney World.

Advertisements.

Video of news anchors.

A What? A Voice Lesson in Emphasis

A nail that sticks up gets hammered down.

Japanese proverb

The Point: When students read, they often don't deliver their message with the power of their natural speaking voice. The following activity helps to transform a "reading" voice into a "telling" voice. The pauses and repetitions also teach students the power of emphasis while gently jolting the speaker to clarify meaning. In persuasive writing, the writer begins to imagine a reader who is actively questioning the words. As a result, the writer chooses words more deliberately, anticipating the need for clarity.

Teaching it:

To be performed in pairs (one, the writer; the other, the interrupting partner).
Each writer selects a chunk of writing, a piece that can be read aloud in a couple of minutes.

Instructions to the writer/performers:

1. With a highlighter or pen, writer marks spots where "A what?" interruptions would be appropriate. (After key words or phrases would be good.)
2. Partner, looking over the shoulder of the writer, says "A what?" at those spots in the reading.
3. Writer repeats those words/phrases and continues.

Debriefing:

Are the interruptions irritating?
No more than two interruptions work well if the piece is serious.
More interruptions seem okay if the piece is light and funny.
Why is there a difference?
At what point does listener interaction stop adding and start detracting?

Example :

A piece marked for performance:
"Last week outside of school, I learned that you can't always get what you want even if you beg.// My mom told me I couldn't go to the mall with Candace, my cousin. I was furious // because I was good all that week just because I wanted to go. I did homework, I washed dishes, I even babysat horrible kids // for her three times. I didn't even talk back once. When Friday came, and I asked her very nicely, // "Mom, can I go to the mall?" she said no!! I have no idea why. I did everything right.//"

The same piece, with the voice play:
"Last week outside of school, I learned that you can't always get what you want even if you beg. (If you what?) If you beg. My mom told me I couldn't go to the mall with Candace, my cousin. I was furious (What?) furious…because I was good all that week just because I wanted to go. I did homework, I washed dishes, I even babysat horrible kids

(horrible what?) Horrible kids! for her three times. I didn't even talk back once. When Friday came and I asked her very nicely (very what?) Very nicely "Mom, can I go to the mall?" she said no! I have no idea why. I did everything right. (you did what?) Everything right! -Patricia Hernandez, 8th grade

Spin-offs:

• Paraphrase: When the writer hears "a what?" he or she should answer with a paraphrase of the original words, and then continue on with the reading.

• Try having the writer mumble just before the highlighted part.

• Use the Gettysburg Address as the piece of writing. (Fourscore and what?) Notice how the humor actually makes the point of speech better. Example "(all men are created What!) Equal !

• Write a humor sketch where the characters keep hearing different words than what they say.

For Younger Writers:

• Try this activity with a fairy tale. Example, "Once upon a time," a what? A time. Practice increasing your volume when you reply.

• Try it with the Pledge of Allegiance.

• Try this activity with a third person who answers the "a what" question with a similar sounding word. *Example*" One nation, under God, indivisible (what?) third person (Amelia Bedevil) " He said Invisible…"

Resources:

Example below. Tape families' or kids' conversations.

Amelia Bedelia books.

Glasser, William. *The Quality School.* Portsmouth, NH: Heinemann, 1989. This book reveals the theory behind students' innate need for belonging and fun.

Moffett, James. *Teaching the Universe of Discourse.* Boston: Houghton Mifflin, 1968. This book covers the interplay between discourse and socialization.

Hopkins, Mary Frances and Beverly Whitaker Long. *Performing Literature.* New York: Prentice-Hall, 1982. This book is a gold mine for strategies for responding to literature through various kinds of re-shaping exercises within literary texts.

Carroll, Joyce Armstrong and Edward E. Wilson. *Acts of Teaching.* Englewood: Teacher Ideas Press, 1993. Written by the directors of the New Jersey Writing Project in Texas, this amazing collection covers both theory and practice.

I'll Say It Again: Contradictions

Never believe anything until it has been officially denied.
Claud Cockburn

The Point: In strong communication every word, every fact, every idea counts. One way to highlight this to students is for them to hear a contradictory voice and be made to repeat a word. This fun lesson helps students to see the footsteps their words leave and learn to step harder.

Teaching it:

Divide students into groups of three (one, the writer; one, the interrupting partner, and one the silent listener).

Each student selects a "chunk" of writing, a piece which can be read aloud in a couple of minutes.

Instructions to the writer/performers:

Preparing the piece:
1. The writer highlights five or six nouns, adjectives, adverbs, or prepositional phrases, or any words that look like they might be contradicted *(see example below)*.
2. The interrupter looks at those highlighted words or phrases and writes contradictory words or phrases above them.

Performing:
1. As the writer reads to the silent listener, the interrupter interrupts and injects the contradictions.
2. The writer shakes his/her head, gives "looks" and repeats the original words before going on.

Debriefing:

What are the effects of contradiction? Short-term? Longer-term?
How and why does it happen?
How can we detect it in ourselves?
How could using this mentally help when you're writing?

Sample:

Before:
"Last year I was very furious. I got a call from a music store that said I won a *sixteen-inch stereo* for my birthday, and my friend Josh received the call. He didn't tell me about it and he kept the stereo. A few weeks later, the store called and asked if I liked my stereo. I said, "What stereo?" They said the one I got for my birthday. They said my friend went to go pick it up. I told them I hadn't gotten anything. *When I got off the phone,* I went straight to my friend's house and he didn't hear me knock. I went *around back* and looked into his room, and what do you think I saw? He had a brand new radio playing loud. I got my radio and left. After that day we *never spoke to each other again.*"
    Oscar, eighth grade

After:

"Last year I was very furious. I got a call from a music store that said I won a sixteen-inch stereo (no, a cassette player) for my birthday, and my friend Josh received the call (it was Dave). He didn't tell me about it and he kept the stereo. A few weeks later, the store called and asked if I liked my stereo. I said, "What stereo?" They said the one I got for my birthday. They said my friend went to go pick it up. I told them I hadn't gotten anything. When I got off the phone,(the next day) I went straight to my friend's house and he didn't hear me knock. I went around back (you went in the side door) and looked into his room, and what do you think I saw? He had a brand new radio playing loud. I got my radio and left. After that day we never spoke to each other again (you talked to him this morning)."

Oscar, eighth grade

Spin-offs:

• Leave out the second reiteration by the writer while performing. Notice how that changes the credibility of the writer.

• Do this exercise, using the Declaration of Independence or other formal document as the writing.

For Younger Writers:

• Make a drawing that contradicts itself with words. For example, a picture of the sun and a label beneath it that reads, MOON. See how many contradictions you can put into your drawing.

• Break up into pairs and create a dance called the moving contradiction. In the dance you make steps but have to contradict them. What would this look like on the dance floor?

Resources:

The song, "Yes, I Remember it Well," from the musical *Gigi*. Sung by Maurice Chevalier.

Jefferson's Contradiction

Uh-huh, Really, Wow:
Tuning in to Confirmation

It takes two to speak the truth – one to speak and another to hear.
Henry David Thoreau

The Point: All strong writing is a conversation with one silent partner. This lesson attempts to help the writer hear a kind-hearted confirming audience. Students insert friendly-listener sounds, so that a monologue becomes a conversation. For persuasion, disagreements from a listener cause a speaker to prove herself or himself. The beauty of this exercise lies in the new confidence that appears in the speaker's voice when the listener actively agrees with her or him.

Teaching it:

To be performed in pairs (one, the writer; the other, the reacting partner)
Each student selects a "chunk" of writing, a piece which can be read aloud in a couple of minutes.

Instructions to the writer/performers:

Preparing the piece:
1. Find a piece that tells about something that you did, or something that happened, or an opinion piece.
2. Highlight five or six places where you can imagine a listener reacting in some way.

Performing:
1. Read/say the monologue to your partner.
2. At the highlights, the partner should say "uh-huh" or "mm hmm" or "wow" or something similar.

Debriefing:

How does a live reactor change the piece?
From the writer's viewpoint?
From the audience's viewpoint?
How difficult was it to react in pre-planned places?
When you write about things that happen, do you mentally hear someone reacting?

Sample:

Joseph, my boyfriend, just moved to another school // and I feel really bad because I miss him. I hope that he doesn't flirt // with other girls. But he is coming over on the weekend. // I can't wait. He is really cute. I've been going around with him since fifth grade. // We might go to the movies // this weekend.

Spin-offs:

- Try inserting the vocal reactions in places where they don't naturally belong and performing this. If the listener tries to look sincere while reacting in strange spots, it's comic! (Part of comedy is off-balance timing.)

- Joseph, my boyfriend, just moved // to another school and I feel really bad because // I miss him. I hope that he doesn't // flirt with other girls. But he is coming over on the // weekend. I can't wait. He is really cute. I've been going around with him // since fifth grade. We might go to the movies // this weekend.

For Younger Writers:

- Invent a new interjection to use, instead of "Uh-huh…", perhaps a trendier one like "Awesome!" or "Sweet!", or perhaps a deliberately strange one like "Rampant!" or "Rank!"

- Make a drawing that illustrates real communication. What's it look like? (See example below.)

Resources:

Cuyler, Marjorie. *That's Good! That's Bad!* New York: Henry Holt & Co, 1991. This picture book features a story about a little boy and a balloon. Each event in the story is followed by a reaction (That's good!) which is then contradicted to show how the opposite is true. It's a perfect model for embedding this dialogue pattern into a children's story.

"Finishing My...." "Sentence?"

When ideas fail, words come in very handy.
Goethe

The Point: In real-life conversations, people often finish each other's sentences. It's a phenomenon that does not happen in monologues or in single-voiced writing. This exercise explores another way to turn monologue into dialogue in a way that occurs naturally. Persuasive writers who can "hear" the audience finishing their sentences will feel more free to use rhetorical devices such as repetition or rhetorical questions.

Teaching it:

To be performed in pairs (one, the writer; the other, the interrupting partner)
Each student selects a chunk of writing, a piece which can be read aloud in a couple of minutes. For this exercise, narrative or gossip works best.

Instructions to the writer/performers:

Preparing the piece:
1. Find a piece that's chatty.
2. Highlight around the piece you want to use, leaving out any of the beginning or ending that you like.
3. Underline the ends of some independent clauses.
4. Edit out any you want to.

Performing:
1. Read/say the monologue to your partner.
2. At the underlined parts, grope for a word....
3. Partner will take over and pronounce the underlined parts.

Debriefing:
What happens when someone finishes your sentences for you?
Why does it happen?
Does it help? Does it irritate?
What makes the difference between help and irritation?
Did your partner complete the basic gist of your sentence or did he change the meaning entirely?

Student sample:
"I've never loved anyone as much as I love Joe. He means... a whole lot to me. He's the nicest, most caring, and loving guy I... ever met. When he doesn't have any money, we still go out at least to the park, or we'll just stay...home and watch TV. I've never...felt that way about anyone before.

Spin-offs:

- Try the finishing sentence game with your students. Explain that they probably know you well now and that people who know each other often complete each other's sentences. See how good they are and enjoy the funny contradictions that occur.

For Younger Writers:

- Create a five-headed oracle. All you will need is a large blanket and five students. A five-headed oracle is a very wise entity that can answer any question posed to it. (After all, you know the saying, five heads are better than one). The next step requires the class to ask questions to the oracle. Each head of the oracle gets to say one word and must make a sentence by listening to the preceding words. Tip: if the oracle is stumped, it's okay to have it say next…..question….please.. This is a fun gag for a talent show.

The Five-Headed ORacle

The Most True Sentence

The badness of a movie is in direct proportion to the number of helicopters appearing in the first 30 seconds.
    Dave Barry (stating a truth)

The Point: The sound of a voice helps contribute to the meaning of words. A different voice pronouncing the very same words can convey different nuances of meaning. In this exercise, the writer chooses a sentence which seems the "most true," and a different voice pronounces this "most true sentence." The resulting emphasis helps the writer hear that sentence more clearly, almost like audio highlighting. For persuasive writing, this exercise can help pinpoint the most important statement in a piece, which can be enlightening if the writer needs help finding his or her position statement or significant evidence.

Teaching it:

To be performed in pairs (one, the writer; the other, the alternate voice)
Each student selects a "chunk" of writing, a piece which can be read aloud in a couple of minutes.

Instructions to the writer/performers:

Preparing the piece:
1. Read your piece to yourself.
2. Find the sentence that you think is the most true, the one which holds the most truth. Highlight it.
3. Copy (and highlight) this sentence at the beginning.
4. Copy (and highlight) this sentence at the end.
5. Highlight any other words or phrases that you feel like, the ones that stand out to you.

Performing:
1. Read the piece, all except the highlighted parts. Someone else should read the highlighted parts.

Debriefing:
Did the repetition bother you?
Did it make the piece MORE powerful? Or less powerful?
For the writer: What great or subtle changes took place with choosing a sentence and repeating it?

Sample:
I guess it does matter to me what other people think.
If I know there's going to be an audience already, how do I think up something that's going to work? Or that they'll be interested in? Or that I won't feel stupid for people to know that it's true?
    When you hear someone's reading, you know what subject their mind's going to, all by itself. What subject would be okay with me if people knew I thought about it a lot? I can hear it, "Oh no, she's always thinking about Matilde." *I guess it does matter to me what other people think.*

I guess it does matter to me what other people think.
Ms. Bernabei , teacher

Spin-offs:

- Replace the sentence with a word or phrase. Mark several places for this word or phrase to be spoken or whispered or shouted.

- Videotape some commercials, and after playing them back, pull the "most true" statement out of them. Tip: It often appears near the end.

For Younger Writers:

- Take a "most true" statement out of a persuasive essay and make a poster of it.

- Make a small book called "Things I Have Learned". On each page write and illustrate a truth about the world.

- Add pictures or photos to illustrate your book. (See example below.)

Resources: **Appendix 17**

Appendix 17, "Confronting Racism." Try doing this activity with a part of this essay.

On a trip to Arizona, I learned to never kick a cactus.

Voices in Stereo

The Point: When students read their work it often sounds like a monotone, when really the piece can be full of different characters or moods. Enlisting a second voice can help the writers to hear their words in stereo. This lesson turns monologue into dialogue in a completely different way and helps students physically hear possibilities for double-voiced writing.

Teaching it:

To be performed in pairs (one, the writer; the other, a second voice)
Each student selects a "chunk" of writing, a piece which can be read aloud in a couple of minutes.

Instructions to the writer/performers:

Preparing the piece:
1. Take your piece of writing. Read it.
2. Listen to your partner read it.
3. Listen for two different voices.
4. Highlight where the "other voice" speaks.
5. Listen to it again with the two voices.
6. Change the writing if you need to, so that it makes better sense.

Performing:
The two students read the two parts.

Debriefing:
Did two different personalities emerge with the two voices?
How did another voice change the piece?
What different criteria did different students use to hear two separate voices? (How did you know where to switch?)

Student sample:
        "Yesterday, I called my ex-boyfriend, *Salvador.* He picked up the phone and said *Hello,* then I said Salvador and he said *What?* Then I said what are you doing and he said *Watching TV.* Then I said Margie wants to talk to you, and he said *Who is Margie?* So he said *Yes, I do remember her,* and then Margie took the phone away from me and started to talk to him."
        Cathy, sixth grade

Spin-offs:
- Try adding more voices. One could be narrator.

- Try organizing your voices around the parts of speech. In teams students read pieces, each person responsible for their part of speech. Some are noun people, some verb people, etc...

- Use this as a lead-in to teach punctuating dialogue and paragraphing.

- Add Hot Truth (theme) line: Pick out the one sentence in the writing that holds the most truth. Copy that sentence at the beginning and the end. Have a narrator perform the first and last lines, with the other two frozen.

For Younger Writers:
- Perform poems out of Paul Fleischman's award-winning book, *A Joyful Noise*. Practice varying the sound of the voices to give the poems different interpretations.

- Write your own poems for two voices that explore two persuasive positions. Use chart below.

Resources:

Fleishman, Paul. *A Joyful Noise*. New York, Harper Trophy, 1988.

Stone, Ruth. *Poetry Alive*. St. Paul, MN: Consortium Books, 2000. These two books contain poems for two voices.

Two Voice Poem Chart		
Voice 1	**Voice 1 & 2 Together**	**Voice 2**

Rewind

Just because your voice reaches halfway around the world doesn't mean you are wiser than when it reached only to the end of the bar.

Edward R. Murrow

The Point: Repetition can help readers hear their words and their effect on an audience. Yet often students don't reread their work enough or the work of others. What if we could do in real life what we can do with our VCR remotes? For persuasive writers, this exercise can clarify sensory images and the need for transitions.

Teaching it:

Divide class into pairs (one, the writer; the other, the partner who holds a "remote").
Each student selects a "chunk" of writing, a piece which can be read aloud in a couple of minutes.

Instructions to the writer/performers:

Preparing the piece:
Mark two spots on the piece, one where the rewind button is hit, and one where it backs up to.

Performing:
When the writer reaches the preplanned spot, the remote-holding student pantomimes (with large arm action) pushing the rewind button. The writer screeches backwards to the preplanned spot and continues.

(Student sample, marked and ready to perform)

I think you should buy the * entertainment book because it is a great deal.//
 It's not just for going to eat; * if you want to go bowling, there are
coupons // for bowling. If you buy * the Panther Gold Card, // it limits
where you can go. With the entertainment book, there's different * kind of
places to go: Italian, fast, Chinese, // any kind. You're probably thinking
they're cheap coupons, * right? Well, // skimming through, I saw $8 off
coupons. Three of those, * and you get your money's worth // and some.   *
So if you still think the Gold Card is better, buy it. // But those days
when you're * craving Carraba's, think of the variety you lost. // (Mark
Zamora)

(How the student sample would sound, performed)
I think you should buy the entertainment book because it is a great deal...
entertainment book because it is a great deal. It's not just for going to
eat; if you want to go bowling, there are coupons...if you want to go
bowling, there are coupons for bowling. If you buy the Panther Gold Card,
the Panther Gold Card, it limits where you can go. With the entertainment
book, there's different kind of places to go: Italian, fast, Chinese, kind

of places to go: Italian, fast, Chinese, any kind. You're probably thinking they're cheap coupons, right? Well, right? Well, skimming through, I saw $8 off coupons. Three of those, and you get your money's worth and you get your money's worth and some. So if you still think the Gold Card is better, buy it. So if you still think the Gold Card is better, buy it. But those days when you're craving Carraba's, think of the variety you lost craving Carraba's, think of the variety you lost.

Debriefing:

Would you like to be able to do this in real life, in real conversation? How would that make things easier/harder?

Spin-offs:

- Bring in a real VCR and a tape of a speech by somebody. Play the speech to a place where the audience applauds or to any sustained pause. Rewind the line several times and talk about what happens when we listen to a line again and again.

- Look at a taped political stump speech and notice the places where the speaker pauses for the applause of the audience. Politicians underline such places before they begin a speech so they know where to pause. Try the same with your speech. Cue the audience with an applause card, or by freezing, in case they are slow.

- Read a poem in unison. Then pick favorite lines to repeat. Turn the normal poem into a chant poem. Script it for a few voices.

- Tape a political campaign speech on C-SPAN. Notice the lines where the politician pauses for the applause of the audience. A good political speech contains many such lines, and a good speaker knows to pause after he says them so the audience can react.

For Younger Writers:

- Create a poem where each line repeats three times. See the *Teachers and Writers Handbook of Poetic Forms,* by Ron Padgett. Talk about how rewinding helps us to hear the true meaning of the words.

- Write a chant poem like those found in Carolyn Graham's book, *Jazz Chants for Children.* Try varying who says the repeating line or lines: sometimes one person, sometimes three, sometimes the whole class.

Resources:

Graham, Carolyn. *Jazz Chants for Children.* New York: Oxford University Press, 1977. This wonderful teaching book uses jazz chants to teach English as a second language. The chants are great models for the chanting classroom.

Padgett, Ron. *Teachers and Writers Handbook of Poetic Forms.* New York: Teachers & Writers Collaborative, 2000. Many poetic forms such as the chant poem depend of repetition. Use this book with your students.

Knowing the Rhetorical Moves

In the 1970's Johnny Most announced the Boston Celtic basketball games. Johnny Most had a way of talking about basketball that helped you see the game in your mind—as long as you knew something about the game to begin with. He also had nicknames for all the players. Listening to the game on the radio, you would hear phrases like "Hondo goes baseline, SWISH, Jo Jo takes it inside and he is mauled and the shot is…YES…. Satch...top of the key…Bang!"

If you knew nothing of basketball, Most's colorful words would sound a bit like a code, and you would see little of the action till someone helped you crack the code. The same can be said for persuasive writing. There are historical rhetorical moves that can help writers to see the game they are playing in a colorful and exciting way. Though some of these devices may appear in a persuasive argument of a writer who knows nothing of them, a little knowledge of these devices can help a writer build a powerful repertoire of choices to use in many different persuasive situations.

The lessons in this chapter explore a few basic rhetorical moves and help students to recognize them in their own work and in the work of others. Each of these moves only becomes valuable to writers at the moment they can use it in their own writing. It's important not to teach these lessons as ends in themselves but as means to an end, a polished argument. In basketball, knowing the difference between a lay-up and a jumper can help a player decide what move to make. In a persuasive essay, the same could be said of knowing the difference between a logical argument and a logical fallacy. Use these lessons to create vocabulary of argument for you and your students to share and play the game with style and flare.

Beyond the 3 B's

If you can't be a good example, then you'll just have to be a horrible warning.

Catherine Aird

The Point: As we have mentioned many times in this book, students come to school with an entire arsenal of persuasive techniques. Before we show some historical persuasion it's a good idea to reflect on our own personal historical modes. This first lesson asks us to reflect on what we know already and contrast it with what an expert like Alan Dershowitz knows about the most effective persuasion.

Teaching it:

How do you persuade members of your family? How do you win an argument? Any ideas? What if we were to write a book called "Top Ten Methods to Get Your Own Way." What would the table of contents look like?

(Make a list of some of these techniques on the board with your class.)
If your class is anything like Louise Van Schaack's fourth graders, the list will be like the one beneath, heavy on what we may call the 3 B's : Begging, Bribery and Bullying. Though these methods might have some effectiveness in family arguments, they fall short of what we might call civilized discourse, and ultimately they are not the most persuasive.

Alan Dershowitz says, "Persuasion is not making someone think what you think. Rather, it's leading them to reality." How does this comment relate to some of the methods on our list? Many of our methods seem to be more coercive and less persuasive than the way Dershowitz describes persuasion. (See appendix 42.)

Come up with ten more methods for persuasion without bullying, bribery or begging. Build a second top ten list including these more refined techniques.

Debriefing:

What's the difference between the two lists?
Which type of persuasion works best in real life? Which on paper?

Student Examples:
Ten Methods of Family Persuasion:

10 Use puppy dog eyes and pout with lower lip.
 9 Say, "Please, please, please" (shameless begging).
 8 Get on hands and knees.
 7 Say you'll clean your room (empty promises).
 6 Clasp hands in front of you and smile in a saintly way.
 5 Paper halos.
 4 Fake tears.
 3 Whine and say, "Pretty please with sugar on the top".

2 Bribe with flowers or candy (beer works with Dad).

1 Try to find a real reason (this one was influenced by the teacher).

Top Ten Better Methods of Truthful Persuasion:

10 Know your point of view.

9 Listen to the other side.

8 Don't editorialize; rather let your facts speak for themselves.

7 Be kind and courteous to your opponent.

6 Nagging works sometimes.

5 Don't be afraid to use your imagination along with the facts.

4 Pretend you are the audience whenever things get confusing.

3 Use humor to make your point where appropriate.

2 Don't force your argument on them; show them the truth.

1 End with your best point re-stated in a more eloquent way.

Spin-offs:

• Write the book for six-year-olds where one character persuades another to do something. Use Frog and Toad as a model.

• Write a poem entitled "Recipe for Arguing." Start by bringing in recipes from home. Make lists of recipe verbs: beat, whip, and mash. Talk about the grammar of a recipe: a list of ingredients and a narrative that tells you what to do with them. Pay particular attention to the relationship between the quantities of ingredients. Some things that are very important you should have in great quantity, but with other less important things, you may want to add only a pinch. Write your recipe poems for arguing on index cards and share them with the class.

For Younger Writers:

• On separate pages collect and illustrate each of your best points and create a classroom cahpter book called "How to Argue or How to Get Your Own Way Without Them Knowing It." (Come up with your own title.)

• Make a classroom poster titled, "Fifty Ways to Get Your Own Way."

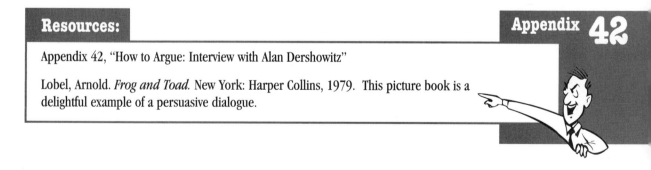

Resources: Appendix 42

Appendix 42, "How to Argue: Interview with Alan Dershowitz"

Lobel, Arnold. *Frog and Toad*. New York: Harper Collins, 1979. This picture book is a delightful example of a persuasive dialogue.

Digging Below A Position

I think we can come to a meaningful solution that suits both parties.
Henry Kissinger

The Point: Persuasive writers, like good mediators, know how to dig beneath an entrenched position and find the common interests which lie below. This is a skill used by international diplomats with warring powers as well as by crafty teenagers with stubborn parents. This lesson teaches a basic formula for digging and gives students a way to talk about real persuasion.

Teaching it:

(Draw a diagram on the board like the one below. Talk about how good persuaders can move their audience from positions of conflict to the common interests which lie beneath.)

Persuasion is the art of digging beneath a position and responding to the common interests which lie beneath. In some ways all conflict begins in the stubborn refusal to do this. As Alan Dershowitz says, "Persuasion is not forcing someone to believe what you believe, but rather, it's leading someone to the truth." In an entrenched conflict the most powerful persuader will be the one who can take one step back and see the other person's point of view. The persuader then can craft an argument with the opponent foremost in his or her mind.

Now let's role-play a scene in front of the class where one character moves another from conflict to interests. (See illustration, appendix 43.) I am going to ring this triangle whenever one character digs beneath the position to an interest of the other character. I'll make the raspberry sound whenever they simply promote the conflict, through more bullying, bribing and begging.

Example:
  Child: Dad can I have a friend over?
  Dad: No. I need the house quiet.
  Child: Please, can I have a friend over?
      (raspberry—begging)
  Dad: No. I told you I have a lot of work to do.
  Child: We will play outside and be really
      quiet.(DING!)
  Dad: I'll think about it.

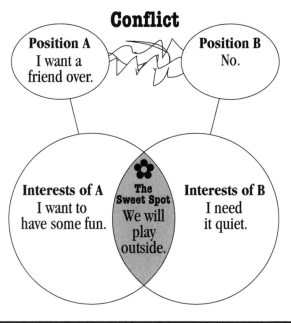

Now let's break up into pairs and improvise a similar scene. Write your conflicts as short plays that begin with a big disagreement, then try to dig at the common interests beneath.

Teaching it:

(As students perform their skits, ring the bell whenever one of the characters is able to make a point that addresses the other side's interests, and do a raspberry for the 3 B's. After doing this a few times, put a student in charge of the bell.)

Whenever you are stuck in an argument, you have to dig deeper to find the common ground beneath. These points of agreement are often where your strongest points lie.

Debriefing:

Did you get more persuasive when you dug beneath your partner's argument?

Can you see the parts of your arguments that rely on the 3 B's (see last lesson) and the parts that are truly persuasive?

Why do we all have such a hard time putting this skill into practice?

Spin-offs:

- Using the Internet or newspapers, research a trouble area in the world such as Northern Ireland or Israel. Map out the areas of conflict, then list common interests. Draft a peace agreement which might persuade both sides to agree.

- Ask students to find a basic source of conflict in their own family. It can be some minor contention like a member of the family not screwing the top on the toothpaste tight enough, or something more heated like when bedtime should be or who should use the family car. Ask them to pretend to be a mediator with no vested interest in the argument. Using the model above, ask them to dig beneath positions and find the common interest.

For Younger Writers:

- Create a play or sketch where a conflict arises and a third party teaches the two conflicted parties to find the common interests.

Resources: Appendix 43

Should There Be Zoos? A Persuasive Text, by Tony Stead, New York, Mondo Publishing, 2000. This book models student voices showing pros and cons of zoo life for animals, using plenty of interesting sources. The last few pages are position paper essays written by children. It's a great model for action papers.

Classifying the Opposition

I would not want to be a part of any club that would have someone like me as a member.
Groucho Marx

The Point: One way to throw the opposition off balance is to classify their position. This is a debating technique which makes the opposition's argument seem less important because it's fueled by a personal bias which your side defines. Practicing the classifying voice can help your students develop a powerful tool for elaborating the flaws on the other side. It can also provide practice in meaningful elaboration.

Teaching it:

What does it mean to classify something?

Let's classify something now.

Start with a label and then zoom in to describe it better with specific detail.
For example, we'll start with this label: Types of Hand Shakers.
Now we'll zoom in to the categories with specific details.

1. Bone Crushers: These people are trying to prove something. They squeeze you.

2. Limp Noodles: You reach for their hand if it dissolves like clammy spaghetti in your palm.

3. The Wilting Rose: The hand extends to you but withers and dies when your hand comes into contact with it.

Now let's try this out on an argument. How would it look if we classified the opposing view to your opinion?

Example: There are three types of people who are in favor of school uniforms: ex-military types who are still acting out their boyhood GI Joe fantasies, parents who fear their children's individuality, and Republican politicians who use any issue that sounds hard line to get elected.

Now you try. If you need help here are some ideas:
There are three types of people who oppose_____.
Four reasons to oppose _____ are _____ _____ _____ and _____.

Debriefing:
What effect does it have when you classify the opposite side?
Is it helpful? How does it enhance your argument?
How might it detract from it?

Spin-offs:

- Use the diagrams below with your students to make pie slices of any arguments they may be making. Each piece is a different group of people who think a particular way because of a personal bias. For example, one group opposing school uniforms could be clothing store managers who realize their sales will be affected. When students are done, ask them to incorporate a few slices of the pie into their essays.

For Younger Writers:

- Try classifying school lunches. Draw pictures to add to your classifications.

- Read a *Book of Hugs* by David Ross and try adding some of your own classifications.

Resources: Appendix 44

"Types of Nose Pickers," Appendix 44. Classifying anything, even Nose Pickers, gives us practice playing the classifier.

Ross, Dave. *A Book of Hugs.* New York: Harper Trophy, 1999. This book is a perfect way to look at easy classifications: buddy hugs, grandfather hugs, people hugs, etc.

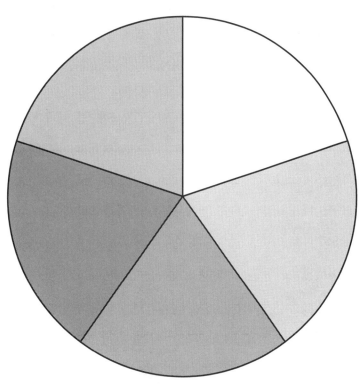

Point of View Pie

Everybody Knows I'm Right

I'll not listen to reason. Reason always means what someone else has to say.
Elizabeth Cleghorn Gaskell

The Point: Golf is the most boring game known to man. This kind of blanket statement is a classic example of overgeneralization, probably the most common fallacy in persuasive writing. Here's a fun lesson to help your students recognize it and know what to do to fix it in their writing.

Teaching it:

Has anyone ever told you that all students need at least eight hours sleep to do well in school? Can you think of some other blanket statements that people might use to try to convince you they're right about something? *(Create some overgeneralized statements and put them on the board, and label them "Before.")*

These statements are made in the heat of passion but work against the writer by oversimplifying the point. Now try rewriting each overgeneralization with a more moderate phrase. *(Create a list and label it "After.")*

Let's compare these lists. What words do you see in the second list which act as "softeners," or "moderators"? *(Make a third list and label it "Moderators for blanket statements")*

Examples: Sometimes…
　　　　　　Some people think…
　　　　　　Often there is a link between…
　　　　　　Imagine what it would be like if…

Does this activity doesn't mean we can't have strong opinions? Of course not. But it helps us to see that when we moderate an over the top opinion, we edge closer to truth.

Debriefing:

What do you think of a person when you hear them say overgeneralized statements?
What happens to a speaker's credibility?
Are all blanket statements bad?

Student Samples, before:

All kids should pick their own bedtimes.
Capital punishment is the only way to stop the rising murder rate.
Women are bad at giving directions.
All men are bad at asking for directions.
Golf is the most boring game known to man.
Pokemon cards are really dumb.
No one over 30 should be allowed to wear Spandex.

Student Samples, after:

Some kids are responsible enough to pick their own bedtimes.

To someone like me who has never played, golf appears the most boring game on the planet earth.

Sometimes I wish there were a law that said no one more than 20 pounds overweight should be allowed to wear Spandex.

Spin-offs:

- Find an advertising slogan that overgeneralizes. Now try moderating the statement with qualifying language.
  Example: Ford has a better idea.
  Qualified: In most cases, Ford has a better idea.
              Ford's Edsel was an exception.

- Look for overgeneralizations in your own writing and wherever possible share them with each other.

- Collect overgeneralizations from your reading and write them in your journal.

For Younger Writers:

- Create bumper stickers for your overgeneralizations and display them in the classroom.

- Make a list of statements that are always true.

Resources:

Web English Teacher. 14 May 2001. http://webenglishteacher.com Besides being an incredible resource for any English teacher, this site contains links to many formal persuasive writing programs, such as the one at Dartmouth. There, you'll find the developmental descriptions of how students' arguments change as they develop as critical thinkers, beginning with William Perry's "cognitive egocentrism," or black-and-white thinking. There's a great handout from Harvard, "What is argument?"

Split Multinationals Not Atoms

BUMPER STICKER

Cause by Association

As scarce as truth is, the supply has always been in excess of the demand.
Josh Billings

The Point: One very deceptive fallacy is the one that associates facts with an idea that doesn't quite logically fit them. In the courtroom such arguments are labeled circumstantial evidence. In writing they are often called false analogies or simply muddy thinking. Here's a quick lesson for making your students aware of the problem .

Teaching it:

People can distort the truth by providing facts in strange ways. Sound confusing? Listen to this:

Milk is Dangerous

Important warning for those who have been drawn unsuspectingly into the use of milk:
1. More than 98 percent of convicted felons are milk users.
2. Fully HALF of all children who grow up on milk-consuming households score below average on standardized tests.
3. In the 18th century, when virtually all milk was consumed at home, the average life expectancy was less than 50 years; infant mortality rates were unacceptably high; many women died in childbirth; and diseases such as typhoid, yellow fever, and influenza ravaged whole nations.
4. More than 90 percent of violent crimes are committed within 24 hours of drinking milk.
5. Primitive societies that have no milk exhibit a low incidence of cancer, Alzheimer's, Parkinson's disease, and osteoporosis.
6. Milk is often a "gateway" food item, leading the user to "harder" derivatives such as butter and even cheese.
7. Most American milk users are utterly unable to distinguish between significant scientific fact and meaningless statistical babbling.

In light of these frightening statistics, we propose the following broad restrictions:
1. No sale of milk to minors.
2. A nationwide "Just Say No to Milk" campaign, complete with celebrity TV spots and bumper stickers that read NOT MILK!
3. A 300 percent federal tax on all milk to pay for all the societal ills we might associate with dairy-related illnesses.
4. The establishment of "milk-free" zones around schools.

Now use this model to create your own set of fallacies based on something you would like to outlaw. For example: Homework erodes moral character.

Debriefing:

How does false association work?

Can you see places in society where information is presented in similar ways?

What does this make you wonder about the use of statistics in persuasion?

Spin-offs:

- Create your own wacky statistical study and present the results to the class. Some possible topics:

    Homework Leads to Severe Brain Damage.

    Gym Class: The Death of Reason.

- Get a newspaper and find a statistic that is trying to prove something. Assume it is a false association and tell the class why.

- Ask students to look for false associations in their own writing.

Resources:

Paulos, John Allen. *Innumeracy.* New York: Random House, 1990.

Paulos, John Allen. *A Mathematician Reads the Newspaper.* New York: Doubleday, 1997.

These two books deal with the everyday distortion of mathematical facts in American society. They provide good tips on how to create false associations or see through them.

Either/Or... What About...

Either those curtains go or I do!
reported last words of Oscar Wilde

The Point: One common fallacy is the "either/or." The author presents the reader with two possible alternatives and forgets the many others. By making the argument too simple, the author leaves it wide open for attack by the other side. This lesson teaches how to see the simplicity trap and how to create complexity.

Teaching it:

Sometimes things appear too cut and dried. You know what I mean. People try to make it all seem so simple. Here are some examples.

> If guns are outlawed, only criminals will have them.
> If we don't drill for oil in the wilderness of Alaska, the Arabs have us over a barrel.

1. Brainstorm your own list of "either/or" opinions using the pattern below as an aid.
   Either _____ or _____ .

2. Now pick a statement and seek other points of view on both sides. Use the words "what about" to prime the pump.

   For example, what about other ways you can express yourselves besides the clothes you wear? What about all the kids who can't afford the fancy clothes; what about their personal expression?

3. Now try rewriting your original to contain a "what about." Try starting with "Some say…"

   Example: Some say we must abolish school uniforms if we want self- expression. I say look around you. People dress based on their economic standing and the clothes they can afford. Should we then give poorer people money so they too can express themselves more freely?

Debriefing:

What happens when we move past "either/or"?
Does our argument get stronger or weaker?
Where in the real world do those either/or statements make real trouble for us?

Student Samples:

Either we abolish school uniforms or we lose all individual expression.

Either we get rid of guns in this country or we face another century of Columbine High School headlines.

Either we let kids chose their own bedtimes or we face another ten years of whining pajama clad children.

Spin-offs:

- Look in the newspaper's op-ed page and extract a few "either/ors" from the world or local political scene. Put them to the "what about" test and see what solutions you come up with.

- Look for "either/ors" in your own writing and see if you can't improve them by including a "what about."

- Find a Web site that has a radical liberal or conservative point of view, like www.nra.org. Extract statements of absolute truth then put them to the "What About" test. Discuss how moderating radical truths on either side leads us to truth.

- Make your own "But what about sign" to remind you to think.

For Younger Writers:

- Role-play an "either/or" situation between a parent and a child. See if the child, with the help of the class, can move the conflict past "either/or."

Resources:

National Rifle Association. 7 May 2001. <http://www.nra.org.> Groups like the NRA promote an either/or attitude towards gun ownership in America.

Million Mom March. 7 May 2001. http://www.millionmommarch.com. This organization, on the other hand, promotes gun control in America. These two political opponents could make for fascinating study in either/or structures.

But what about...

When Do Analogies and Metaphors Go Bad?

What Einstein was to physics, what Babe Ruth was to home runs, what Emily Post was to table manners…that's what Edward G. Robinson was to dying like a dirty rat.

Russell Baker

The Point: One of the most powerful ways to make a point is to create an analogy to something unrelated. However, analogies can be tricky, because they don't always work out the way we want them to. This lesson teaches students to recognize the bad apples and either toss them or repair them. That last analogy was a sour one. Did you catch it?

Teaching it:

What are analogies? Why do we use them? Why don't we just say what we mean? Read Webster's definition below.

Analogy: A similarity or likeness between things in some circumstances or effects, when the things are otherwise entirely different.

(Read the following analogies to the class.)
School uniforms relate to schools, the way seeds are important to flowers. They may all look the same to start with, but as they grow and develop, their individual shapes and colors will inevitably emerge. We need not worry about wiping out our individuality if the seeds look the same to start with.

A world where children pick their own bedtimes is a world where parents get to pick the time they get up and go to work.

Can you see the power of an analogy? It starts you thinking in images or ideas that get away from the original argument. A good analogy is like making a movie of your argument. It casts your ideas in vivid images. Unfortunately, movies sometimes fail do justice to the original story. There are many ways that analogies can fail. Here are some of the most common.

Too exaggerated:
Before: Mandatory drug testing of students involves the same WW 2 Gestapo tactics that stain twentieth century history books with blood.

After: Though mandatory drug testing does not involve the same tyrannical approach to civil rights that infected Nazi Germany, it's hard to see how these testing practices reflect true democratic values.

Clueless and disconnected:
Before: Mandatory drug testing is like Groundhog Day, except if the groundhog doesn't come out, they drag him out.

Teaching it:

After: Fundamentally, mandatory drug testing is about distrust and is a betrayal of a basic human rights that we even give animals. You don't see them giving urine tests to Punxsutawney Phil on Groundhog Day. Who knows what he could be doing in there all winter?

Debriefing:

How do analogies fail?
How do they succeed?
What advantage is there to creating analogies?
How do exaggerated analogies make you disbelieve the author?

Spin-offs:

- Make a list of statements in your journals. Pick one and create a false analogy to prove. Try repairing the analogy or creating a better one. Talk about what makes it work and what makes it fail.

- Find a three dimensional object, like a block of wood, a salami, a stick of butter, or a hat. Now write an extended metaphor using all your imaginative qualities to connect the object to the position you are arguing for. For example, those who oppose gun control are like large salamis; they all have the same shape, and when you cut them open and look inside, you see more fat than meat.

For Younger Writers:

- Make a list of things on a piece of paper. On the other side write a list of big ideas like love, hope, fear. Now make a metaphor connecting items from one list to the other. "Beauty is a box of tissues."

Resources:

Lane, Barry. *51 Wacky We-search Reports*. Shoreham, VT: Discover Writing Press, 2001. In this book you'll find a section about creating comic analogies which make serious points.

If the Federal budget was your family's budget, the first three floors of your house would be filled with weapons and there would be a line of children at the fridge and not enough food inside to feed them. Concerned friends would say, "What's with all the guns?" You'd reply, "You never know..."

Ralph Nader

Making Straw Men and Adding Wind

It's not what we don't know that hurts; it's what we know that ain't so.
Will Rogers

The Point: One way to disarm the opposition in a debate is to create their position in your own image as a straw man and then blast it apart. This is called a "straw man," because unlike a substantial argument it can be easily pushed aside for your point of view. The trick is to create a convincing straw man so that your audience does not sense the writer is stacking the deck. Here's a lesson which will talk students through building an essay like this.

Teaching it:

(Bring in a scarecrow if you want to make it more dramatic.)

What are the qualities which make a scarecrow? For one thing, they have a hard time standing up on their own. They usually are propped up with a pole. In other words, they are not like a real person, though from a distance they could pass for one. We're going to organize their essays around a scarecrow or straw man, and watch how the wind can blast it apart. I'll demonstrate.

Begin by writing one sentence that directly disagrees with your point of view.
For example: If I believe in school uniforms, I might write:

Many people feel school uniforms are the worst thing that could happen to education.

This is our personal straw man, but at this point he is pretty undeveloped. The more elaborate we can make him, the more powerful our refutation of his point of view will be. So let's add a few sentences to stuff him with a bit more straw.

Many people feel school uniforms stifle creativity and deny students a basic human right of self-expression. They profess ideas about civil liberties and the students' basic rights. These views resonate well with our American constitution and our basic desire for life, liberty, and the pursuit of happiness.

Now let's begin unraveling him:

But upon closer observation there is something seriously wrong. Consider the 14-year-old girl who must sit next to the 14-year-old boy wearing a coed naked Rugby shirt; or the Jewish boy whose lab partner is a girl who has a safety pin through her nose and a Swastika on her arm. What we wear can also infringe on the civil rights of others.

Debriefing:

Why is this straw man strategy better than just ignoring the opponent's point of view?

Would this strategy have been impossible in primitive societies?

How would it have looked?

Spin-offs:

- Create a poem for two voices. One is the straw man, and the other is the voice which pushes him away. Try acting including body movements and blocking.

- Revise the lead of your essay to include a straw man. In the second paragraph blow away the straw man.

For Younger Writers:

- Create a dance called "The straw man and the wind." Act out the pattern of dressing as the other side and then showing your true cards.

- Draw the straw man and the wind of truth.

Resource:

Lane, Barry. *The Tortoise and the Hare, Continued.* Shoreham, VT: Discover Writing Press, 2001. In this retelling of Aesop's fables, each new addition is a straw man that is blown away by the next addition.

Hare Whips Tortoise in Rematch.
World Searches for New Moral.

Playing with Four Patterns of Thought

The reverse side also has a reverse side.
Japanese proverb

The Point: Once students are fluent with the different aspects of their position and its opposition, it's time to experiment with different patterns of organization. The following lesson helps us to see some crucial choices students can make to reorganize their essays.

Teaching it:

There are many ways to organize the points of your argument. Today we are going to explore how to trace and retrace our patterns of thought. Below are four basic patterns of organization. After I tell you about them, try writing your essay following one of them.

Basic One-Two
(First point) The United States is the world's number one producer of greenhouse gases and is one of the few nations not to sign the Kyoto agreement. This is not the kind of behavior we should expect from a world leader.
(Second point) Global warming is a reality, and every industrialized nation must do its part to cut back on its carbon dioxide emissions. We must send a message to our congressmen to sign the Kyoto agreement. The US must take its place once again as a world leader, not cower in the shadows of big business.

Strawman and the Wind
(Strawman) In a year when the stock market has faltered it doesn't seem unusual that the US president would not sign the Kyoto agreement limiting greenhouse gases, citing it might hurt American businesses.
(The Wind) After all, American businesses, which are responsible for one quarter of the world's carbon dioxide emissions, must not sacrifice profit for anything as inconsequential as the environment. So what if there is no earth left for future generations. The most important gains are the stock market points we gain today.

Give an Inch to Get a Foot (Crafting the opposing argument in your own voice; noting the concerns of the other side and agreeing with them)
(Giving an inch) Many people in business say that the environmentalists are killing us with regulations, edicts, laws that protect a species of owl by stopping logging on a thousand acres of forest. It's not difficult to see why unemployed loggers may harbor hostility to tree-hugging granola-heads whose lawyers put them out of work. In the case of the Kyoto agreement, the American president has sent a clear message to the world on the side of the unemployed logger. Business as usual is more important than concerns for protecting nature.
(Getting a foot) Okay, I'll grant you that, but business as usual will lead us to a bleak, barren industrial landscape. One has only to look at the environmental nightmare that is Eastern Europe to see where greed and power without just centralized regulation can lead.

Teaching it:

Ace in the Hole
(Position) The United States should sign the Kyoto agreement. It's the only responsible thing to do.
(Lesser reason) The US produces one quarter of the world's greenhouse gases.
(Lesser reason) European nations have already agreed to sign it under great duress and political pressures not to.
(Major reason) If the US is to remain a world leader we need to sometimes take a stand that puts the world above our own personal interests.

Debriefing:

What are the strengths and weaknesses of each pattern?
Which one do you use most often?

Spin-offs:

- Invent your own pattern of thought, using the elements in the patterns above. Try making it as unique as you can. For example, four bad reasons and one good one.

- Draw a picture that shows the shape of your essay. For example, it may be apple tree with the biggest apple at the top and less important ones at the bottom.

For Younger Writers:

- Get a stack of big index cards. Call them reasons-why cards. On each card, write one reason that proves your point of view. For example, let's say recess has been cancelled for the year by the principal and your job is to convince her to bring it back. Your cards might say:

  Running around at recess helps us to sit still and pay attention later.
  Recess is fun.
  Recess helps us learn to play and work with others, a skill that also can be used in class doing projects.

Collect many reasons why, then experiment arranging them in different ways. When you find a pattern you like best, write your essay.

Resource:

Appendix 51

Appendix 51, Pattern Planner For The Essays.

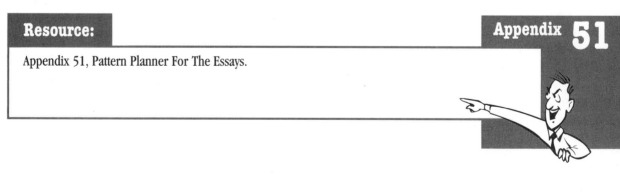

Beginnings and Endings:
Thickening the Stew

There is a connection between the beginning and the end that can help a writer get a handle on what it is he or she is trying to say.

Too direct and boring.

The New York Times reports that 83% of all stories end where they begin.

We made that up.

Once upon a time there was a writer who got the crazy idea that all stories and essays don't have to begin with "once upon a time" or end with "and they all lived happily ever after"…

Better.

Writers make choices all the time, and some of the most important ones are where to begin and where to end. Textbooks often seize on this fact and create formulas to simplify a complex process into a few stock sentences. Begin with an introduction that states your position, follow with a body, then a conclusion. Say what you're going to say, say it and then say it again. Follow all topic sentences with three supporting details. Though such instructional templates can sometimes help students grasp a basic understanding of the structure of an essay for a timed writing assignments, they fall far short when it comes to crafting a complex argument into a lively, readable piece of prose, whatever the purpose of the writing might be.

In other words, when it comes to writing, one size never fits all. Each essay is as individual and complex as the writer who puts the words to paper, and because of this we need a box of varied tools to help shape these essays to fit our own voices and our own messages. The lessons on beginning and ending in this chapter illustrate diverse ways of starting and concluding a persuasive essay. View them as a start and build on them with your own additions. Make it clear to students that all writing is a bubbling stew, and that as their teacher you can show them a few herbs and spices for their simmering work in progress. They will decide when and how to add these ingredients, and in time they will serve it up to the world.

Playing with a Title

I'm very suspicious about titles. Until I get the title, I don't know what type of book I'm gonna write.
Larry McMurtry

The Point: Titles can help us strike a unique tone that complements our point. Playing with titles can also help us to see the many possibilities at our disposal. This lesson will help your students see the value of choosing the right titles.

Teaching it:

Today we are going to talk about the value of a good title. A title is more than just a label for a piece of writing. It's the first thing a reader sees and it sets the tone for what will come next. For example, you all know a traditional fairy tale like *Goldilocks and the Three Bears*. If we give it a different title it may show us a different point of view about the story.

Here are some new titles:
"Break-in at Three Bears House Police Suspect Human Girl" (crime story)
Fighting Your Inner Bear (self-help book by G. Locks)
"If You Like Hot Porridge Try Three Bear Café" (restaurant review)

Here are a few possibilities for titling the same persuasive essay:
"We Must Stop Global Warming Today" (direct statement of position)
"Palm Trees in Vermont?" (funny image that makes the point)
"We Need More Oil, Now" (dressing as the other side)
"US Produces 1/3 Greenhouse Gases" (title states fact)
"Can We Continue Business as Usual?" (start with a question)

Choose a position on a particular issue and write five titles.

Debriefing:
How does each title change the tone of your essay?
What are the first titles that pop into your mind? Why do you think they do that?

Spin-offs:
- Take a title of any book and try changing the title several times to give it a different tone.

- Go to the library and list titles. Bring them to class and categorize them into different types.

- Create a title board in the classroom. Next time you go to title a piece look to the title board for ideas.

For Younger Students:

• Make a list of everyday events and give them a title.
  For example:
  Getting up: Eight A.M. and He's Still in Bed
  Breakfast   Not Eggs and Bacon Again!
  School: Mona's Gerbil Ate my Homework

• Bring in photos from home. Give each several titles or headlines. (see below)

Resources:

Editorial pages of newspapers.

Bookshelves full of titles at the library.

1. **Lakota Hoop Dancer Kevin Locke spreads message of the oneness of humanity to local children.**

2. **"We are one family," says Kevin Locke.**

Once Upon a Time, You Were Wrong

You don't have anything if you don't have the stories.
Leslie Marmen Silko

The Point: One of the best ways to make a point is to tell a story. Chances are, if you are a teacher, you do this already on a regular basis. For example, you can say to your students, "If your homework is not done, you'd better have a good excuse." Or you can tell a story about how the boy whose dog ate his homework fared when it came time to compute his final grade.

Stories are the best way to make a point, because they can put the audience in your shoes, guide and gently coax them to listen. Leading with a story can be a powerful tool for learning.

Teaching it:

Here are the beginnings of two pieces of writing. One begins with direct assault on the reader's views; the other tells a story.

Once upon a time in a land far away, there was a kingdom where everyone dressed the same. It all started as great idea. After all, girls and boys were spending hours deciding what to wear each day, and some girls and boys could afford expensive clothes while others could not. Dressing the same helped everyone to feel equal and good about themselves, until one day they had to leave school. What would they wear to that job interview or that date? Some of the young women showed up in blazers and ties; others wore jeans in a statement of their newfound freedom. Not really having sartorial experience, they all made terrible first impressions, and all the jobs went to students from schools where there were no dress codes. There was one exception, however; these were the students who joined the army. They packed their real clothes away for another three years.

School uniforms are a dumb idea.

What's the difference between these two leads? *(Let students discuss a comparison.)*

For example: If you want to convince your parents to lend you the car for a trip to a rock concerts you could demand, beg or plead with them or perhaps tell them a story about the time you ending up taking a ride with an upperclassmen who drove on the wrong side of the road.

Rewrite the lead to your essay as a story.

Read some of Aesop's fables and notice how he extracts a moral from the story. Create some of your own fables. Try starting with the moral first or the story first.

Debriefing :

What is the difference between a straight lead and a story lead?
When would a story lead be more effective, when not?
Which is more effective, a humorous story lead, or a serious story lead? Always?

Spin-offs:

- Videotape the evening news or an evening magazine story and bring it in to class. Play part of a news story and ask your students to give it a moral. For example, a new study shows that 65% of all Americans are overweight....

- Moral: Eat a Twinkie at your own risk!

- Tell a story to your class and ask them to tell you the moral. Have your students do the same for each other.

For Younger Writers:

- With your class, make a list of morals. Now write stories to go with them.

- Do the last activity as an improvisation performance exercise. You can do it in teams as a quiz show. Each team has three minutes to create a story after being given a moral. Create a panel of independent judges to observe and rate the competition.

Resources: Appendix 53

Appendix 53, Fables by Aesop.

Aesop's Fables: Online Collection. 6 May 2001. <http://www.aesopfables.com>
Download versions of your favorite fables.

Carroll, Joyce Armstrong, and Ron Habermas. *Jesus Didn't Use Worksheets.* Houston: Absey & Co., 1996. A master educator and a theologian join to present a thought-provoking discussion of the teaching methods of Jesus. This book is full of insights and samples about why stories or parables are so effective.

and the moral of tonight's news
broadcast is "Be afraid,
Be very afraid."

Start with Facts

Get your facts first, then you can distort them as you please.

Mark Twain

The Point: Facts speak for themselves and lead the reader to a thesis before the writer can state it. But facts are not ends in themselves. They can be enhanced or exaggerated by a clever writer to achieve an effect. Here's a way to play with facts and learn about their power in the process.

Teaching it:

Facts speak for themselves. No doubt you have heard this before. What does it mean? It means a well-chosen fact can say more than a dozen well-chosen opinions. For example, listen to the following facts and see if you can guess the opinion of the writer who is quoting them.

Example:

1. Europeans spend $11 billion yearly on ice cream, $2 billion more than what is needed to provide clean water and safe sewers for the world's population.
   (Author wants more money into protecting the earth's water.)

2. Americans and Europeans spend $17 billion yearly on pet food, $4 billion more than the estimated annual additional food needed to provide basic health and nutrition for everyone in the world.

3. In 1993 handguns were responsible for 37,184 deaths in the US.

4. The estimated cost of achieving and maintaining universal access to basic education for all, basic health care for all, reproductive health care for all women, adequate food for all and clean water and safe sewers for all is roughly $40 billion per year or less than 4% of the combined wealth for the 225 richest people in the world

Now collect some facts of your own to prove the point you are trying to make in your essay Pick one and state it in your lead sentence. Next write your lead, stating an opinion.

For example:
Fact: In 1993 handguns were responsible for 37,184 deaths in the United States.
Opinion: There is no excuse for the legal sale of handguns.

Debriefing:

Which lead is stronger? Why?
Do you think listeners identify facts and opinions to themselves as they hear them?

Spin-offs:

- Look at the snapshot section of the *USA Today* newspaper. It can be found in the lower left-hand corner at the beginning of each section. Create your own snapshot and graph using a statistic from your argument.

- Take your opinion and invent three fictional facts to support it. Next, go to the library to find real facts to support the fictional ones,

- Find a numerical statistic and create another one from the original statistic.

- Read newspaper articles and extract three facts from them. Write leads using these three facts.

For Younger Writers:

- Try these facts instead of the ones in the lesson above:
  1. On Super Bowl Sundays Americans consume an estimated 14 tons of high cholesterol potato chips.
  2. Thirty percent of all children of working parents go to bed later than 9:00 P.M.
  3. Students at schools that require uniforms get 30% higher grades than students at schools that don't require uniforms.
  4. Children at schools with one-hour recesses do 10% better on standardized tests.

Resources:

World Almanac for Kids 2001. Mahwah, NJ: World Almanac Books, 2001. Can there be any better collection of facts?

Clement, Rod. *Counting on Frank*. Milwaukee: G. Stevens Children's Books, 1991. In this picture book a child writes a series of compelling leads based on the mathematical facts.

Experts agree, most people couldn't care less about experts.

The Blunt Beginning

What is true is what I can't help believing.
Oliver Wendell Holmes, Jr.

The Point: One way to start is to just spill your opinion onto the page and then work backward to prove it. This is the traditional academic approach, but it can work especially well when the writer is simply trying to get complex ideas down on the paper in a direct way. If it seems too straightforward, then after a draft is completed the writer can always go back and change the lead to something subtler. Here is one way to teach the blunt beginning to your students.

Teaching it:

I'm going to read you the beginning line of a couple of papers.

> School uniforms are a bad idea.
> All guns should be outlawed in America.
> School recess should be longer.

Would you say that the authors of those statements are hiding their point? Or being blunt?

When is blunt better? Below are a few possible answers.
1. When you want to be clear and direct.
2. When the point you're making is a complicated one and you don't want to confuse the reader.
3. When you are in a hurry and need to finish fast, like in a timed testing situation.

Debriefing:

What's the difference between a blunt lead and a less direct lead?
What is the reader's possible reaction?
What would happen if people walked up to each other and started off conversations with their "bottom lines" like this?

Spin-offs:

• Find any newspaper and look for front-page hard news stories. Read the lead to these stories and point out how the direct approach allows readers to browse the page and find out a lot of information just by reading the leads.

• Practice writing blunt statements about everything. Let your opinions get bold and far-reaching. Here are some examples.

> All schools should offer a choice of chocolate or plain milk.

> All bread should be toasted till it makes cracking noises when you butter it.

- Write a letter of complaint about a specific product. Spell out your concerns clearly in the first sentence.

- Write a letter of appreciation about someone who works near you. Spell out your admiration clearly in the first sentence.

For Younger Writers:

- Write a newspaper article about something that happened to you today. As all news articles do, bluntly spell out what happened in the first sentence.

- Write a shocking tabloid newspaper article about something that happened today.
  KIDS GET UP LATE, ALMOST MISS BUS; MOM SCREAMS AT THEM

- Find a headline that means one thing, then illustrate it to mean another. Below is a headline from the *London Times* about lamb price war.

Resources:

Sample letters, Chapter 10.

Fears grow of "lamb war" with France.

56   The Myth-Blasting Lead

It would be better not to know so many things than to know so many things that are not so.

Felix Okaye

The Point: A great way to put your reader off-guard is to blast apart a commonly held belief in the very first few sentences of a piece. This makes for interesting reading and also can give an historical dimension to your argument.

Teaching it:

(Create some myth-blasting leads following the model of these examples. Share them with your class and discuss the power of taking apart a commonly held belief.)

Listen to two examples of myth-blasting leads:

> Everyone knows that the right to bear arms is protected by the Constitution, but did you realize that at the time in America when the law was created, there was no such thing as a police department?

> School uniforms will greatly reduce school violence and create a better learning environment. If you believe this, you haven't seen the research.

Now, tell me: what makes a myth-blasting lead? *(Some commonly held belief, and then opposition to it.)*

Let's make a list of commonly held beliefs or truths:

> Sex leads to reproduction.
> Breathing keeps us alive.
> There was less violence when there was prayer in the schools.

Next, let's turn these statements into myth-blasting leads which let the reader in on the big secret that only you know about.

> Example:
> We all know that babies come from sex between males and females. If I were to tell you that it has never clinically been proven, you might not believe me, but it's true.

> You think that if you stopped breathing tomorrow you would die. But don't tell that to Katwon Aswami, a Tibetan yogi who hasn't breathed for two years.

Debriefing:

What is the effect of a myth-blasting lead?
What might a good time to use it?

Spin-offs:

• In your notebook collect basic truths about the universe, then look for facts to disprove them.

For Younger Writers:

- Read portions of a book called *Lies My Teacher Told Me* by James Lowen. Lowen blasts apart myths in American history by giving us other sides of the story. Create a myth-blasting lead using unique information.

- Do a research survey in your class to gather information on a topic of your choice. Then write a lead based on your most revealing piece of information.
  Example: If you think that all third graders love pizza, think again.

Resources:

Boller, Jr., Paul F. *Not So! Popular Myths about America from Columbus to Clinton.* New York: Oxford University Press, 1995. Each chapter blasts apart another myth about American history.

Lowen, James. *Lies my Teacher Told Me: Everything Your American History Textbook Got Wrong.* New York: Touchstone, 1995. Lowen shows you the other side to one dimensional history textbooks.

Lowen, James. *Lies Across America.* New York: Touchstone, 1999. In his sequel to *Lies My Teacher Told Me,* Lowen travels across the country showing us all the untold stories behind historical monuments. Both books are great myth-blasting resources.

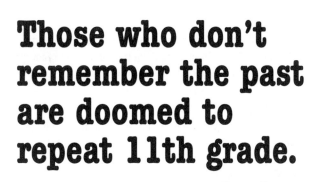

Those who don't remember the past are doomed to repeat 11th grade.

James Lowen

Shine the Light of a Question

We do not write what we know; we write what we want to find out.
Wallace Stenger

The Point: A question can be a light that shines the way down through a persuasive essay, yet many times it's used in a mechanical or formulaic way. This activity helps students to find probing beginning questions.

Teaching it:

(Bring in a flashlight to class and turn the lights out.)
A question is like this beam of light. It points in a particular direction and illumines certain parts of an argument when you try to answer it. Finding the right questions to begin with can help organize your essay by showing you which details to include and which to leave out. Questions also help to illuminate all the angles.

For example, here is a list of questions about the school uniform issue. Try answering them and you will begin to develop a point of view on the topic.
Jot down a quick answer to each one.

Do you hate school uniforms?
What will school uniforms do to children's sense of individuality?
When in history and in what countries are school uniforms standard?
Who stands to benefit from school uniforms?
Why is the question of school uniforms an important issue?
If teachers wore uniforms, how would it effect the school?
Which of those questions show the most about your point of view? Which question brought out the least information?

Avoid meaningless robot rhetorical questions which writers sometimes ask in an attempt to write inquisitively without actually asking anything. I'm not talking about a good rhetorical question that gets you thinking, rather the mindless question that seems to be just taking up space. There is a temptation to write this way on tests. Here are some examples.

Do you have a favorite season? Well, I do!"
Have you ever wondered why people believe in school uniforms? Well, I'll tell you.
Do you have a favorite person?

This type of question does not expect the other person to answer.
Now break into pairs and make your own lists of real questions.

Pick one question to make as the lead to the essay and freewrite for nine minutes.

Debriefing:

Were some questions more interesting to you than others?

Did you find that questions brought out a different reaction in you than statements would have? Can you explain why that happens?

Spin-offs:

- Find a persuasive essay and read it. Afterwards try writing the one question which the essay answers. Talk with your students about how questions are often the driving force in writing.

- Practice turning facts into questions, and questions into facts.

- Take the words to a popular song. After each verse write lists of questions that get raised in your mind. See if the later verses answer these questions.

For Younger Writers:

- Make your own book of questions. See resources for models.

- Make a poster of a question. Write the question on the poster, then choose images, perhaps ones that begin to answer the question beneath it. (See below.)

Resources:

Stock, Gregory. *The Kid's Book of Questions*. New York: Workman Publishing, 1989.
This book provides great question-asking modeling.

Start with a Quote

I hate quotations.
Ralph Waldo Emerson

The Point: Whenever we try to make a point, the audience can always fall back on the fact that it's only our own opinion. This is why it is a great idea to get quotes from famous people to make our opinions seem like commonly held beliefs. This lesson aims to teach students to develop an eye and an ear for good quotes and how to begin using them to help create an argument.

Teaching it:

Quoting famous people, like finding a strong fact, is a way to make your argument without it sounding like it's your own personal opinion. Choosing or finding the right quote can be a time-consuming experience, but it can be a very effective tool.

Take a quote and tell what it could be used to prove.

For example:
A penny saved is a penny earned. -Benjamin Franklin
If you earn a lot of money and spend it all you are worse off than someone makes less but manages to save it.

All that glitters is not gold. –Shakespeare
We must not always judge beauty by what is immediately seen as pretty.

Debriefing:
What's it like to explain quotes?
Can you use quotes to good effect in your persuasive essays?
Why is it that people give more credibility to something if someone famous said it, than if "just you" said it?

Spin-offs:
- Collect many quotes from the Internet and other sources. Arrange them thematically and do a small illustrated manuscript called "My Favorite Quotes," or make your own title.

- Choose an interesting quote and try freewriting about it. In your writing connect it to a story in your life.

For Younger Writers:

• Create your own book of quotes as a class that you add to as the year goes on.
The quotes can be from books read, visitors to the class, words heard on TV or radio.
Have a quote box at the front of the room where students can add the quotes throughout the year. At the end of the year, put the quotes all together as a farewell gift book.

• Listen to everyone around you and jot down whatever memorable things they say. Collect these, with the speaker's signature and date on each one. Publish them at the end of the year!

• Collect proverbs and paste them on the wall in your class. For fun, give them new endings. (See below.)

Resources:

Bartlett's Familiar Quotations. 6 May 2001. <http://www.bartleby.com.>

Bartlett, John. *Familiar Quotations.* Boston: Little, Brown and Co., 1980.

Famous Quotations Network. 6 May 2001. <http://www.famous-quotations.com>.
These Websites have great information on quotes.

Quoteland.com: Quotations on Every Topic, By Every Author, and in Every Fashion Possible. May 5, 2001. http://quoteland.com. This site is one of many that break down quotes thematically. This makes them much easier than trying to find one by an author that fits your theme.

Give a man a fish
   and he eats for a day.
Teach him to fish
   and he's gone every weekend.

Anonymous Michigan Teacher

59 End with a Scene

Too many pieces of music finish too long after the end.
Igor Stravinsky

The Point: A dramatic scene can be an unconventional way to end a persuasive essay. Drama brings a moment into focus for the reader and the writer. If we can effectively dramatize our point, the reader will be drawn in to our stance before he can reject it.

Teaching it:

The best book on drama exercises for the classroom remains Viola Spolin's *Theatre Games for the Classroom.* Use this book to create a playful atmosphere for drama in your class for theater. Here are some good ideas to try.

Pick five students to be an acting troupe. The class gives them a position to act out, and they have three minutes to huddle and come up with a way of dramatizing that point of view. To prepare the troupe, try acting out a point of view yourself with four other students. The whole class can make suggestions.

A variation of the last would have the students choose a position in secret and then act it out. The class would have to guess their position from the scene.

To make it even harder, no talking aloud.

Now go back to your writing and try ending your essay with a dramatic scene that makes your point.

Spin-offs:

- Bring in dramatic TV commercials into class. Talk about how in 30 seconds of drama a position is created. Try making a TV commercial for your stance. If possible, tape the commercial.

- Pick a position at random from a list and with a few partners take a few minutes to dramatize that position in a scene. Stop. Now take the opposite of that position and turn that into a scene.

- Find a persuasive essay or letter from the editor. After you extract the point of the letter, try turning it into a scene.

For Younger Writers:

- Take a fairy tale and pick a point of view within it Assuming that no characters think of themselves as wrong, rewrite the scene from a character's point of view.

- Choose a photo of a scene like the one on the next page. Choose characters within the photo and write a scene.

Resources:

Spolin, Viola. *Theatre Games for the Classroom*. Evanston, IL: Northwestern University Press, 1990. Like her Bible, Improvisation for the Theatre, Spolin's book will give you dozens of ideas and warm-up activities to turn your class into an actor's studio.

Glynn, Carol. *Learning on Their Feet*. Shoreham, VT: Discover Writing Press, 2001. www.discoverwriting.com. This comprehensive book is filled with dozens of activities for using drama to teach across the curriculum in math, science, language arts and social studies.

PHOTO: JESSIE LANE

End with an Image

Don't write endings; find them.
Thomas Williams

The Point: Another way to solidify a point in the reader's mind is leave him or her with a palpable image to carry away from the essay. In other words, I can tell you what to think about global warming and you can agree or disagree with me. But if I leave you with a picture of palm trees growing at the North Pole, you will have to agree with me until you can rid your mind of the image I have created there.

Teaching it:

Any argument can be turned into an image by imagining a picture to prove your point of view. Use some the examples beneath to make your point.

Handguns should be illegal in America.
Image: Imagine if handguns had been illegal since 1960. Imagine a world where Mark Chapman can't shoot John Lennon because they wouldn't sell him the weapon. John Lennon gets his left arm broken by Chapman's baseball bat. John Hinkley can't shoot Ronald Reagan. And 100,000 more people are alive because the guns they were slaughtered with haven't been sold.

Capital punishment is cruel and inhuman punishment. It should be forever outlawed.
Image: Imagine it is your son or daughter who has been convicted of the crime. They say they are innocent and you believe them, but now there are only four hours to go before the lethal injection will pulse through their veins. The governor has said no to the appeal, and you are eating a last meal with them in their cell.

Debriefing:

How is an image different than an opinion or statement?
What is the power of ending with an image?

Spin-offs:

- Make a list of opinions and create an image for each opinion. Try throwing some funny ones in.

- Bring in images from advertisements and ask students to write a sentence for each image that shows what the image is saying about the product.

    The Marlboro man might say "Cigarettes will make you macho."

    Now come up with your own opinion about the product and create your own image.

For Younger Writers:

- Draw your opinion on a piece of paper. The only rule is no words. Other students must guess your opinion by staring at the image you create.

- Bring in a photo like the one below. Give an opinion to a figure in the image.

Resources:

Lane, Barry. *Reviser's Toolbox.* Shoreham, VT, Discover Writing Press, 1999. Chapter three in this book has many examples of snapshots, which are images that enhance a character, a setting, or an opinion.

Humans are very strange creatures.

Summing It Up—Looping It Up

And to end the news here are the main points once again....
BBC World Service Newscaster

The Point: In conclusion, let me say that one of the best most traditional ways to end an essay is to summarize the main points. Though this book often promotes less traditional ways of crafting the persuasive essay, we also accept that each essay is different. A traditional summary can sometimes be the best way to end. This lesson is about how to determine if a summary is the best way to conclude and how to write one.

Teaching it:

Read the following ending to your class and ask them what the essay was about. When they tell you all the key points, ask them how they could know so much when all they read was the last paragraph. Discuss the power of the summary ending. It is like a study guide that reviews the key points. One way to write a summary is to make a simple list of the key points in your argument and then turn that list into a paragraph.

Sample ending:
In conclusion, school uniforms are bad for three reasons. They lower a student's self- esteem, they promote mindless conformity, and they create the shallow illusion that everything is ok because everyone's in ties and dresses. Schools should be preparing people for the real world where even your boss might be wearing a T-shirt. Let's stop judging books by their covers and start teaching the things that really matter.

Debriefing:
When might summing it up be the best choice for an ending?
When might it not be?

Spin-offs:
- Write or rewrite the ending of your essay as a summary.

- Write a poem called "In conclusion" and draw together a summary of your life.
  Example: **"In conclusion"**
    The sun will burn out
    The earth will turn into a chunk of ice
    Slurpee machines will be rendered useless.

- Create the latest dance sensation, not the Jerk or the Mashed Potato, but The Summary!

For Younger Writers:

- Preachers are told to make three points in their sermon. Extract three points from an essay you've read or even a TV commercial. Now write a summary ending using the three points. *Example* In conclusion, Colgate will make your teeth whiter, breath fresher and stop cavities.

- Make a summary poster which, through both images and words ,sums up the main points of your argument.

- With three classmates create a summary poem. Each classmate can take a part of the argument. Perform your poem for the class.

Resources:

Seuss, Dr. *Green Eggs and Ham.* New York: Random House, 1960. This classic children's book models the summing it up pattern. The power of the summary is that nothing is left out. The reader is continually brought back to the main points.

(summary poster)

In Conclusion

1. The planet is heating up.

2. The U.S. won't join the world in taking responsibility for greenhouse gases.

3. The U.S. values short term profits over what we leave our children. This is madness.

Elaboration:
The Fire not the Fog

Paper fails Reason: insufficient elaboration.
-from a failing state test paper

What do the students need to do — put in more adjectives?
-overheard from a high school principal

Details are the walls, not the wallpaper.
Barry Lane

I f we think of student writing in scientific terms, a thesis statement or position statement is like a hypothesis. Elaboration is the proof. In life, the proof is in the pudding. In writing the pudding is the details, the facts, the stories and whatever else makes the point.

This truth is especially noticeable in testing situations where students are sometimes asked to show their thinking about subjects they care little about. Companies who market test-oriented writing programs often present elaboration in these situations as the ability to use big and educated-sounding words for that authoritative voice. They'll help your students plant three multi-syllabic adjectives in alternating paragraphs or spin topics and sub-topics into a whirling dervish of crochet patterns for building an essay.

And in the end, with all their bland topic sentences followed by their three supporting details marching neatly in single file behind them, they'll help your students to sound less like themselves and exactly like the people who wrote the tests.

Luckily, in most states today this nonsense will usually not be recognized as exemplary writing (even though such approaches are routinely adopted). Why? These tests, in the end, are read and scored by human beings, who after hours sitting in a hard chairs reading stultifying essays, relish the clear impassioned prose of writers who know not only how to play the game, but also how to bend the rules to fit their own voices. If you or others doubt this, arm yourself William Zinsser's On *Writing Well,* or Ken Macrorie's *Searching Writing.* Simple, clear and truthful language will beat out abstract, complex and deceptive every time.

They test for gold with fire, not fog; and when we write, the detail is the fire that shows us our gold. In this chapter the first lessons help to eliminate the fog; the next lessons help find the fire and develop ways of igniting it even when you don't have any matches.

Robots Lose: Use Your Own Words

"Oh Frederick, can not you in the calm excellence of your wisdom, reconcile it with your conscience to say something that will ease my father's sorrow?"
"What?"
"Can't you cheer him up?"

from *The Pirates of Penzance* by Gilbert and Sullivan

Never choose a big word when a small one will do.
George Orwell

The Point: Choosing details begins with choosing words. When writing gets too formal, the big show-off words take over. Writing that packs a wallop is usually full of small words, simply stated and clearly understood. The following lesson teaches the power of direct simple diction in presenting and elaborating an argument.

Teaching it:

Sometimes in our writing we try to sound more important by using big words or pretending we know all the answers. We call English teachers literary educators, and custodians building maintenance specialists. Though it's okay to use big words, often times we can make our writing stronger by choosing a simpler way to say it.

Below are some examples of real writing using big words. Find some examples of your own or just rewrite some of these.

Quitting smoking now greatly reduces risk of heart disease, lung disease and emphysema. (from the US Surgeon General's Warning)
Translation: Smoking will kill you.

The IRS Mission: Provide America's taxpayers top quality service by helping them understand and meet their tax responsibilities and by applying the tax law with integrity and fairness to all.

From St. Phillip's College Code of Conduct: College personnel with administrative authority may initiate disciplinary proceedings against a student accused of scholastic dishonesty. "Scholastic dishonesty" includes, but is not limited to, cheating on a test, plagiarism and collusion.

From SAISD Parent-Student Handbook: A teacher may remove from class a student who (1) has been documented by the teacher to repeatedly interfere with the teacher's ability to communicate effectively with the students in the class or with the ability of the student's classmates to learn; or (2) whose behavior the teacher determines is so unruly, disruptive or abusive that it seriously interferes with the teacher's ability to communicate effectively with the students in the class or with the ability of the student's classmates to learn.

Debriefing:

What was the process you went through to write less like a robot?
How can this help your writing?

Spin-offs:

• Find a passage from a difficult science or social studies textbook and rewrite it for a six-year-old. Notice how small words can break down the thought process.

• In your own writing look for places to shrink words and sentences.

For Younger Writers:

• Rewrite the Pledge of Allegiance in your own words. Replace big words like "indivisible" with your own thoughts that explain it. Illustrate your writing.

• Practice robot writing. Take a really simple sentence like "The dog brought the newspaper in the house" and write it like a robot with many big words that cover up the meaning. See how many more words you can add to the sentence. Tip: if you use a thesaurus you will find words like "canine," instead of "dog," to help make your writing worse.

• Create a Mr. Robot character. Draw his picture and make him talk in robot language that is hard to understand. (See below.)

Resources:

Find robot writing. Look in computer manuals. Read the fine print on airline tickets, contracts, or the disclaimers they write about the side effects of drugs.

Fist-Pounding, Bell-Ringing Detail

Don't write that school lunches are gross; write about yellowing vanilla pudding and gobs of cool whip that coat the roof of your mouth like latex paint.

Barry Lane

The Point: All persuasion depends on proving it to a doubtful audience. The more we listen to this other side and fight against this doubt with strong, well-reasoned arguments elaborated in fine detail, the more our writing improves. Yet sometimes it's hard to see or hear this when we listen to a piece of persuasive writing. The following lesson aims to teach students to hear the best details.

Teaching it:

Have you ever tried to put up a tent in a windstorm? If you have, you'll know the value of stakes that you pound into the ground. Each new stake stops the tarp from flapping away. It can be the same way with an argument. A big idea is like flapping tarp. Each concrete fact or specific detail nails it down just a little more. Today we are going to learn how to pound stakes to nail down flapping opinions with fist-pounding, bell-ringing detail.

(Get or make a good fist-pounding lectern, and find one of those bells you ring by slamming your hand down upon it. Practice pounding or ringing.)

1. We'll start by learning the difference between an opinion (what I think or feel) and a fact (something that has been proven or recorded by a third source).

   Opinion: Contrary to what the NRA says, handguns do not protect American citizens; they endanger them. (I can't pound. This is the wind or hot air.)
   Fact: A study of all gunshot deaths in the Seattle area found that out of 743 deaths reported that the majority occurred in homes where guns were kept, and more than half were accidental. (Pound, Ring a ding ding.)

   You can't pound on an opinion, only on a fact, but it doesn't have to be a documented fact like the one above. It can be simple— an anecdotal or story fact.

   For example, "TV is sometimes educational." (I can't pound on this because it's too general and may just be my opinion.) Now compare it to this: "The other night I saw a documentary on sharks on the Discovery Channel, and I learned that they have three rows of replicating razor-sharp teeth." (Pound, Ring. Can you see how this nails down the idea?)

2. Now look at a piece you have written and draw an X at the places where you could pound your piece or ring your bell. Read your piece with a partner, practicing the pounding parts.

(Read the piece to the class, fist-pounding or bell-ringing whenever they get a fact or detail that nails down an opinion.)

Teaching it:

3. Now let's add a new voice: the doubting audience. Whenever we write, our audience often doubts our words, but they keep those doubts silent. Today we are going to make them audible. Let's practice. I'll read the beginning of my piece and when I pause, you doubt me.

Contrary to what the NRA says, guns don't protect citizens; they endanger them.
Doubting chorus: No way! Guns protect us from gun-toting criminals!

4. Read your piece to the doubting chorus and add your fist-pounding or bell-ringing to it.

Debriefing:

Who won? The writer or the doubters?
Was there enough fist pounding or bell ringing, or does the writer have to work on this more?
How would you write for bell-ringing and fist-pounding?

Spin-offs:

- One person reads their own writing in front of the whole class, pausing after each sentence. The class doubts the writer's assertions.

- Take a piece of published non-fiction, perhaps a letter to the editor or an editorial. Someone reads it to the class, pausing to let the doubting chorus chime in. Who wins?

For Younger Writers:

- Take a piece of writing that is really boring non-fiction writing, like an old basal reader. Have someone read it to the class, pausing for the chorus.

- Try rewriting it to make it more truthful and interesting by answering the doubting chorus's questions.

- Get a copy of the school handbook and using the doubting chorus, rewrite parts of it in your own words.

- Take the school handbook and pick five rules. For each rule, create a story that proves why the rule is important.

- Go to the Web site www.dumblaws.com and pick a few dumb laws. Pick a few stories that go along with them.

Resources: Appendix 63

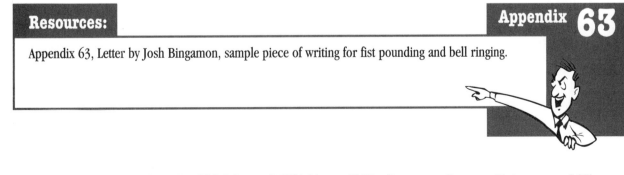

Appendix 63, Letter by Josh Bingamon, sample piece of writing for fist pounding and bell ringing.

Made You Look
(Elaborating With Humor)

Superman don't need no seat belt.
> Muhammad Ali, to flight attendant as he refuses to buckle up

No, Mr. Ali— Superman don't need no plane!
> Flight attendant who knows this lesson

The Point: In the real world a great skill is simply to persuade people to pay attention to what you have to say. Have you ever watched flight attendants on a plane? They have an announcement to tell passengers what to do in an emergency, and yet nobody seems to pay attention to them. Only one airline, Southwest, has learned the secret of convincing people to listen to them. The following lesson takes Southwest Airline's lead and teaches students how to elaborate with joy and humor.

Teaching it:

1. Have you ever been on an airplane? Pretend for a minute you are all on a plane and I am your flight attendant whose main job is to insure your safety. Now I'm going to read you some announcements that could save your life. *(Read announcement below in a robot nasal voice. If you want, ham it up by pinching nostrils together.)*

Please pay attention while important safety information is reviewed.

Federal aviation authorities require that passengers observe all lighted signs and posted placards.

In the event of an emergency, aisle path lighting will illuminate aisle and lead you to the exits.

Your seat belt has a metal end that fastens into the buckle. To fasten, insert metal end into the buckle and adjust low and tight around your waist. To release, pull back on the buckle.

Your cabin is equipped with two lavatories, one in the front of the aircraft and two in the rear. All lavatories are equipped with smoke detectors. Federal law prohibits tampering with or destroying any smoke detector.

In the rare event of a water landing you'll find a life preserver beneath your seat. Place it over your head and fasten the straps around your waist. To inflate the vest, pull down on the straps. You may also inflate the vest manually by blowing into the tubes. Please do not inflate your vest till you have exited the cabin. Your seat cushion will also serve as a flotation device. Remove it from the seat and place both arms through it.

In the event of a loss of cabin pressure, an oxygen mask will appear from the panel above you. Pull down on the cord to release the flow of oxygen, place the mask over your nose and mouth and breathe normally. If you are traveling with a young person, place the mask over your face first, then secure their mask.

2. What do you think? Are you ready to snap into action or are you falling asleep? I bet you are falling asleep. Only one airline, Southwest Airlines, encourages their flight attendants to rewrite the announcement so

Teaching it:

people will pay attention. This is both fun for the flight attendants, because it relieves the monotony of a robot-like job, and fun for the travelers who often have been on many plane rides that all seem the same.

For example, instead of "Your seat cushion serves as flotation device to be used in the rare event of a water landing," on Southwest, the announcement becomes: "Should our flight suddenly evolve into a cruise, you'll find that the seat cushion serves as a flotation device. Your plastic tray table detaches to make a handy shark repellent."

This flight attendant made you look with humor, and yet the information is there for you to understand and take to heart.

3. Now it's time to have some fun. Take any one of the statements from above and with a partner, rewrite to make it less like a robot and more like a human being. The only rule is, you must include the same information. However, you can embellish it any way you want.

For example: Place the mask over your nose and chin and breath like this (Deep Darth Vader Breathing) "LUKE, I AM YOUR FATHER."

Tip: It helps sometimes to read the statement to a friend and have them react. Then see if you can put their reaction into your rewrite.

Example: Your seatbelt has a metal end that fastens in the buckle.
Friend's reaction: DUH.

Rewrite: If you haven't been in a car since 1950 you might not know that your seatbelt has a metal end that fastens into the buckle.

Spin-offs:

• Look at your own persuasive essay. Is there a place where you can take a robot voice and make it sparkle with humor and animation?

Resources:

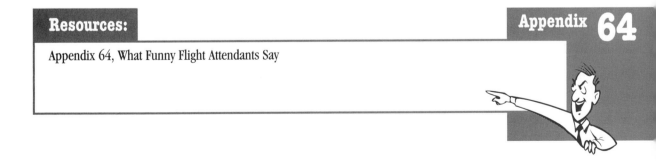

Appendix **64**

Appendix 64, What Funny Flight Attendants Say

Where My Opinions Come From

It takes a great man to make a good listener.

Arthur Helps

The Point: Sometimes students need a back door into fresh ways to think about elaboration. This exercise gives them practice at looking at opinions from a different perspective, while embedding rich visual detail.

Teaching it:

Think of three people in your life who have had strong beliefs about the best way to live. Choose one of these people.

On a blank piece of paper, write down some words you can remember (or imagine) hearing that person say. (Take about two minutes.)

Next, enclose those words into a word bubble. Draw a simple drawing of the speaker.

I'm going to ask you a few questions. For each, take about a minute, and on your paper, answer each one with a complete sentence.

1. What is one thing you knew that they believed about life?
2. When they said those words in the word bubble, what did their face look like? (Eyes sparkling? Eyebrows scrunched up? Devilish smile? What?)
3. When did they say that? (When you were five?)
4. What is their body language? (Are their hands on their hips? How do you picture them standing/sitting as they say that? Feet up on the couch?)

Now here's the challenge. See if you can combine all that information into one sentence with no drawing. You have five minutes.

Student Responses:

My brother always tells me, "Nobody can be loved more than you can," as he gives me a hug and smiles, wiping his frown off his face and replacing it with a grin. -Kati M., 9th grade

As my mother holds her Bible, I sadly look at her gentle face, knowing that like every time before, she'll tell me, "Just trust in God; it will all work out." -Kristen S., 9th grade

Yesterday when Stephanie and I went to the mall, she saw a pink leather shirt and began to spin with it, and as her face lit up, she looked at the price tag and gave out an unpleasant noise, saying, "This is craziness!" -Brittany R., 9th grade

Debriefing:

(After they finish, have them share their sentences.)

Now, on the bottom of your paper, answer in just about one minute this question: Are these sentences different from what you usually hear from yourselves? How and why?

(Have them discuss THIS. This is where the truth about elaboration comes out in discussion: opinions come from somewhere; and helping someone else see your vision makes a thought really stick.)

Spin-offs:

• Rearrange the words and phrases into an "Ode to _____." An ode is a poem that praises.

For Younger Writers:

• Draw a picture to go along with your statement.

• Take the opinion of your person and make it the chorus of a song. Create your own melody or simply take the melody of a song that already exists.

• Bring in a photo of someone in your family or yourself. Then write an opinion beneath the photo.

Our family has unique talents.

Anchoring Feelings: "Fine. You?"

"And how are you this evening, Mrs._____"
telemarketer showing limited concern

The Point: Have you noticed how students answer the question, "How are you?" Within themselves lies every bit of information needed to turn a one-word answer into a fully complex, multi-part, detailed answer, but they rarely take the time or energy. Practicing that answer can help students articulate parts of a whole, increase specificity of language and complex sentence structure. Awareness of feelings can also help them to read an audience, an important part of persuasion.

Teaching it:

On a scratch piece of paper, in the next minute or two, answer this question. How are you feeling right now? Not physically, but emotionally? How are you feeling?

Now look at what you wrote. See whether you identified the source of your feelings. (That means tell where that feeling came from.) Add that if you want to. Put these sentences aside for a few minutes.

Now, I'd like for you to look through your journals and find a place when you had really strong feelings. You're going to write a sentence and tell in that sentence, these three things:
  1. When this was.
  2. What your feeling was.
  3. What made you feel that way.
Write your sentence on a sentence strip, and don't write your name on it unless you would like to. You have about six minutes.
(Pick them up and share some aloud.)

Is there a volunteer to read how you answered the question I asked you a little while ago? "How are you feeling?" (Hear some responses.)

How are the sets of answers different? What does that mean?

Student Responses:

Before

I feel depressed and upset.

My feelings consist of being exhausted, fortunate, upset, uneasy, and asking the question 'why.' All these feelings come from life itself and all the situations that I've come across.

I feel happy with so much energy.

Why We Must Run With Scissors © 2001 Discover Writing Press · www.discoverwriting.com

After

Last night I felt angry because I didn't have my house keys, and my mom wasn't home.

On Valentine's Day I felt overwhelmed with love when everyone showed me how much they appreciate having me around.

In January I felt great because when I went to a party at my cousin's house, my friend brought me roses, balloons and a card.

It kinda made me feel disappointed that morning when people started comparing me to cartoons.

Samples of Student Reflections:

At first, the sentences were more like "Life rocks," or "Life sucks," and nothing else but blank silence. The other sentences were more like packed.

It seems like adding all these three things together into one sentence is easy. But then when you hear it, it sounds like something you would hear in a book instead of just from us.

Is this another way you're turning us into writers?

It's easier to write more about strong feelings than about feelings that are just blah. You remember where you were and stuff, like what made you feel that way, when it's a stronger feeling.

Spin-offs:

- For fun try telling a friend how you really feel when they casually ask you "How's it going?" This works best with good friends, but you can experiment with telemarketers who call at dinnertime and begin their conversation, "And how are you today?" Post the speech by the telephone.

  Well, to tell you the truth the day started with a bad case of diarrhea and went downhill from there, and then this telemarketer called at lunchtime, and there's nothing worse than getting calls from telemarketers when you are trying to have a nice relaxing meal. So tell me, what are you calling about?

For Younger Writers:

- Place your forearm of your hand on a big sheet of paper and create a feelings tree. Write the name of a feeling in the middle and describe a moment when you felt the feeling for each finger.

- Write a Go-inside-a-feeling poem. Begin by brainstorming a list of feelings on the board with your students, then write the words "Go inside" on the board. Now you are ready to Go inside a feeling. Write a poem that tells you what's inside.

  Example:

  "Go inside MAD"   "Just wait, You wait!"
  feet stomping   nostrils flaring
  bottles cracking   fists pounding
  "That's mine, You idiot" I'm not coming back here

Filters and Intensifiers:
A One-Sentence Rewrite

You are somewhat like a hound dog
Crying most of the time...
                                    a less emphatic Elvis

The Point: People use filters to soften the meaning of a sentence. Here's an example: "I am somewhat happy today." Verbal filters often weaken the writing unnecessarily. Teaching students to replace filters with stronger words serves two purposes: to understand more clearly the need for and nature of verbal filters; and to strengthen diction in writing. This lesson helps students to read their emotions more accurately and chose the right words to describe them.

Teaching it:

When someone is telling how they feel about something, they mostly "soften" the feeling when they put it into words. On the board are two sentences (Write: "She is kind of mad at her boyfriend" and "He was unhappy at work"). Work with a partner if you'd like to, and rewrite these two sentences, making them as intense as that girl and that employee REALLY are. Use a thesaurus if you need to. You have about five minutes.

(Share/post examples of rewrites that the students produce.)

On a slip of paper, explain to me about brains and mouths and filters and intensity. What's the point here? How does it work?

Student responses:

She was kind of mad at her boyfriend.
She was furious with her boyfriend.
She had animosity for her boyfriend.
She was aggravated with her boyfriend.
Her fury towards her boyfriend was intense!

He was unhappy at work.
At work, he was continually sorrowful.
He felt growing dissatisfaction at work.
He was miserable every time he clocked in.
He felt catastrophe over him every day at work.
He hated his work.

Some student reflections about brains and mouths and filters and intensity:

Today we learned how to intensify words, taking the shield off the words. We don't always tell the whole truth or use the right words to express ourselves. It's human nature.

It is better to use filters, because you wouldn't put yourself in a position where people would judge you. You would want to keep it to yourself.

Intense words are very descriptive words that you use to show your exact feeling without being filtered at all. Filtered words make you take your feeling away to make a "boring" sentence with your untrue feelings with the feeling taken away as much as possible.

Debriefing:

How do intensifiers and filters work in writing?
When are they necessary?
When do they weaken the writing?

Spin-offs:

- Draw a cartoon depicting a thought bubble versus a word bubble. Which one has the filtered words? Which one has the intense words?

- Make and post a classroom list of de-intensifiers, or words which will always minimize a feeling (example: "sort of").

- Look for places in your work where de-intensifying language can help soften a point.

For Younger Writers:

- Work further on the intensified sentences to add figurative language. (How aggravated was she? She was as aggravated as a _____ in a room full of _____s.)

- Create a skit where one person offends another. In the first skit have the offended person get very mad and express their feelings directly. In the second skit have them use filter words to soften their feelings. Note the difference.

Resources:

Robbins, Anthony. *Giant Steps: Small Changes to Make a Big Difference.* New York: Fireside Book, 1994. Self-help guru Tony Robbins says some notable things about how language effects our feelings. Are you devastated by my behavior, or are you peeved? The language we choose frames our world.

The Good, the Bad, and the Ugly: Elaborating People

No one can have a higher opinion of him than I have, and I think he's a dirty little beast.

W. S. Gilbert

The Point: Which are easier to list: qualities you like in a friend, or qualities that make someone an ex-friend? Both categories are accessible to students, and they make a perfect entry to writing convincing elaboration. This brainstorming activity will produce a useful list in each category.

Teaching it:

What characteristics do you really despise in a person? What are some things that you might see in a person that might convince you that they will NEVER be your friend? Or that they would be a HORRIBLE person to work with? Number your scratch paper 1-10 and in the next minute or two, make a quick list.

Next, on the back of this scratch paper, number again 1-10. This time, list good qualities. What are some qualities that you find valuable in a friend or a co-worker?

Student Responses:

The Bad	The Good
Liar	Hard working
Conceited	Honest
Self-centered	Selfless
Lazy	Dependable
Dishonest	Polite
Rude	Quiet
Mean	Funny
Backstabbing	Original
Hardheaded	Generous
Bossy	Respectful
Greedy	Entertaining
Disrespectful	Energetic
Boring	Genuine
Fake	Level
Moody	Caring
Dream stealer	Compassionate

Now we are going to learn to make a few negative assertions about people and back them up with the facts and evidence. But I don't want to encourage bad-mouthing each other here; rather I want you to be good judges of character, so we will prove our assertions with what we have observed in the life of this fictional person.

Here's a novel; pick a page and point to the name of the first character you see and give him or her a negative quality from our list.

Let's all pretend that we know someone named......*[glance into any novel you just opened and find a name]* ...(in our case)...Pinky. Choose one of the words from this list of horrible characteristics. For practice, let's use the first word on the list: liar. Pinky is a liar.

Imagine someone right there, arguing, "No, Pinky is NOT a liar."

Prove that Pinky is a liar. Tell something you saw Pinky do one time that proves that Pinky is a liar.

"Pinky lies to his mom and dad. Every time he says something, it is almost always not true. He says he can stop lying, but he still does it anyway. Just the other day he told them he was going to the movies, when he really just wanted to go hang around the mall."

Now choose another word from the list. Write a statement first that says "Pinky is _____ (that word)." Then prove it with an incident you have seen Pinky do.

Debriefing:
How does Pinky change when we elaborate reasons for his attitude?

Student Responses:
Pinky is mean. Pinky stole $400 from the safe at her last job and blamed it on me. - Ernest Morgan

Pinky is extremely selfish. All she does is think about herself. It's always about her. She is never willing to lend a helping hand. She always wants to do things her way. One day I asked her to do something and all she said was, "What do I get out of it?"
   - Josephine Serrano

Pinky is a bossy person. If you start talking and working with him, he is going to start bossing you around. If you like to work with him, you are going to be doing everything he tells you. Man, Pinky is so bossy! I don't like Pinky bossing me around.
   - Vangie Garcia

Spin-offs:
• Make a few positive perceptions about Pinky and prove them with evidence.

• Make a negative assertion about yourself and back it up with evidence. Example: "I'm such a slob". Proof: Yesterday, when I got home I couldn't find my bed.

For Younger Writers:
• Pick a villain from a fairy tale and make and prove negative assertions about them. Example: " The Wolf is big and bad because he eats children!"

• Pick a villain from a fairy tale, make a positive assertion, and prove it. Example: The Wolf is nice because he only eats enough food to survive and is an endangered species.

Virtuous Assertions

They say such nice things about people at their funerals that it makes me sad to realize that I'm going to miss mine by just a few days.

Garrison Keillor

The Point: Who gets enough positive feedback? Nobody. This lesson will demonstrate the absolute personal power of elaboration. Students will now apply the skills from the previous lessons to write assertions about their actual classmates' positive qualities, and to elaborate fully, by telling actual, truthful incidents they have witnessed. Three of these comprise the body, the most meaningful part, of a letter of recommendation.

Teaching it:

Use the bank of positive qualities that the students have brainstormed and the virtues list from the last lesson. Have students think about another student they know and admire and then fill in the blanks in the statement: (Name) is (characteristic), appendix 68. Then employ the doubting chorus to show how proof is easy to find. On a piece of paper, have the student start off by writing down the statement. They will continue with the proof. Get a volunteer to model the process aloud like this:

Ms. B: Edgar, who is someone you want to say positive things about?
Edgar: Chris.
Ms. B: Okay, great. What's one characteristic from the list that is true about Chris?
Edgar: He's peaceful.
Ms. B: Okay, so write 'Chris is peaceful.' Got it? Okay.
          Now...how do you know he's peaceful? I think he's not peaceful at all.
Edgar: Yes, he is.
Ms. B: No, he's not. What have you ever seen that tells you he's peaceful?
Edgar: Lots of things. He doesn't get mad at anyone, and he doesn't yell or curse...
Ms. B: Okay, he's peaceful. There's your proof. Can you write what you just said, after your statement?
          Now you have a character opinion with proof.

Everyone, choose a person. Fill in the blanks. Prove your statement. We'll share in about 10 minutes.

Debriefing:

What did you learn about your person?
Were you surprised by what you uncovered?

Student Responses:

Chris is peaceful. This whole year that I have known him, I have never heard him curse nor raise his voice at anyone. He is always saying sorry or thank you. If you look mad or something he will check in with you to see what's wrong. He will even try to calm you down. -Edgar Nunez

Angie is helpful. Just the other day she helped me in an assignment that I couldn't understand. She took the time to explain the assignment step by step until I understood it. -Isabel Vasquez

Raymond is responsible. He always keeps his priorities straight and has never let any of his peers down. One time during school when I needed him to bring something from home for our class he didn't let me down. He brought it, and it was very important to my grade. He was there for me. -Travis Brinkley

Spin-offs:

- Take *The Family Virtues Guide* to class and have your students pick a virtue that they or one of their classmates exhibited. Write about it and share.

- Write a spoof political commercial where one candidate praises the other, unlike most ads where candidates rip each other apart.

For Younger Writers:

- Write an ad for a person you interview. Like all ads, put the most important positive quality up front. Take a photo or draw a picture of them for the ad. (See below.)

Resources: **Appendix 69**

Appendix 69, Handout for (Name) is (characteristic).

Popov, Linda. *The Family Virtues Guide.* New York: Plume, 1997. This is a very practical book that can help teachers and parent do the most important thing, identify and label good behavior, then figure out how to practice it themselves, so that the next time you're cut off in traffic you can shout at the Yo Yo who pulled in front of you, "I'm practicing detachment now!!"

If you're feeling down, Andy Green will lift you up.

Letter of Recommendation for Someone I Know

Working with Julie Andrews is like getting hit over the head with a valentine.

Christopher Plummer

The Point: When students can write opinion statements and prove them, the logical choice for publishing is to have them write a full-fledged letter of recommendation for one of their peers. Collecting letters about themselves is great training for students who are preparing for the world of work.

Teaching it:

(Sell students on the idea, and then review them in formal letter form. Look at some letters of recommendation of your own, or from other sources, to decide on the opening and closing they want to use. After they've had a chance to write them, these make a wonderful read-around. See if your students aren't floored by the actions they've taken which other students describe as "proof" of their positive characteristics.)

Do your teachers know all about you? Who knows you best? Do you know each other's good qualities in ways that teachers or supervisors don't? In fact, you're the experts when it comes to knowing the best characteristics in each other.

Think of a student in this classroom that you admire. It doesn't have to be someone who is your friend. It might be someone you've noticed for other reasons, someone who might even be surprised to hear that you admire them.

Next, pick from our list three characteristics which are actually true about that person. Go ahead and write a letter about that person, naming these three characteristics and backing each one up with proof.

Assertiveness, caring, cleanliness, compassion, confidence, courage, creativity, detachment, determination, enthusiasm, excellence, faithfulness, flexibility, friendliness, generosity, gentleness, helpfulness, honesty, honor, humility, idealism, joyfulness, kindness, loyalty, moderation, modesty, orderliness, patience, peacefulness…

Spin-offs:

- Write a full-fledged letter of recommendation for someone, using three positive character opinions along with an opening and closing, in letter form.

- Write a letter of recommendation that won't get them the job. Include details like some of those included below. Have fun!
  Examples:
  Even though he never gets to work on time, he always walks in with a smile on his face.

Rudy is so easy to talk to, it's like talking to a stick, because he doesn't answer back.

He's a cool guy, even when he's trying to copy off me.

She may talk about you behind your back, but she is still a good friend.

For Younger Writers:

- Write an imaginary letter of recommendation that you would like for your future children to write about you.

- Write a letter of recommendation about a character in a piece of literature you've read, or from a movie you've seen. Write as though you are another character.

- Write a letter of recommendation for one of your parents (or someone else in your family), using positive parent characteristics.

- Write a letter of recommendation for one of your teachers or a staff member at your school. (They will most likely put it into their professional portfolio.)

Resources: **Appendix 70**

Appendix 70, Sample letters of recommendation.

To Whom it May Concern,

I'm writing to recommend Prince Hamlet of Denmark for a position in your Philosophy Department. As his beloved uncle, I have known Mr. Hamlet for several years now and have found him to be an extremely thoughtful young man with a keen sense of justice and a unique ability to see all sides of any given situation. He is also very fond of foreign travel so moving to Tazmania won't be a problem.

Please don't hesitate to call if you have any further questions. I may even be able to pay for his travel.

Sincerely,
King Claudius

Tips For Standardized Tests:
Writing a Letter About an Issue

This is only a test. Had this been a real emergency…

(test of Emergency Broadcast System)

Millions of students throughout the United States face tests which ask them to write a letter to someone in authority, presenting their position on some issue. No matter what state, what test, or what rubric, those tests ask students to jump through several hoops Everyone knows the hoops which are stated within the test prompts. As we mentioned in the last chapter, plenty of help has been published elsewhere, showing sample prompts, scoring guides for various score points, and practice of different kinds within the confines of what is stated on the test prompts. This chapter voices the "unstated hoops."

First, there's the issue of voice. Can a student write with a clear and compelling voice? The voice does not even have to be the student's own personal voice, but that's not stated within any prompt. Authenticity of character is no part of any rubric, but "appropriate voice for the audience" is. Clearly, this can liberate many students who completely understand how to play a role.

Second, is the issue in the prompt really one which the student might care about or have a valid vote for? Sure, test-makers may try to offer a prompt which in some way resembles some feature of the student's real world, but the unspoken truth is this: it is not an issue; it's a test. The issue is picked out of a hat, and students have every right to imagine that they have a whole history with that hat, or that issue, when addressing it.

And finally, who is this audience? Someone in authority? No. A pretend person in authority. What if the prompt says, "Write a letter to the principal of your school"? The student knows that the letter is not actually going to be sent to the principal of a school. The test is not to see how effectively the principal would actually be swayed (though that's an idea worth thinking about). Instead, the test measures how well the student would know what to say IN THE EVENT that they were actually writing to a school principal.

In some respects, the test measures the student's ability to assume a role as much as it measures the student's ability to write. Tests teach drama as much as writing. This chapter explores these unspoken rules inherent in writing for a test. We've included some lessons designed to point out common pitfalls, too, or habits which cause a student to fail. The last lessons teach skills which will make an adequate paper stronger.

Ironically, when students flex their muscles for some of these tests, they pick up skills which will make them much stronger spokespersons when it's not "only a test." These muscles can even be used to speak against the test or other issues of injustice or ignorance that afflict them.

Writing For A Test: Real Vs. Fake

You can't judge Egypt by <u>*Aida.*</u>
Ronald Firbank

The Point: If you're about to move from real-life persuasion to writing persuasively for a test, then a discussion of the differences can help students. Here's a five-minute freewriting exercise that teaches the distinction to your students.

Teaching it:

Imagine you're asked to write a persuasive piece for a test. Is this kind of persuasion different from real-life persuasion? How? What, in your view, are the true differences? Are the goals different? Are your techniques different?

Explain yourself as clearly as you can.

Student Responses:

Is writing on a test different persuasion from real-life persuasion? Yes, because writing for the test is like writing about what that sheet of paper said. You have to imagine yourself. Real-life persuasion is like what you were doing at home or on the street, wherever you go. -Mondo Lugo

Writing a persuasive essay is much harder. My goals are different also. Sometimes on a test your opinions are not at all truthful. Your techniques are different. You try your best to make the highest score where when you are being persuaded in real life, you either say yes or no, and that's the bottom line. You have a conversation with another person either on the phone or face to face, but in an essay, you have no idea who this person is. -Louise Tovar

Real persuasion is different and better. With persuasive writing, you don't get to use tone of voice or facial expressions. With writing, you only state facts. With real life, you can use life experiences to back you up. Like when you try to persuade someone to do something you've already done, you tell them, "Well, remember when I did this and nothing happened." -Edgar Nunez

Debriefing:

What strategies will help you succeed on the test?
How are they different than life?
If you could design a better test, what would it be?

Spin-offs:

- Pretend you are the state and are designing a test you really want people to fail because you are mean. What might the topic be?
  Sample topics:
  Make an argument for the importance of cleaning out belly button lint.
  Summer should be shorter. Explain why.

Research your state's test at the Web site www.fairtest.org . Write a persuasive letter describing a non-testing alternative which would help people know what students are learning.

Read a few pages from Alfie Kohn's persuasive essay, The Case Against Standardized Testing. Write a letter to the state commissioner proposing an elimination of high stakes testing in your state.

For Younger Writers:

- Convert this lesson into a class discussion.

- Talk about times students have been persuasive at home. Then ask them how that may differ from writing about a topic which may not interest them, such as school uniforms, or whether we should have a vending machine in the cafeteria, etc.

- Make a T shirt slogan that speaks to the eliminating of tests.
  Sample slogans:
  High stakes are for tomatoes!
  You don't fatten a pig by weighing it!

- Design and write your own writing test for your parents or your teacher or your state's governor.

- Since the unstated goal of tests is to show parents and state governments what you are learning, one way to get rid of tests is to simply write a letter telling parents and state agencies what you learned this year. Make some lists on your own, and then write a letter or a poem or create a large poster showing them what you learned this year.

Resources:

Seuss, Dr. and Jack Prelutsky. *Hurray for Diffendoofer Day.* New York: Alfred A. Knopf, 1998. This book spoofs boring tests and gives the message, it's okay to think.

Kohn, Alfie. *The Case Against Standardized Testing.* Portsmouth, NH: Heinemann, 2000. This slim volume provides essential information about why tests often are divorced from true learning. Read it and use it as ammunition with parents who think test scores are the best measure of their child's learning.

Finchler, Judy. *Testing Miss Malarkey.* New York: Walker & Co., 2000. The teachers, principal and parents tell students that "the test" isn't important, but the hoopla surrounding testing day will sound painfully familiar!

Fair Test: The National Center for Fair and Open Testing. 5 May 2001. <http://fairtest.org>. This Web site will keep you informed on the anti-testing movement in the country and will show you how your state's test stacks up against others.

Teacher Information Network. 5 April 2001. <http://www.teacher.com>. Want to see the state testing in Alaska? In Alabama? From this home page for the Teacher Information Network, you can look up any of the education departments in the country.

Imagining a Different Face

What is this, an audience or an oil painting?
Milton Berle

The Point: When students take a test, they usually don't think much about the audience. They write to an anonymous throng of faceless evaluators. It's no wonder their voices dry up and their own faces grow tense and expressionless. Here's a lesson for freeing voice by imagining a different reader face.

Teaching it:

When you take a test, they send your essay to someone to read. Can you imagine the worst possible person in the world to read your essay? Draw a picture of the person you hope does NOT get your essay…the most boring, the most bored reader!

Now draw a picture of the same audience after they've read the most wonderful essay.

Debriefing:

Would imagining the second audience make any difference when you take the test?

Student samples:

Dante Washington

Student samples:

Niko Laven

Stanley Hayward

Robert Medrano

Spin-offs:

- Make a class quilt of the faces. Call it the Bored Reader Quilt.

- Call a test company on the phone and ask what the qualifications are to score the test.

- In many states students are not given their tests back. Write a letter to the state department, asking for a copy of your essay.

For Younger Writers:

- Make paper-plate drawings of caricatured audience members; hang these in your classroom to use as audience.

Secret Weapon for a State Test: Pretend It Matters

You just gotta save Christianity, Richard! You gotta!
Loretta Young to Richard the Lionhearted in the movie *The Crusades*, 1935

It is not whether you really cry. It's whether the audience thinks you are crying.
Ingrid Bergman

The Point: The persuasive essay on any state test is a hypothetical situation. It's not real. It may seem real, and it may be about something real, but it's not real. Students may be asked to write a letter to someone who really exists. But here's the key: Will that letter actually be mailed? NO. It's a test. Prompted tests are like an acting test. The key word is "IF." IF a student heard of a situation which concerned them, how WOULD they go about showing that they can be articulate and civilized?

Students and most other human beings tend to be honest creatures. They can sabotage their own performance and fail the test if they admit that they don't have an informed opinion, or that they really don't care about the subject matter, even if it's true, or that they can actually see both sides of a situation.

Here's how to help: Teach your students to pretend it matters.

Teaching it:

What's the difference between a real letter and a hypothetical one?
What's the difference between a letter you write to someone in the real world and one you might be asked to write for a test?

(Discuss the difference with students.)

Pretend that this issue is real.
Pretend that you have been having some thoughts about it.
Lots of thoughts.
Pretend you've been listening to many heated conversations about it.
Everyone you know is upset about it.
Your family and friends, everyone in your neighborhood are all standing behind you, pushing you, nudging you, saying, "Go on! You've gotta tell them how we feel!!! You've gotta tell them NOW!"
Imagine yourself feeling so urgent about the issue that you must pound your fist on the table as you talk.
What would you say?
Notice how your language changes.

Examples: Wishy-washy: I think that it'd probably be a bad thing.
Fist-pounding: I urge you to reconsider!

Debriefing:

Can you imagine hearing a position change in a paper with an urgent tone?
How does the language become more specific when the tone is more urgent?

Spin-offs:

- As the test draws near and students write practice papers, use one to demonstrate how to take a lukewarm position and fire it up by pretending that the issue is crucial.

- Read some opening paragraphs from a low-scoring paper (from chapter 10). Translate these into fiery statements.

- For a spoof, write and perform a fiery speech which begins with one fervent opinion and ends with the opposite opinion, just as fervent.

For Younger Writers:

- Make a list of passionate verbs that might replace the phrase, I am upset about.... (see below)

- For example: I'm irked!
                I'm appalled!
                I'm outraged!

Resources:

The letter to the editor page of your local newspaper. Hunt for passionate letters.

List of Passionate Verbs

upset	confused	scared
appalled	bewildered	terrified
outraged	flummoxed	frightened
		panicked
_____	_____	_____
_____	_____	_____

Listen to the Doubting Bullies

Those who know only their side of a debate know little of that.

John Stuart Mill

The Point: Question: What is the main reason that kids fail a persuasive essay on state tests?
Answer: Failure to elaborate.

Saying "Don't forget to elaborate!" or nagging them doesn't usually work, but teaching them to hear an unreceptive audience can help them to see the holes in their arguments.

Students know the sound of dissent. They know the sound of an argument. But hardly ever in real life is an argument presented in the form of a monologue; it's almost always, ALWAYS, dialogue. If nobody disagrees with you, the argument is finished.

That's the secret. If nobody disagrees with you, the case is closed. The argument is over. No elaboration is necessary.

So if you want students to elaborate, it helps to insert disagreements. You can practice this orally, until students catch on to the sound of disagreements and pretend that someone is disagreeing with them. Then the process goes internal, and they can reproduce it in a written composition.

Teaching it:

An essay is a conversation where you only hear one speaker. The audience is invisible. What if students imagined a bully, a nay-sayer, a jerk, belittling their comments? It might sound like this:

> "Football makes a lot of money for our school."
> "It does not."
> "It does too."
> " You don't know what you're talking about."
> "Football DOES make money for the school."
> "You don't know that."
> "It DOES."
> "Prove it, Einstein."

> "Well….how do I know it?….hmm….well, last weekend I went to a game with three friends. By the time we had each paid for admission, programs, and popcorn and sodas, we'd spent about $10 each. You could just look around the stadium at thousands of people eating popcorn and looking at programs and know that a huge amount of money had been spent at that ONE game."
> "That shuts me up."

The point here is to imagine there's some bully standing near you, always disagreeing and challenging you to prove yourself. Your goal is to react to that voice, and "shut the bully up" with proof.

Debriefing:

If everyone knows how to prove themselves, then why is it unnatural to do it on paper?

Student Responses:

Every time I wrote a reason on why I wanted a specific thing, I remembered the bully, and hearing "No, you don't want that!" "That's not true!" or "That's not right!" And it made me explain myself. -Travis Brinkley

...you pretend like some jerk is on your shoulder and he keeps saying negative things and that makes you feel like you don't know what you're talking about. But that's the point: to prove him wrong. It makes you explain more about what you're talking about. I really think that the jerk system is a pretty cool system and it really helped me. -Roxanne Gonzales

Spin-offs:

- Take a published persuasive essay from chapter 10 and read it to your class. Have the students play the doubting bullies. Pause at certain moments and show them how the author chose to answer these questions.

- Take the first verse of a popular song and play the doubting bully after you sing it. Notice how the song often answers the bully.

  Example : Yesterday, All my troubles seemed so far away; now it looks as though they're here to stay. *What troubles? Why are they here to stay? What's wrong with you, buddy?*

- Get editorial pages from the local newspaper. Pick one editorial and read it while a classmate plays the doubting bully. Do this twice, then find a place in the editorial to answer the bully. Does it improve the argument?

- Draw a picture of your personal doubting bully.

Resources:

Park, Barbara. *Junie B. Jones and the Stupid, Smelly Bus.* New York: Scholastic, Inc., 1997.
The whole Junie B. Jones series features a child protagonist who is constantly "talking back" to her readers, as though they're arguing with her.

Editorial page of the local newspaper.

Quick Way to Fail #1: the "Inappropriate" Category

The first human being who hurled an insult instead of a stone was the founder of civilization.

attributed to Sigmund Freud

The Point: In some states, in order to graduate, students must demonstrate "audience awareness" while persuading. One way to interpret this is to show students that there is social value in the ability to debate over heartfelt issues, using the rules of citizenship.

This lesson is best delivered as an awareness talk while teaching students how to score a paper, without specific practice afterwards.

Teaching it:

In our state, the citizens want you to know some things before you graduate.

They want you to be able to do the most important, most sophisticated job you will have to do as a citizen. Do you know what it is that they value this highly? Think about it. What is the single greatest problem in our country? (violence, killing) What is the single greatest right we have in this country? (the right to voice our opinions, free speech)

In all seriousness, the adults in this state, your parents, your grandparents, your neighbors, ALL want you to be able to express an opinion that is diametrically opposed to someone else's, and to express it passionately, without anyone resorting to violence. They care so deeply about this that they will not give you a high school diploma unless you can do this. That is one of the reasons that you can count on persuasion to be your assignment.

If, in your persuasive speech or letter, you threaten to break a law or use any form of violence, you will automatically fail the test. It sounds simple, but it does happen. I've seen a paper where a student laid out a position, with reasons, well elaborated, and ended it with "And Sir, if you DO pass this law, just wait until you get out to the parking lot and take a look at your car....just kidding." The readers would not laugh. This paper earned a failing grade, just because of that statement. Yes, the test is hypothetical, but it is the place to show that you know how to play the role of impassioned CITIZEN.

Name-calling is another form of inappropriateness. . You can say "This is an idiotic idea," but if you say, "You are an idiot," you will fail. Name-calling isn't persuasion. It backfires. Doesn't it backfire when someone uses it on you? Sure it does.

Debriefing:

Is there really a relationship between civilized behavior and language?

Is there really a violence problem in our country?

Spin-offs:

- Find an incident in the newspaper that illustrates a person committing an act of violence. Make an "I should've said" exercise to create a speech for the perpetrator of the violence, prior to the incident. Feel free to invent details.

- Take a high-scoring essay from chapter 10. Write one sentence to add to this essay, which would ruin the essay's score because of inappropriateness. See who can do it with the fewest number of words.

For Younger Writers:

- Think of a time you saw someone hit or kick someone. Instead of kicking or hitting, what could they have said out loud to express the same thing? Pretend you are that person; write a short speech to express what they needed to say. If you don't know what was bothering them, make something up.

- Draw a picture of love facing hate. (See below.)

Resources:

Teaching Peace. Brewerton, NY: Red Grammar Rednote Records, 1988. On this kids' album there is a wonderful song called "Use a Word," that should be studied by violent offenders.

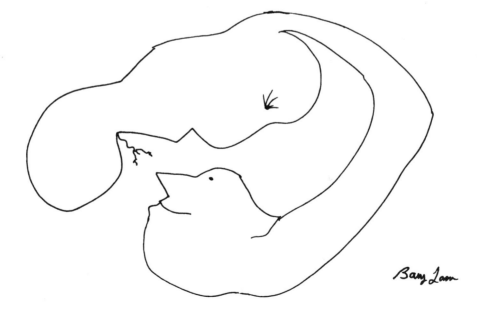

Bany Lam

Quick Way to Fail #2:
Filibustering with the Position

Calvin Coolidge didn't say much, and when he did he didn't say much.

Will Rogers

I'm sorry this is a 20-page letter. Had I more time I would have written a one-page letter.

H.L. Mencken

The Point: "How long does it have to be?"

"Well, a really long paper can fail!"

This exercise demonstrates that you can state a position and restate it so many times that you can fill up a whole lot of paper without ever moving into the argument. It happens all too often. Exaggerating it is fun, and students see the point more clearly.

Teaching it:

(Read the sample below as dramatically as you can and ask students to tell you what you said. Then re-read it and show them, using asides, how it's a simple case of restating the position over and over.)

In a persuasive essay test, is HOW MUCH you write the most important thing?

Listen to this paper and be prepared to tell me why it would fail the test.

Sample:
Dear Principal,
I have been thinking about the new cafeteria policy that has been proposed, that we should have nothing but liver for lunch every day. I think this is a bad idea. It is a really bad idea. In fact, I feel strongly about it. This idea has me very upset. Liver for lunch every day? No choices? I mean no disrespect, but I cannot think of a worse idea. Sir, I am against this new policy. It is the worst idea I have ever heard. It's the worst idea that anyone has ever heard. Everyone I know thinks it is a bad move. My mother even thinks it is a lousy idea. My sisters and brothers think so too. We do not think you should accept this new policy. The liver for lunch idea should not be passed. I appreciate your taking the time to hear my point of view. Please do not allow this to happen.
> Sincerely,
> A student

(Second read-aloud)
Dear Principal,
I have been thinking about the new cafeteria policy that has been proposed, that we should have nothing but liver for lunch every day. I think this is a bad idea. (What did I do? Stated the position, right?) It is a really

Teaching it:

bad idea. (What did I do? Just repeated it.) In fact, I feel strongly about it. This idea has me very upset. Liver for lunch every day? No choices? I mean no disrespect, but I cannot think of a worse idea. (All this did what? Just restated the position. I'm still against it.) Sir, I am against this new policy. (What's this? The fourth re-statement?) It is the worst idea I have ever heard. It's the worst idea that anyone has ever heard. (More re-stating) Everyone I know thinks it is a bad move. My mother even thinks it is a lousy idea. My sisters and brothers think so too. We do not think you should accept this new policy. (Anything new here? Nope.) The liver for lunch idea should not be passed. (Here the position is being used as a conclusion.) I appreciate your taking the time to hear my point of view. Please do not allow this to happen.

   Sincerely,

     A student

Debriefing:

In a persuasive essay test, is HOW MUCH you write the most important thing?

What did you hear over and over?

How many words would it take to do a great job of stating a position?

Spin-offs:

- Take any position statement and have a contest to see who can stretch it out the longest without ever stating one reason.

- Write a bad poem where each line says the exact same thing in a different way.

    Example:
    I hate spinach.
    Spinach is something I despise.
    What I really dislike is spinach.
    Don't give me spinach, please.

- Pretend you are running for President. Find a simple message like "Americans need a tax cut." Now write a speech that says this message over and over again.

Resources:

Find examples of filibustering persuasive essays or write some yourself.

Quick Way to Fail #3: The Wyatt Earp Model of Redundant Reasons

What luck for rulers that men do not think.
Adolf Hitler

The Point: When students respond to a persuasive prompt without any planning, often the resulting writing may not show separated, distinctly presented reasons. Showing them how to spot the problem is one task for the teacher; showing them how to fix it is another. Sometimes handing students a graphic organizer or an outline form doesn't help. What if students merely fill in words that are repetitive?

A wonderful solution to this was devised by Belinda Licea, a teacher from Jefferson High School in San Antonio. Her students listen to a paper and draw pictures which illustrate each of the developed sections of the essay. When students have practiced hearing three distinctly drawable "reasons" in an essay, they are likely to transfer this idea to their own writing before they start composing.

Teaching it:

(Discuss with students the need for distinctly different reasons in a persuasive essay. Demonstrate with them the use of graphic icons to prevent repetition.)

In the 60's, there was a television show called *Wyatt Earp*. The theme song went like this: *"Wyatt Earp…Wyatt Earp…brave, courageous and bold…"*

Now let's see. Wyatt Earp had some mighty good qualities. First, he was brave. That's a good thing. Secondly, he was not only brave, but he was also courageous. And if those two weren't enough, he was also bold!

What happened here? Did I tell you three things about him? No!

Here's another example. From Shakespeare's *Much Ado About Nothing*:

Don Pedro: Officers, what offense hath these men committed?
Dogberry: Marry sir, they have committed false reports. Moreover, they have spoken untruths; secondarily, they are slanders; sixth and lastly, they have belied a lady; thirdly, they have verified unjust things: and, to conclude, they are lying knaves.
-Act V, Scene I

Look at what each one of those means, while we read it again.

In a persuasive essay, if you tell your reader that you have several reasons for your opinion (which you should), how can you be sure that you really do?

Draw three cartoon squares onto your paper. Label them 1, 2, and 3. Ready? I'm going to read you a paper about eliminating the football program. Listen to the first part and see if you can draw a picture to go with it.

Teaching it:

(Read the first part, below.) Now listen to the second part and see if you can draw a picture for it. (Read second part.) Now the third. (Read third part. Have students share their responses.)

First part:

The football program plays a very important role. It's a form of entertainment. People look forward to games because it gives them a chance to socialize and to see the talent many of their friends do not display in class. Being involved in football, I know how important this is. Knowing that your friends come to watch you play makes you feel good about yourself and boosts your confidence. People like to show off, whether they admit it or not. Football and other sports help students to accomplish that state of mind.

Second part:

Second, some students dedicate their whole life to a sport such as football. It may be their dream to play professionally one day. By terminating the program, you seize their chance to live their dream. In order to play football for college or professionally, you must have a high school football background. This time period of playing is critical because it gives you a chance to learn new techniques and increase your knowledge of a certain sport. In some cases, students rely only on their football talent to get themselves into college. If you drop the football program, you may actually be crushing someone's chance for a college education.

Third part:

I realize the only reason you would indeed be shutting down the football program is because of budget costs. We have a strong sports booster club at our school with many loyal parents. I suspect we could receive large donations and even have a fundraiser for the football teams to pay for costs concerning football. The parents enjoy watching their children play a sport they love. I know they would gladly support us with donations. Perhaps we could even get a loan for the costs and pay it back after a successful fundraiser.
(From a paper by Tom Willet, Sophomore, Mr. Roediger's class, O'Connor High School)

Student reaction, after taking the state writing test:
One tip that really helped me was learning to draw pictures like a little comic strip. That helped us identify the reasons and helped us write them in detail. –Michelle Echevarria

Spin-offs:

- Listen to any paper from the appendix and draw it.

For Younger Writers:

- Create a planning sheet (outline or pre-writing) using only pictures, no words.

- Fashion a storyboard modeled from *A Christmas Carol,* by Charles Dickens . Have students build an argument using the past (development of the problem), the present (state of disarray), and the future (clear badness of some kind) if their advice is not heeded.

Grace L.

1- Past
Life was hard but people like Old Fezziwig knew how to lighten the load.

2 - Present
Bob Cratchett has a tough life and you make it tougher.

3 - Future
What will happen to your name after you die? What will they say about you?

Resources:

Shakespeare, William. *Much Ado About Nothing.* New York: Cambridge University Press, 1988.

See blank form on next page

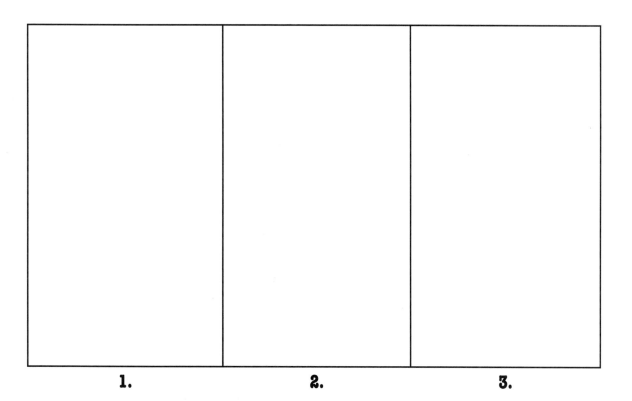

1.   2.   3.

It's Good! Good for You! Only $1.99! (Ray's Story)

All good things come in threes.

Barry Lane

The Point: This bottom-line pass-fail strategy helped one student pass. Use it as a last ditch method with the students who need it.

(Share the following story with your students. Have them try out Ray's three categories on any issue to see if they are adaptable for your students.)

It was crunch time for Ray. A twelfth grader taking the Texas TAAS writing test for the fifth time, he was desperate. He knew how to read a prompt. He knew how to take a position on an issue. He could discuss it reasonably. The problem was organizing his thoughts into well-elaborated reasons. He had made a failing score point "1" four times already, and none of the other strategies was working for him.

As he approached for another round of tutoring, I took a magic marker and wrote on a cardboard box, the following:

> **It's good!**
> **Good for you!**
> **Only $1.99.**

He recognized it as a commercial for some product and realized that he was looking at three reasons to buy something. Could he use that structure on any prompt? Sure. Why not?

Here's how Ray Rodriguez describes his success on the State writing test in Texas.

"These three things helped me to pass the TAAS writing because it was like hearing a commercial on TV. They're trying to sell something but the customer wants to know why they should buy it. So the TV ad tells them something that sounds good to them, like 'buy this product...it tastes good.' This right here can be a reason on the writing test. Then just elaborate like they do, by proving it tastes good, having backup like 4 or 5 people all saying 'it tastes good!'

"Then saying it's good for them and having researchers' or doctors' approvals, telling the customers it's fat-free or low-cholesterol. This is also another reason to sell the product, and the backup of doctors' approvals and again, elaborate.

"And what gets the customers to buy it is that the price is only $2.00. Then the customer says 'Yeah! I'm going to buy that. People say it tastes good, and the doctors approve of it, and it's cheap – just $2.00.'

Teaching it:

"So my point of all this is if you get the reader's attention by telling them three reasons you feel about whatever the question is about and elaborate on them, you get them to believe you, like the customer believed the commercials.

"This idea helped me. I think it will help anybody pass it because I thought I wouldn't pass it and I did. I tried tutoring and studying, but nothing seemed to work. This idea did. It's magic. Use it. It will help."

-Ray Rodriguez

Spin-offs:

- Make a list of ideas to sell. List at least three details for each idea. Then put the details in order of importance. Experiment putting the best details first, then last then in the middle. Discuss the difference.

- Bring in ads from magazines. Try to find at least three selling points in each ad. Talk about how the advertiser prioritized them.

- Pretend you are selling an old car that no one would want to buy. Find three selling points.

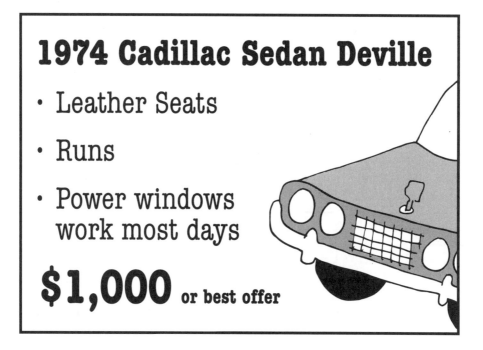

1974 Cadillac Sedan Deville

· Leather Seats

· Runs

· Power windows work most days

$1,000 or best offer

Plan Sheets

Self-expression must pass into communication for its fulfillment.

Pearl S. Buck

The Point: Teachers have long recognized the importance of pre-writing as a critical step in the writing process. For state writing assessments which involve persuasion by presentation of a position and elaborated reasons, students are helped by learning to plan for these elements before composing a single word on their paper. Without this pre-writing step, students might realize too late that they have sat right down and composed an argument with potentially deadly holes. The planning sheets, or graphic organizers, make the holes easy to spot and pain-free to fill. They can take any number of forms.

Different plan sheets appeal to different students. Below are thumbnails of two particularly useful ones, the "Think Sheet" developed by students at Jefferson High School in San Antonio, and the "Plan Sheet," used by Geri Berger and Laura Lott and their students at O'Connor High School in San Antonio.

Teaching it:

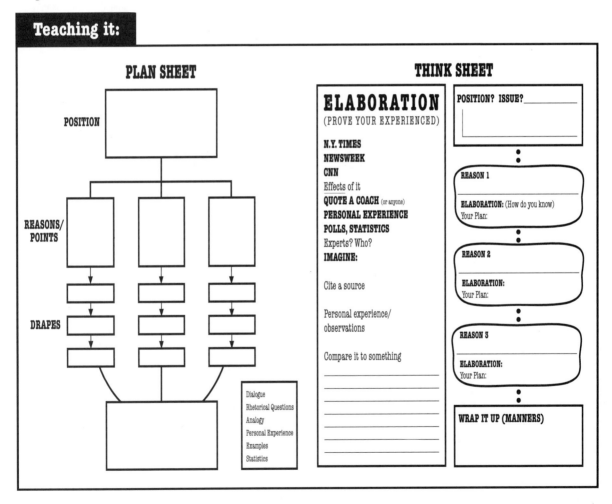

Spin-offs:

- Listen to an essay read aloud, and decode the outline by noting what you hear on the plan sheet. Then prescribe the next steps for the writer.

- Get a topic and develop a plan or think sheet for the topic. Don't write the essay. (Why not practice just doing the thinking part?) (see Barry's Pie Chart Plan Sheet below)

Resources	**Appendix 79 a b**
See appendix 79a and 79b for enlarged sheets	

PIE CHART PLANNER

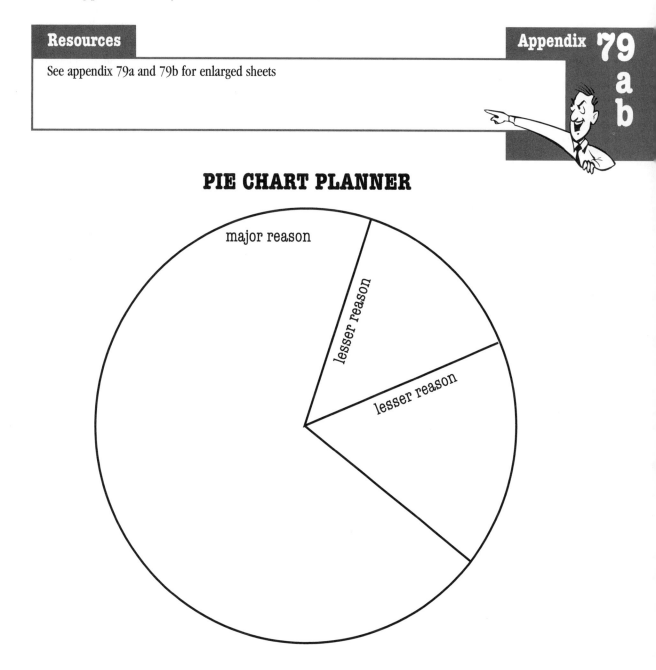

80

DRAPES – Building Elaboration

He can compress the most words into the smallest idea of any man I ever met.
Abraham Lincoln

The Point: The single most common reason that Texas students fail the TAAS persuasive composition is "lack of elaboration." They may have a position and they may enumerate reasons for their position, but without elaboration, the paper receives a failing score.

Geri Berger, an English teacher at O'Connor High School, teaches her students to choose elaboration methods using "DRAPES," an acronym for six elaboration strategies. She says any acronym can be devised, but this one works well for her students.

Teaching it:

(The students should already have an issue, a position, and several reasons. Perform the process below to develop each reason. A process that usually works well is to practice one together before asking students to apply this lesson to their own individual papers.)

Today you're getting a gift, a tool to use for elaboration. You have an issue: abolishing football. You have your position, for or against. You have reasons.

Could I get a volunteer to give me one of your reasons?
(Football is a big money-maker.) Now what's the next step? Once you've explained that reason, if it needs explanation, what's next? Proving it is next. That proving is elaboration.

(Write DRAPES vertically on the board.)

How would you prove that football makes money? How do you know that?

(Gather answers and apply them to the appropriate place next to DRAPES, as illustrated below.)

How many DRAPES should you use for each reason? *(Two or three would do well.)*

From now on, DRAPES will be the next planning step after you have reasons, and before you begin to write.

Memorize DRAPES and what the acronym stands for.

> **D – Dialogue**
> **R – Rhetorical question**
> **A – Analogy**
> **P – Personal experience**
> **E – Example**
> **S – Statistic**

Teaching it:

Football makes money. How do I know?

D (Dialogue): Scott Brady, our athletic director, said, "Last year, profit from football tickets alone made $18,000 for the school."

R (Rhetorical question): Do you know how much an average spectator spends at a game?

A (Analogy):   Football games bring in cash the same way that rain brings in crops.

P (Personal example): Last Friday, my friend Dottie and I went to a football game, and here is what we spent...

E (Example) One example of profit is in concessions. Chocolate alone brings in...

S (Statistics) 62% of our student body bought at least one ticket to a game this month, at the cost of $3 each.

Spin-offs:

- Listen to an essay, and fill out a "Drapes Report" on the piece you hear.

- Develop a coloring legend and have students underline their DRAPES.

    D = blue
    R = red
    A= green
    P = purple
    E = yellow
    S = orange

- Post papers to see the trends, visible through the color patterns.

Resources:

Appendix 80

Elaboration stationery, appendix 80. Created by Jann Fractor's students at O'Connor High School, the images on the side of the page show "the ways we know things." Students can look at the images and be reminded of the DRAPES.

Transitions: Driving for the Comfort of Your Passenger

Lord Ronald said nothing; he flung himself from the room, flung himself upon his horse and rode madly off in all directions.

Stephen Leasock

The Point: Knowing where you're going can increase a test score. And showing your readers that you know where you're going is just as important. In Texas, a paper which would earn a score point of 2 may be boosted to a score point of 3 with clean organization and smooth transitions.

Students mostly already know the functions and tools of transition. The driving metaphor gives them access to their natural abilities!

Teaching it:

(Explain the driving metaphor. Then show students a paper which has no transitions. It is probably written as one paragraph.

Then show them a paper which is organized clearly and ask them to find the "brakes and blinkers," or any signals of changes in the road. Make a class chart of words or phrases that they find.)

Imagine you're sitting in the passenger seat of a car. You can tell that the driver is about to turn. How? (You feel him slow down, you sense the blinker being turned on...) You see a stop sign ahead. You're relaxed, because you can tell the driver sees it too. How can you tell? (You feel the brakes slowly being applied, well in advance of the stopping moment.)

Have you ever ridden with a driver who stopped suddenly? Who made turns suddenly? Who changed lanes suddenly? How would you describe your comfort level? (Your hands grip the seat; your body stays strained for coping with sudden unexpected changes.)

The same thing happens in writing. When you're talking (in your piece) to your audience, it's as if you're driving them to your destination. You're going to shift from point to point. Use all the brakes and blinkers you have, in order to show your passengers changes are coming.

Debriefing:

What signals do you find?

- Words like first, second, third, furthermore, finally.

- Spaces, like indentations, which give the reader's eye a clue.

Spin-offs:

- Use highlighters in traffic light colors to show transitions for slowing, accelerating, or stopping.

- Create a list of transitional words or phrases that can help glue together your essay.

- *Example:* Moreover,
  Consequently,
  In the past.

Resources:

Score point three student samples, Chapter 10

Texas Education Agency, Division of Student Assessment. 3 Feb. 2001.
<http://www.tea.state.tx.us/student.assessment>. Want to see the prompt they used last year on Texas's eighth grade essay? This Web site posts released tests for every grade level tested in Texas.

Zesty Words and Compositional Risks

The difference between the right word and the nearly right word is the same as that between lightning and the lightning bug.

Mark Twain

The cherry tomato is a marvelous invention, producing as it does a satisfactorily explosive squish when bitten.

Miss Manners (Judith Martin)

The Point: In language, specificity is power. In life, students understand and embrace enthusiasm and spice, and their understanding can be transferred to powerful writing with the concept of zesty language. In state testing terms, zesty language can make the difference between a passing score point and the higher score points. In fact, zesty language, on the simple rubric, is one of the two differences between a score point three and four. If you point out to students their own zesty language, you train their ears to listen for it. In turn, listening for it becomes using it, because the writer anticipates that the reader will be listening for it too.

Furthermore, students are encouraged to use their knowledge of prefixes, roots and suffixes to invent words if they need to, just as Shakespeare did.

Teaching it:

(Explain the concept of specificity to students. Then look together at student samples from your class or from the appendix, finding the zesty words and phrases. The most powerful examples will come from your own students' writing. Build word walls or sentence banks in your classroom.)

Do you know one of the tricks that stand-up comedians use? Specificity. Food at the store is nowhere as funny in a joke as frozen fish sticks at the Piggly Wiggly. Why? Is it because it zooms the audience to the exact place and view that the comic sees? I don't know how it works, but it does.

The same is true in persuasive writing. And the zesty words don't even have to be big, difficult words. *Examples?*

Someone I know versus my neighbor, Alicia Narvaez.
Recently versus last Tuesday.
He wanted me to go versus he goaded me into going.

Do you ever use simpler words because you don't know how to spell a zesty one? In many state tests, spelling doesn't count. The essays are graded as drafts, not proofread, polished copies. Pull out the stops and fire up your most sparkling, vivid language. (And if spelling does count, use a dictionary!)

A student named Anez made a score point four in her essay, and her final line used the phrase "students in the new millennium." She misspelled the word "millennium" and added about 10 extra vowels. Did it matter? No. The readers could tell she meant millennium. Nobody's going to read your test essay except the readers.

Student Responses:

I am writing to you concerning the motion the school board just passed that revokes students' rights to drive to school. -Jennifer Knoupp

After hearing the proposal to discontinue student parking, I felt it imperative to voice my opinion. Those students will be unable to accommodate the unflexible bus schedule. -Paul Pan

Traffic congestion and overcrowded parking lots are two major problems. I believe that not allowing students to drive to school will cause a chaotic uproar. -Brynn Clark

Taking away the students' privilege to drive to school will not reduce traffic congestion. A school population of 2,700 cannot rely on just buses and family to go to or from school. -Sofia Jordan

I find this proposition appalling and grossly unfair. However convenient this proposition may seem to the environment, it proves to be a huge disadvantage to the student body. -Selin Silva

This inflexibility of transportation would also hinder the fine arts programs and other extra-curricular activities because the children would not be able to stay after school for practices and rehearsals. -Jayme Burket

Spin-offs:

- Read a class set of student essays, highlighting zesty language. Share some of these examples with your class, out loud, naming the student writers.

- Compile and distribute "Fourmaker Phrases" lists from your students' writing.

- Look through their essays, scanning for vague words like "thing" or "bad idea" or "people." Highlight these and replace them with zesty words.

- Look at the sample essays in the appendix. Zesty language is marked on some of them.

For Younger Writers:

- Onto sentence strips, copy your best line from an essay. Post these on the wall.

Resources:

Appendix 82

List of "Fourmaker Sentences" in Appendix 82.

Haunting Aftertastes: Debunking "In Conclusion"

Anyone who says you can't see a thought simply doesn't know art.

Wynetka Ann Reynolds

The Point: Vivid imagery helps any writing; on a test, it can make the difference between a strong score and the highest possible score. Organized but mediocre writing often ends with a summary of what has been said; truly persuasive writing leaves a reader with what Joyce Armstrong Carroll calls "proprioceptions," physical body reactions to the writing. Some examples of proprioceptions include a lump in the reader's throat, eyes welling with tears, a smile, or a "gut feeling." If a writer has full command of his reader's vision (and a writer does), why not use that power to leave the reader with a feeling that will last far beyond the last word? Images do this.

This is one of the elements present on papers which earn a score point four, but not a score point three.

Teaching it:

(First, debunk the myth of the "conclusion." [See chapter 6.] Conclusions do NOT need to restate the position and reasons; in fact, in many cases, only really boring formula papers do this. Next, show them how to make their reader have a physical reaction with a haunting image at the end of their paper. Then practice.)

How should a persuasive essay end? *(Freewrite for one minute flat and share answers.)*

How do the best commercials end? *(Compare student answers.)*

If you give an argument by presenting your position and giving well-explained reasons, the reader will mentally say, "Yeah, yeah, okay." If you give them a powerful, moving image, the reader will get goose bumps and say, "Wow." It's the "wow" that does the real convincing.

As a writer you have the power to invoke images. You can make your readers visualize anything you want. How? Just by telling them to. Yes! You can. How do I know this? Our brains cannot STOP themselves from connecting things. They connect things to other things all the time. They can't help it. Want an example? Can you remember not knowing how it felt to read? Having to ask your mom to read you a billboard or a word on a cartoon? Now, can you look at THAT (point to some large word in the room where you are) and NOT READ IT? You can't.

Want another example? Your brain will not let you NOT connect an image I tell you to picture. Want proof? Okay…try right now NOT to picture….a zebra. *(Pause and look at their faces.)* See that? What happened?

It's magic. USE this magic in your paper. Why would you end with a boring summary of "this is what I told you….thank you for your time…." when you COULD end with a powerful image that will continue to do its work long after you've finished your words? Go ahead. Haunt them!

Teaching it:

How would you command an image? Say the words: "Picture this…." or "Just imagine…"

(Then share with the students Becky Pineiro's closing image in the argument not to eliminate the football program, below.)

Example:
"So I hope you decide NOT to cancel the football program next year. But if you don't, just imagine. You're driving down the freeway on a Friday night in September. Your car approaches Alamo Stadium. You glance over your shoulder, out your window and what do you see? The parking lot is dark and empty. The stadium lights are dark. The quiet is deafening. There are no school buses, no crowds of parents, no shouts of cheerleaders, no bands playing. As you drive past, you will wonder…where is everyone? Sir, don't let this happen. Sincerely, Becky Pineiro"   (inspired by Becky Pineiro)

Debriefing:

Why do you suspect teachers have taught you to end with "in conclusion"?
Is that always a poor way to end?

Spin-offs:

• Look for haunting images in the essays in the appendix. Mark them with something sparkly.

• Pick a feeling, then describe a place through the filter of that feeling without telling the reader what the feeling is. Notice how your emotions come through in the details you choose to describe. This is a skill that will help you create a haunting aftertaste.

For Younger Writers:

• After taking an essay test, write about how you did it; what helped; what problems you encountered. Share these on a voluntary basis with each other, or you could pass them in to create a pool of successful strategies.

• After creating a new rule you think is important, imagine the "worst case scenario" if your rule is not implemented. Draw on vivid imagery and sensory details in your description.

Resources:

Silverstein, Shel. *The Giving Tree*. New York: Harper & Row, 1964. The final image in this picture book of the old man sitting on a stump says more than any sermon on conservation could.

Piven, Joshua and David Borgenicht. *Worst-Case Scenario Survival Handbook*. San Francisco: Chronicle Books, 1999. This clever book, written like a first aid manual, will show you how to deal with extreme situations in a logical way. Use it as a model for imagining extreme examples for an essay.

Persuasive Test Triage:
Medicine Bag of Devolved Essays,
Rubrics, and Other Tips and Tools

I think there's always a little bit of glee in destroying something.

Sue Shoopman

What if the essays were our patients? We'd have to look at them to assess their condition. Some essays are barely alive; in some, we can hear a heartbeat. Some exhibit muscle tone; some glow with good health. But whatever the condition, medicine is available for all.

This chapter begins with a generic rubric or scoring guide for first-draft persuasive position letters. This rubric is most useful when you use the icons that go with it. You can keep the medical metaphor and use any stamps you have handy, or you can use different colored highlighters for the various features which comprise the score points. Any metaphor will work, as long as it's one that students can match up with these meanings:

1 not good enough
2 adequate
3 pretty darn good, better than average
4 incredible

Following the rubric, you will find a series of papers written by high school students. Some are annotated with explanations for the scores.

Using Devolved Essays

How does this collection differ from commonly published scoring guides? The first group of four essays is actually the same essay. It has been "devolved." That is, we started with a student essay that would make the top score, and then we ruined it, little by little, until it was a three, then a two, then a one. You can do the same thing with your students' papers, and teach them the process too! Imagine THAT conversation:

"Hey James, excellent paper!"
"Thanks!"
"Do you mind if I show it to other students as an example?"
"Naw, that's fine with me."
"Would it be all right with you if I messed with it some?"
"Huh?"
"I want to see what it looks like without some of its brilliance."
"Huh?"
"I want to take out some of the zesty language and haunting images, and see what it looks like as a three."
"Oh. Okay." A big grin follows.
"And then, I'm going to remove all your transitions and see how it looks as a two. Is that all right with you?"
"Sure! You'd better take out a little specific language, while you're at it."
"You're right; I will."

"I know, you're probably going to mess it up to make it be a one, huh?"

"You know it. I'm going to mess it all the way up."

"You would."

"But know what, James? Your '4' paper is the only one I'm going to keep your name on."

"Good!"

What do other students learn from looking at these? They learn that any paper can become any score. It's all within their reach.

After the devolved sample comes a slew of score-point-four papers. We use these routinely to acquaint students with the sound of excellent persuasive voices. With each practice round for any given test, students produce a whole new crop of excellent models. Models from any book can never be as effective as models produced by the guy who sits a row over from you.

After modeling the excellent papers, its time to look at papers that need more. What do they need? And how do we fix what's wrong?

Triage

We used the "triage" metaphor because it focuses on some of the surgical work of teaching writing:

Looking at a product and moving the process along from one stage to the next.

Reading a paper and scoring a diagnosis.

Identifying successful steps.

Prescribing medicine, all available from the previous chapter, to strengthen the weaknesses. All under the plate-glass group observation deck!

With the state writing tests, teachers definitely sense a no-nonsense urgency, where quantifiable results will always count. Our hope is that these strategies can help convert the tasks to meaningful learning. Without a doubt, it will always be work—hard work. But the work can definitely come from our own students, and it can be wonderful.

Resources:

NPR All Things Considered, Commentaries. 10 Mary 2001. http://www.npr.org/programs/atc/commentaries/2001/may/. Summarizing the daily topics on the National Public Radio's show, "All Things Considered," this site is a rich mine for interesting and fresh topics for persuasion.
For example, "Commentator Stephen Lynch can't believe that some schools around the country are banning dodgeball. He thinks this trend toward making childhood 'safe' coddles kids."

Spandel, Vicki. *Creating Writers:Linking Writing Assessment and Instruction.* New York: Addison-Wesley Longman, 2001. This is one of the must-have resources for anyone setting up a class and who wants to create 6 trait assessment that drives instruction in a positive direction. Vicki Spandel makes assessment enjoyable and includes dozens of students examples to help you do the same. (Visit Spandel's Write Traits Web site at www.writetraits.com for more information.)

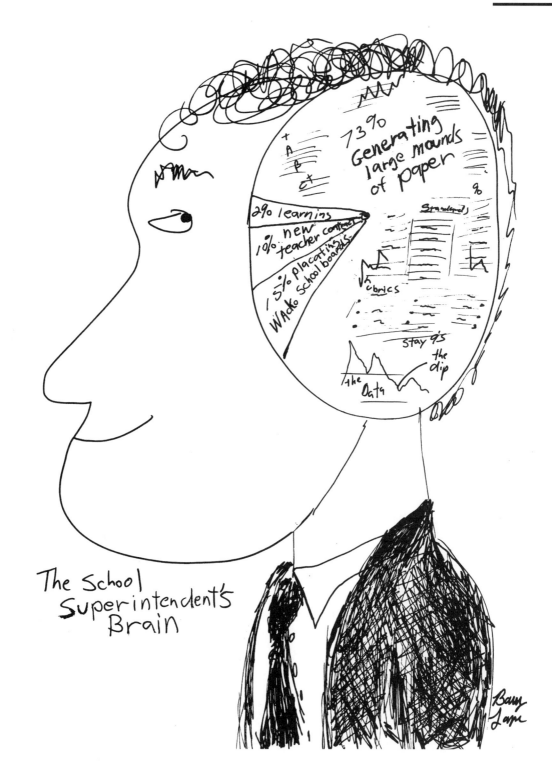

The School
Superintendent's
Brain

Icon Rubric for Persuasive Letter

This rubric looks at content only; language conventions and mechanics are not addressed because the essay is treated as a first draft. Scoring works cumulatively. X stands for all the negative traits of #1. The location of the x forces the reader to identify which characteristic is being pin-pointed.

Score Point	Icon(s)	Characteristics	Description
1	X	Unclear position. Changing position. Insufficient reasons. Reason(s) without elaboration Inappropriate citizenship.	This essay fails to establish a persuasive argument.
2	→ - ★	Clear position Reasons Sufficient elaboration	This essay provides a minimally successful argument; it might have some problems with organization.
3	#	**(In addition to "2" characteristics:)** Transitions Some specificity of language.	This essay provides a convincing, organized argument; it is easy to follow.
4	✳✳	**(In addition to "2" and "3" characteristics:)** Zesty, precise language. Haunting images. Rhetorical devices.	This essay is persuasive and thorough, resounding with conviction and skill.

Sample Score Point 1 – Code blue

January 21, 2000

Dr. Patranella,

It has come to my attention that you are looking into adding a course to the selection our school presently has. It is my opinion that **you should choose a plumbing class.**
Plumbing covers many areas. It would be a wise decision to choose plumbing for a new course because it isn't just focused on one subject. Many people go on to work in other fields because they have learned so much about that field through plumbing, they are able to make a living doing it. Choosing a plumbing course for a new class will be giving students opportunities and interests after they graduate.

Plumbing classes can save students money. Basic plumbing knowledge is practically common sense, but people are not well informed. School's purpose is to educate, and educators shouldn't take common sense for granted. A plumbing class would improve this situation, and improve students' capabilities.

Some students may become plumbers when they graduate. Plumbing for a living offers many things other jobs don't. It sure beats an office job. My point is that by choosing a plumbing class for the new course, you could be affecting somebody's future.

Sincerely,
A student

Position is clear.
*Three different reasons are given, **without** elaboration.*

Sample Score Point 2 – We have a pulse.

January 21, 2000

Dr. Patranella,

It has come to my attention that you are looking into adding a course to the selection our school presently has. It is my opinion that **you should choose a plumbing class.**

Plumbing covers many areas. It would be a wise decision to choose plumbing for a new course because it isn't just focused on one subject, **but actually would be four classes in one: plumbing, ventilating, electricity, and water transportation. Plumber Steve Dobson says, "All students should be taught the very basics of plumbing as a part of their high school curriculum. It covers so many important subjects, it is almost a necessity to life."** Many people go on to work in other fields because they have learned so much about that field through plumbing, they are able to make a living doing it. Choosing a plumbing course for a new class will be giving students opportunities and interests after they graduate.

Plumbing classes can save students money. Surveys show **11 out of 17 people can't fix a leaky faucet,** and 8 out of 9 people can't unstop a toilet. Such basic knowledge is practically common sense, but people are not well informed. School's purpose is to educate, and educators shouldn't take common sense for granted. A plumbing class would improve this situation, and improve students' capabilities.

Some students may become plumbers when they graduate. This possibility is increased by the fact that **you don't have to go to college** in order to become a plumber. Plumbers earn an average of $68,000 per year. Plumbing for a living offers many things other jobs don't, such as **days off,** and it gives you a **variety of job sites.** Every day you have **something different to do.** It sure beats an office job. My point is that by choosing a plumbing class for the new course, you could be affecting somebody's future.

Sincerely,
A student

Position is clear.
Three different reasons are given, with sufficient elaboration.

Sample Score Point 3 – Muscles are present and toned.

January 21, 2000

Dr. Patranella,

It has come to my attention that you are looking into adding a course to the selection our school presently has. It is my opinion that you should choose a plumbing class. **Plumbing offers many opportunities in the real world, and basic knowledge of how things work in the plumbing field can be of great assistance to students.**

First, plumbing covers many areas **like electricity, ventilation and water transportation. This information is valuable for students who have never had the chance to learn what really makes a home run. Every day, plumbers work side-by-side with electricians and they often need to know where water lines are located, so they don't dig into one. Air and water is a large part of a plumber's job. He is responsible for making sure water lines don't break beneath the foundation, and for designing vents.** It would be a wise decision to choose plumbing for a new course because it isn't just focused on one subject, but actually would be four classes in one. Plumber Steve Dobson says, "All students should be taught the very basics of plumbing as a part of their high school curriculum. It covers so many important subjects, it is almost a necessity to life." Many people go on to work in other fields because they have learned so much about that field through plumbing, they are able to make a living doing it. Choosing a plumbing course for a new class will be giving students opportunities and interests after they graduate.

The average plumber charges 80 dollars an hour. With the knowledge a plumbing class would supply, students could avoid this cost. Surveys show 11 out of 17 people can't fix a leaky faucet, and 8 out of 9 people can't unstop a toilet. Such basic knowledge is practically common sense, but **the population** is not well informed. **What are students learning?** School's purpose is to educate, and educators shouldn't take common sense for granted. A plumbing class would improve this situation, and improve students' capabilities. **It may even save them 80 dollars.**

If a plumbing class is added to our selection of courses, some students may become plumbers when they graduate. This possibility is increased by the fact that you don't have to go to college in order to become a plumber. **Furthermore,** plumbers earn an average of $68,000 per year. **Besides the money,** plumbing for a living offers many things other jobs don't, such as days off, and it gives you a variety of job sites. Every day you have something different to do. It sure beats an office job. My point is that by choosing a plumbing class for the new course, you could be affecting somebody's future.

I would like to end by mentioning that, as principal, you cannot go wrong with a plumbing class. Students' futures can be changed. Those who had no plans after high school now suddenly have a career possibility. By choosing a plumbing class as the new class, many people's needs will be met.

Sincerely,
A student

Smooth opening and closing.
Reasons are organized, using clear transitions. Specificity used in elaboration.

Sample Score Point 4 – The aura of glowing health!

January 21, 2000

Dr. Patranella,

It has come to my attention that you are looking into adding a course to the selection our school presently has. It is my opinion that you should choose a plumbing class. Plumbing offers many opportunities in the real world, and basic knowledge of how things work in the plumbing field can be of great assistance to students.

First, plumbing covers **a wide range of activities besides the removal of wastes. It encompasses** the fields of electricity, ventilation and water transportation. This information is valuable for students who have never had the chance to learn what really makes a home run. Every day, plumbers work side-by-side with **skilled** electricians, **who value plumbers for their expertise on the way a house is built, and how to solve problems that arise involving the foundations.** They often need to know where water lines are located, so they don't dig into one. **The transportation and distribution of** air and water is a large part of a plumber's job. He is responsible for the **prevention** of water line breakages beneath the foundation, and the design of vents **that provide sufficient air to different buildings.** It would be a wise decision to choose plumbing for a new course because it isn't just focused on one subject, but actually would be four classes in one. Plumber Steve Dobson says, "All students should be taught the very basics of plumbing as a part of their high school curriculum. It covers so many important subjects, it is almost a necessity to life." Many **plumber apprentices** go on to work in other fields **primarily** because they have learned so much about that field through plumbing, they are able to make a living doing it. Choosing a plumbing course for a new class **will be opening new doors for students, and** will be giving them opportunities and interests after they graduate.

Did you know the average plumber charges 80 dollars an hour? With the knowledge a plumbing class would supply, students could avoid this cost **by fixing minor problems their family and friends encounter.** Surveys show 11 out of 17 people can't fix a leaky faucet properly, and 8 out of 9 people can't unstop a toilet. Such basic knowledge is practically common sense, but the population is not well informed. **Sure, they know how to graph a parabola, or write the formula for acetate, but they can't unstop a toilet!** What are students learning? School's purpose is to educate, and educators shouldn't take common sense for granted. A plumbing class would improve this situation, and improve students' capabilities. It may even save them 80 dollars.

If a plumbing class is added to our selection of courses, **it is inevitable that** some students **who take interest** may **actually** become plumbers when they graduate. This possibility is increased by the fact that you don't have to go to college in order to become a plumber. Furthermore, plumbers earn an average of $68,000 per year. Besides the money, plumbing for a living offers many **privileges** other jobs don't, such as days off, and it gives you a variety of job sites. Every day you have something different to do, **whether it be maintenance, repair, laying lines, or drawing plans.** It sure beats an office job. My point is that by choosing a plumbing class for the new course, you could be affecting somebody's future. **Going to this class could be a turning point in their life, and as an educator, it is your interest to help build futures.**

I would like to end by mentioning that, as principal, you cannot go wrong with a plumbing class. Students' futures can be changed. Those who had no plans after high school now suddenly have a career possibility, **whether it be plumber, electrician, water maintenance technician, or ventilation service person.** By choosing a plumbing class as the new class, **lives will be touched, knowledge will be shared, a foggy subject will be** made clear, students will be better prepared for their future, and your job as an educator will be fulfilled.

Sincerely,
James Alan McGinley,
Sophomore, Mr. Scott Stone's class,
O'Connor High School

Zesty and sophisticated language. Sharp specificity in examples. Rhetorical devices used: metaphor, rhetorical question, strong parallelism at the end.

Sample Score Point 4

Dear Mr. President:

My name is Stephen Mahaffey and while you may never have heard of me, you will now hear from me. I understand, Sir, that you are leaving open for discussion the final destination of a large sum of money that the United States Government has recently acquired. **From the bottom of my heart, I know that** you should spend the money on free admission public skateparks.

We've all seen it. The X-Games on ESPN, the Gravity Games on ABC, and various other television shows staking a claim to "Extreme Sports." This is the up and coming generation of kids and teens who are just that. Extreme. I believe that if you want to keep these kids from causing the violence and rioting that we know they're capable of, you have got to give them something to occupy their TV-twisted minds. When the Vietnam War was in full swing, the new generation of teens did not get what they wanted, and the United States practically fought a war within its own boundaries, with its own inhabitants. All I'm trying to say is this: The new generation, my generation, will stand up to its reputation of being extreme if you force it to, but violence is senseless and painfully regretful, so please, let's all be on each other's side. We'll get along if you just give us something to be peacefully happy about.

Imagine. You just paid half of this month's paycheck to buy yourself a new tennis racket. You're practically going crazy now, returning home from work, as you jump into a pair of athletic shorts and a comfortable cotton shirt. You can't wait another minute to go try out this brand new racket. As you rent a bucket of tennis balls and a ball launcher, you can feel your heart skip beats with anticipation. Alas, as you step onto the court, you can just feel the swing in your arms before the ball even reaches your side of the net. Here it comes! POW! Suddenly, from behind, you're pummeled repeatedly by a police officer who takes your new racket and tells you that if you want it back, you're going to have to take it downtown, to a judge. This is exactly what it's like for many skateboarders who enjoy their hobby and are scolded and looked down upon for it. There are hardly any quality locations to practice this sport without "No Skateboarding" signs on the premises. Sir, just as taxes build parks for football, tennis, basketball, baseball, and soccer, there is now a need for skateparks because despite previous stereotypes and prejudices, extreme sports are now officially a part of America.

Creative is the artist who blends his techniques and produces an eye-pleasing plethora of colors, shapes and emotions. Everyone enjoys being pleased by art. Once again, let us forget all previous prejudices and misconceptions. To me, skateboarding is a form of art all in itself. In fact alone, the definition of art is: any form of human activity that is the product of and appeals primarily to the imagination. I can honestly say from experience that skateboarding in its technical state (beyond the beginning stage) relies very heavily on imagination and creativity in order to please 1) the participant and 2) whoever is watching. Many of today's top professional skateboarders have very complex and intelligent minds. The previous stereotypes suggested differently. It was shown in Transworld Skateboarding Magazine's April 1999 edition, that of all the professional skateboarders in January, 1999, 63% were involved in some sort of creative field of work other than skateboarding. These include photography, musicianship, fine arts, and acting. All 63% had earned a high school diploma, and of the 63% who had passed high school, 22% were beginning or were already enrolled in college courses.

Picture this: the streets of Washington, D.C. are flooded with screaming, raging teenagers who are furious about being told not to skateboard anywhere. The fences and gates of the White House are being pushed back and forth with the demanding sway of the rioters, while you sit inside, wondering "Why didn't I just let them have their skateparks?" Don't let this happen, Mr. President. Build skateparks.

Sincerely,

Stephen Mahaffey, Sophomore, Mrs. Laven's class, O'Connor High School

Sample Score Point 4

Dear Sir:

Sometimes the ruling body or group is called upon to make a decision that will affect the entire group. I am of the opinion that the choice to do mandatory drug testing is one of those decisions, and that it will affect the entire group adversely.

One reason I think that mandatory drug testing will not be good for the school is that it is expensive. It would cost the district threee million dollars a year to test every single graduating student. This money could be put to good use for education purposes. It could be used to increase the number of field trips taken by the various schools, or it could be used to replace worn and damaged books. The drug testing is just another expense and an unnecessary one at that.

The Constitution guarantees everyone the right against unreasonable search and seizure. Searching the insides of one's body on the off-chance that they may have taken drugs recently is an unreasonable proposition if ever I heard one. How would you like it if before you got your paycheck, you were given a drug test? I don't think you would like it at all. If you had taken any strong painkillers lately, such as morphine, codeine, Vicoden, or Demerol, the drug test would detect you as surely as if you had just snorted cocaine.

The best reason that I think they should not allow the school to do mandatory drug testing before you graduate is that it is in violation of your right to privacy. What someone does in the privacy of their own home is their business, not mine, not the school's, not yours. If the government suddenly decided that YOU weren't allowed the right to privacy, how would you feel, knowing that you were undesired, disbelieved, and mistrusted?

Many things have been tried to remove the rights of a group of people. Hitler put the Jews in concentration camps. Our founding fathers made the African-Americans into slaves, and the school is trying to start mandatory drug testing. Please don't let them do it.

David Sharp
Sophomore
O'Connor High School

Sample Score Point 4

Dear President of the School Board,

I am writing in concern over your not allowing high school students to drive to school. I find this proposition appalling and grossly unfair. Before you consider passing this ridiculous rule, I suggest you take in mind reasons against it.

Most high school students have been waiting in anticipation for years to be able to drive to school. I know I have been waiting eagerly for some time, as have many of my friends. We are enrolled in driver's education classes, and it would be wrong to restrict us from utilizing our newly received licenses. Some of our parents have bought us cars for one reason in particular: to be able to drive to and from school. This rule would anger some parents who have already purchased a vehicle for their children. Not only would this rule be affecting students, it would also be affecting parents, both of whom will be angered.

The majority of students attending high school are involved in at least one extracurricular activity, or so it is at my high school. Transportation to and from these activities cannot be dependent on a school bus. It would be easier to be able, as a student, to drive yourself to and from your activities. Some of our parents cannot work around their work hours to drop us off and pick us up from school every time we have a club meeting or athletic event. It would be more practical if the school board would allow us to drive in order to make it easier for our parents.

This rule would also be inconvenient for transfer students. Some of them live far from the school and they must depend on themselves to drive to and from school. If you eliminate student driving, what will these transfers do? They would be forced to depend on their parents or neighbors for a ride to school; however, this may be a huge inconvenience. The enforcement of this rule would provoke disagreement from the parents of transfer students and potentially cause huge controversy.

Now that you have taken the time to review some reasons against this rule, I'm sure you are debating on whether to even consider passing this rule. However convenient this proposition may seem to the environment, it proves to be a huge disadvantage to the student body. You need to find ways to improve traffic and the size of parking lots instead of putting restrictions on our independence. I seriously recommend you consider not passing this rule until you have heard from the compact majority. Thank you for your time in reading this letter.

Sincerely,
Selin Silva
Sophomore, Ms. Eden's class
O'Connor High School

Sample Score Point 4

Dear _____,

Some people think certain lyrics should not be played on the radio, and I am one of them! There are laws, morality, and children's futures at risk. If you look at the facts, you too will agree, controversial lyrics should indeed be banned from radios.

First of all, I'd like to address laws that we have around the country that should be thought of when this subject is at hand. In some places in the USA, Northside Independent School District included, you can be ticketed and fined for using vulgar language in public. What then gives this right to anyone on a national radio? Here is a nonsensical question. Are you allowed to sell illegal things? Then what gives certain singers the right to sensationalize drugs, stealing, and vandalism and make it sound okay? My last point is simple. It is against the law to sell or advertise anything without telling the possible negative effects it can have. Yet I've never heard that done when artists are talking about underage drinking, stealing cars, or cheating on a spouse.

Secondly, promotion. What do vulgar lyrics promote? Violence. An example of this is Snoop Dogg's latest in which the lyrics include "bust a nine on a cop, watch him drop, watch him drop." If anyone were to speak these words in a public arena, they could be arrested for probable cause! The rising dangers of STDs are not being recognized through lyrics like Christina Aguilera's "Genie in a Bottle." Last on my list but definitely not least, songs also promote the use of drugs as if it is free market. A study in St. Cloud, Minnesota showed 83.5% of all the drug users in a downtown high school listened to lyrics suggesting drugs' appeal.

Last but not at all least, what about the kids? Children from ages 5 to 17 have a 75% chance of acting on persuasion rather than their own smarts. So what goes on through the mind of a 6-year-old who is "pretty sure" it's not okay to play with guns but heard that they are cool by a famous guy on the radio? As children grow, they learn new ways to express their feelings and emotions and many turn towards others to find the answers to life's questions, and music is a form of self-expression. If a child needs an answer and the wrong one is given by Lauren Hill and her song "If I Ruled the World," or M & M's "Acid Lick" or Dr. Dres "Buda Lover",who is to blame? You and I for not stopping this while we had the chance. A study was done in Nebraska and 2,000 teens were surveyed and asked if they had ever started a new trend, tried something new, or done something wrong because of an idea springing from the words of a popular song, and 73.9% said yes.

There are a million reasons to protect each other while we still have time. Laws, promotion, lives, children and homes may not be getting the positive attention needed due to lyrics of a song. Do as I say, not as I do! But what do you do when the people you look up to most say the wrong thing? Don't let lies and anger corrupt our lives. Fix what needs fixing.

Sincerely,
Sarah Stephens
Sophomore, Mrs. Lott's class
O'Connor High School

Sample Score Point 1 (Insufficient elaboration) – Metal detectors

Dear Chairperson,

    I am writing to agree with you about installing metal detectors in our school. I think it is a good way to keep violence out of schools, especially after the violence in other schools in the past couple of years. I will go over a few reasons why I agree with this idea.

    I think metal detectors will help enforce the school's rules. Metal detectors will help people to stop bringing cell phones, beepers and other electronics to school.

    Also if we have metal detectors, I think it will decrease absences and students skipping school. The students will be more secure about people not having weapons, and they will feel more safe at school.

    Finally, metal detectors will limit violence. This means people can't bring guns or knives and there will be more police officers free to stop fistfights.

    Overall, I think it is a good idea to install metal detectors, and I am behind it 100%.

Sincerely,
A student

This essay presents a position.
It presents three distinct reasons.

None of the reasons is proven with elaboration.

This essay would be perfect for practice with the doubting bully, with DRAPES, with zesty language, with haunting images.

This essay could be evolved into a 4.

Sample Score Point 2 – Metal detectors

Dear Chairperson,

On the idea of adding metal detectors, my opinion would be that we shouldn't have them. Mainly because it would make the halls more crowded, waste students' time and would cost a lot of money.

My first reason would be that it would cause a lot of traffic problems. Every time you would go up to the metal detectors, there would be a line and if it took so long, we might have to come to school earlier to stand in line.

My second reason is that it's time-consuming. It would take too long to stand in line, and have everyone taking everything out of their pockets. And if your backpack went off, they would have to go through all their stuff until it didn't go off any more. It might also be embarrassing if you were a girl and you had to take all your personal belongings out. If the students were late to school, then they would be even more late to class even more, because of standing in line.

My third and last reason would be cost. Metal detectors are very expensive. In our library we spent about thousands on the detectors and there is only two of them. If they had to put them all over the school, that would cost millions. Hiring more staff would become a problem too. You would have to hire more police to control the metal detectors. And police are paid more, so that would cost more money.

All my reasons can show you why not to put metal detectors in the school. I still believe that they are a waste of time, a waste of money, and they cause traffic problems.

Sincerely,
A student

This essay presents a position.
It presents three reasons, but the first two are really the same.
Inside the second reason is the issue of embarrassment, which could be elaborated
    into a whole separate reason.
The third reason is so well elaborated that it carries the paper into a two category.

To fix it up:
    1. Draw the reasons (to make the reasons more distinctly different)
    2. Using a plan sheet or think sheet, plan out elaboration using DRAPES or doubting-bully-talk.
    3. Add zesty language.
    4. Use a haunting image at the end.
With these steps, this essay could be a 4.

Sample Score Point 3 – Metal detectors

Dear Chairperson,

I have been informed that you are going to be considering installing metal detectors at my high school. In my opinion putting metal detectors in the school will be the biggest mistake the school board will ever make. My opinion is that I am not for putting metal detectors in the schools. I have many reasons to back up my opinion.

Well to start off, one reason would be the cost for putting in metal detectors. Our school already used 56 million dollars on building and getting supplies for the school. Now they want to install metal detectors in the school. But after you pay that off, then you got to think about hiring more staff to look after the metal detectors. Before I went to a school with metal detectors and I did not like it because there was never enough money to get new supplies for the students because they put in metal detectors.

Another problem that will come in effect will be the hassle of getting into the school and time consuming. To be able to get in the school, you have to go through metal detectors and that means waiting in long lines just to get into school. Also it will take a long time to get off your rings, earrings, and watches. Some students do not get to school until 8:40 and they have to go line and get checked by the metal detectors and may cause them to be late to class. I was at a school with metal detectors and it was not fun standing in those long lines and students pushing and shoving just to get in school.

The one thing I think is the most important is that the metal detectors will give the impression that we have a problem. To me this shows that the school is unsafe and parents will send students somewhere else that is safe. If people drive by they might think this school is a bad school. It also may show that students will not learn in this school. If I was a parent and I had a choice where to send my kid, I would send him where it looks safe, but if the school have metal detectors that will draw away the new students.

As you can see, installing metal detectors is not a good thing in high school. So please take my reasons into consideration. Thank you very much.

Sincerely,
A student

This essay presents a position. It presents three reasons, cleanly organized. The second reason uses some specifics.

Why isn't it a four? Minor problems with language control and lack of zest.

So, to make it a four, replace ordinary words with committed, zesty words, and add haunting images. Then read it aloud and see if your ears give you any problems with the language control. Revise as needed.

Sample Score Point 4– Metal detectors

Dear Chairperson,

I feel that metal detectors at schools in our area is a bad idea. Although many others have opted to include detectors in their gun control policy, I feel that our school can live without them.

One major con of metal detectors is cost. We would have to take money out of our general funds. To recover from this huge debt, fund-raisers would have to be created. No student likes to go door to door selling products that they know are cheap and overpriced. If our debt was still not covered, we would have to wait longer to receive new equipment. Those funds should be spent in other areas like installing more doors in the big buildings so students aren't struggling to get to class every day. 45% of students are tardy at least once a week because of overcrowdedness. Why I have to carry a 30-pound backpack is because I don't have time to get to my locker between classes. We need doors much more than metal detectors.

Another aspect of metal detectors is the hassle they create. Have you ever stood in an airport for half an hour just to get through the security check? Well think of the delay when 3,000 plus students arrive all at the same time and are forced to line up single file in a few metal detector lines. Tardies would triple and frustration would abound. I personally don't like having to wait in lines.

Our school already looks somewhat like a prison. Walking through metal detectors on the way to class every day would just worsen that feeling of being confined. Students like to feel free, they don't want to feel confined. 65% of students already feel caged in with all the fences and gates. The learning environment is just as important as the learning itself.

Seeing how our school doesn't have a gun problem or even a history of one, putting metal detectors up would create the illusion that we do have a problem. In fact, the chances of getting injured in a school shooting almost match that of winning the lottery. Plus parents are like a hen laying on her eggs: If they were to think that this school had a gun problem, they might take their kids and enroll them in a safer school.

Metal detectors are a very bad idea. They would cause cost issues, tardies, frustration, a bad learning environment, and the withdrawal of many students. Please take the time to reconsider and decide that metal detectors are not necessary. Not just for you or me, but for all 3,000 students of this school. Thank you for listening to my side of this issue.

Sincerely,
Jason Taylor

Where does this paper sparkle beyond a 3?
Effective use of rhetorical tricks, like parallelism ("Tardies would triple and frustrations would abound") and like the mother hen simile.

Sample Paper (Unscored) – Metal detectors

Dear Chairperson,

   I feel that we should have metal detectors in our schools. I have some serious and important reasons for the installation of metal detectors. Metal detectors increase the safety of the staff and student body as well as limiting the violence. Also students will not fear attending school.

   The installation of metal detectors increases the safety of the staff and students. Recently, students of Columbine High School brought weapons to school. They did not have metal detectors and lives were lost. Do you want to take the risk of your child's safety over some "trashy" looking metal detectors?

   Newspaper statistics show that John Jay High School has had a 40% drop of their violence rate. This is because they have installed metal detectors just this past month. Also students will be persuaded to leave their arms and weapons at home. Metal detectors limit the violence at school.

   Metal detectors will also raise the attendance count. Students will not be afraid to attend school. Last year at my school there was an alleged bomb threat stating that on May 20, 1999, our school would be blown up. Many students worried for their safety did not attend school that day. I remember that in every class, more than half of the students were gone! Teachers were unable to teach us because they were worried that most of the class would fall behind. Wouldn't you come to school if you knew that guns and other weapons were not present during the school day? Let's not make self-defense a required course to graduate!

   I strongly believe that installing metal detectors would be a wise decision for our schools. They limit the violence, increase safety, and reassure students not to be afraid while attending school. I urge you to seriously consider my reasons and hope you decide to make metal detectors the next step in protecting our schools.

Sincerely,
A student

What score would this paper get? Have students score it and discuss their findings. (Then make time for reflections on their process. What knowledge did they demonstrate and use while making their judgments? What does that say about their preparation as test-takers?)

Sample Score Point 1 (Insufficient elaboration) – Cutting sports program

Dear Chairperson,

My name is Jonathan. I am a sophomore at Sandra Day O'Connor High School. During English class an idea of y'all's came in front of us. The idea was to cut athletic funding from all Northside schools. Well I don't agree and let me tell you why.

Well first off, all sports are really popular. And if you were to cut back you might drive that popularity away from sports. Who would want to join sports when they're having to make cuts? And not having enough or the right equipment for the job.

When you play sports, it teaches you responsibility, trust, and how to work as a team. Those are qualities you need to make it in the real world.

Sports also work on your people skills. You learn to talk to a person and to meet people.

Last but not least, if you were to make cuts from sports, you would sooner or later make cuts from other departments. It would end up being a chain reaction. So when you make cuts, everyone would suffer one way or the other.

That is why we shouldn't make cuts from the sports department. I would like to thank you for taking the time to read my letter.

Sincerely,
A student

This essay presents a position.
It presents three distinct reasons.

None of the reasons is proven with elaboration.

This essay would be perfect for practice with the doubting bully, with DRAPES, with zesty language, with haunting images. It would be a snap to turn this paper into a passing paper, by asking 1) HOW do you know equipment make a sport more appealing, 2) HOW do you know people skills could improve, and 3) HOW do you know the results of a chain reaction? Adding that elaboration would turn this paper into a 3, since it's already clearly organized.

Sample Score Point 2 – Cutting sports program

Dear Superintendent,

Recently I have been informed that NISD is considering cutting the funds for athletics, and as an athlete, I would like to give my opinions why they should not cut any funds.

Through high school sporting events, the whole community is brought together. With a high school basketball, soccer, volleyball, or in most cases, football team winning or going to the playoffs, communities get all riled up. Without that, there would be no place to really come together.

Many college scholarships come from high school sports. Most all professional athletes come from college and before that, they were in high school. Without the athletic program, many colleges wouldn't be discovering high school athletes. So professional sports would be ruined as well.

Grades are another reason that should be considered when making this decision. If you think about it, all athletes have to be passing to play. So having the athletic program sets the standards for the grades. It's real simple. If you fail, you don't play. The coaches will push athletes as well because they don't want to lose players.

In conclusion, I feel we should keep the athletic program in full force. It has helped communities come together, kept students' grades up, and even made high school athletes super stars.

Thank you,
Anthony P.

This essay presents a position.
It presents three distinct reasons, with enough discussion to be considered adequate elaboration.

More specific elaboration would bump this into the clear "3" category.

Sample Score Point 3 – Cutting sports program

Dear Superintendent,

    I have been hearing about the debate on whether or not to cut the sports fund. While I have many issues on whether or not to cut it, I have come to the conclusion that yes, you should cut the sports funds.

    My first issue is from personal experience. My freshman year of high school, I had a coach for algebra. He would always refer to football and basketball for examples on problems. This creates a problem itself because it shows his head is somewhere else. It was also not hard to see that coaching came first before algebra.

    My second issue also comes from personal experience too. I think that players get away with a lot of stuff. As an FFA lamb raiser, I have to feed my lambs twice a day and on stockshows. At the time, I was dating a football player who also came up to school on the weekends. Well we turned on to Leslie Road, and he was doing 50 mph, and then 30 in the school zone. He was also dipping and not wearing a seatbelt. And when the cop pulled him over, he saw the football sticker and let us off with a warning. When my brother came up the next day, he was doing 26 mph and he was not dipping, and he was wearing his seatbelt. When the same cop pulled him over, he wrote him a ticket. This happens all the time. I do believe that that was not fair to my brother, nor the rest of the students that drive.

    My last issue concerns all of the student body. Let's admit it, on game days, our minds are not on learning that pi r square. We want to know who's playing what position, and whose leg is broken.

    I hope that you will consider my issues along with everyone else's also.

Thank you,
Amanda C.

Well organized, convincing essay.

Sample Score Point 4 - Cutting sports program

Dear Superintendent,

I have heard through my high school math teacher that you are going to cut athletic funding and thought I should write you my support. I want to share my reasons for backing the proposed plan.

For starters, I have always believed school is for learning. Too much time is wasted on sports. Every day ten minutes is wasted in the announcements describing last night's game. This time could surely be better spent. Sports do not teach any real skill. Athletes are loud and noisy; they lack self-discipline. Statistics show 90% of bullies are in a sport. In general sports disrupts the learning and peace of the classroom.

Sports also cause fights between schools. People are beat up and hurt because of their schools' teams. These rifts are unhealthy and hurt the entire district. In "Sports Stink," they talk about the anger that can cause someone to lash out due to a lost game. It would be better to keep peace in the district than slowly be torn apart because of a silly game.

Finally, the money used for equipment in sports could be better spent. Statistics have proven up to 5 times as much is spent on sports than the arts. With the money for sports, the NISD could build enough buildings to support overwhelming numbers of students. Money for better books is spent on footballs and baseballs. Cash that could hire more teachers for the school is used to maintain the fields. This money could help our school greatly but right now it is being squandered.

Superintendent, I ask you to imagine half the student body out on a schoolnight watching another stultifying football game when they should be preparing for tomorrow's test in an overcrowded classroom. Please, would you want your child to grow up this way? I know that the school would be better off without the sports department.

Sincerely,
Jon Sherette
Sophomore, Mrs. Laven's class
O'Connor High School

Unscored – Cutting sports program

Dear Superintendent,

I was informed that NISD is examining a program that will cut all funding for sports/athletics. I think this is not right, which means I am totally against it. The fact is that I believe the reason why lots of kids do good in school is so they can play in sports. If there was no funding for the athletics any more, the kids would have no interest in caring about their low grades.

Not only will their grades drop, but they won't care into coming to school because they won't be coming to school. Their interests won't be recommended any more. They could just want to skip all the time, getting them into more into bad things. The parents could also start complaining about the program cutting all athletic funds and not all programs. This could also hurt other programs by people complaining that they're still funding those programs but not athletics, which is a very important program to all kids. Also, to parents that can't afford money for their education, those kids need scholarships.

Sports brings motivation and high self-esteem to all kids. It makes them not be a quitter or a person just wanting to go home with nothing to do. The kids that are very talented won't be held back from what they want to be when they grow up.

So may you think about what you're doing before you act. Think about how all these people out in the world would want to be something that they've dreamed of being but can't because of the fact that it won't be funded any more.

Sincerely,
A student

This essay presents a position.
How many reasons can you draw?
How many of these reasons are proven with elaboration?

What score would this paper make?

Persuasive Practice Prompts

(list compiled by Laura Lott)

1. Your best friend is not doing very well in school. Write a letter to your friend to convince him/her why he/she should do better.

2. You want to have a pet. Your parents will let you have one if you can prove that you will be responsible for it. Write a letter to your parents to convince them that you should be allowed to have a pet.

3. A close friend of yours is thinking about running away from home. Decide what is best for your friend and write a letter to your friend convincing him/her to follow your opinion.

4. Your school principal is considering a dress code which would prohibit mini-skirts for girls and earrings for boys. Prepare a speech to be presented at the school board meeting. State your opinion concerning the dress code and persuade your audience to agree with you.

5. Your parents are considering taking away your telephone privileges because you tie up the phone and cannot seem to manage the length or the number of phone calls you receive. Give your position and provide convincing reasons for your position.

6. Recently, your city government prohibited the sale of a certain recording to minors because of its lyrics. In a letter to your city council member, state your position and give convincing reasons in support of or in opposition to the council's action.

7. You have been asked to nominate your favorite teacher for the "teacher of the year" award. Write an essay convincing the administration to agree with your choice.

8. Students must attend school approximately 90 days each semester. Your district is considering implementing an absentee policy that requires students with more than five days of absences to appear before the school board in order to get credit for the semester. Do you agree or disagree with this policy? State your position in a letter to the school board. Include adequate support for your reasons.

9. In preparing the new school year calendar, your school board is considering replacing the five-day spring break with five four-day weeks. You will be addressing the board as a representative of your student body. Choose one of the calendars to support and present convincing reasons for your choice.

10. Animals are sometimes used for instructional purposes in science classes. There is both support and opposition for this practice. Consider both sides of the issue, choose one and support it with convincing reasons.

11. It has been recommended that all competitive sports be eliminated from the school curriculum. As president of the Student Council you have been asked to present pros and cons of this issue. Take a position and support

it with convincing reasons.

12. You have just been hired by a grocery store for a part-time job as a courtesy clerk. You contribute most of your paycheck to the family budget. Your friend feels this is wrong. Consider your parents' point of view and your own. Consider both sides and choose one. Give good reasons to support your opinion.

13. Texas law mandates tutoring for all students who have failed a class. These tutoring sessions have been held during the school day and after school. Prepare an editorial for your school newspaper in which you give your opinion for the best time. Use convincing reasons to support your choice.

14. The state legislature has limited assembly time (pep rallies, performances, meetings, etc.) during the school day. Decide whether you agree or disagree with this regulation and write a letter to your legislator giving convincing reasons to support your choice.

15. Cliques exist in most areas of society. Sometimes students find it difficult to fit in if they don't belong to a certain group in their school. It is very helpful, however for the students to have a place where they belong. Consider the issue and decide if it is better to have these groups at school or not. Choose a position on this issue and give support to it.

16. In your school an unexcused tardy requires the student to attend Detention Hall for the same amount of time as the student was tardy The principal is considering revising this policy. Write a letter to your principal in which you state your position and provide convincing reasons for your position.

17. There is policy in your school which states that students cannot wear hats or sunglasses to school. Do you agree or disagree with this policy? Write a letter to your principal in which you state your position and provide convincing reasons for your position.

18. Your school is trying to make people in the community aware of the need to conserve the earth's resources. Select an earth's resource and write an article for the newspaper in which you try to convince people in the community to conserve this valuable resource.

On the next pages are several 6 trait rubrics designed by Vicki Spandel of the Write Traits Company. One is for teachers and the others for students.

For more information about six trait materials and workshops visit www.writetraits.com.

WRITE TRAITS 6-POINT SCALE

IDEAS

6
- ☑ Clear, focused, compelling—holds reader's attention.
- ☑ Striking insight, in-depth understanding of topic.
- ☑ Takes reader on a journey of understanding.
- ☑ Satisfyingly rich with significant, intriguing details.

5
- ☑ Clear and focused throughout.
- ☑ Strong main idea, thesis, or story line.
- ☑ Authentic, convincing, based on research, experience.
- ☑ Main idea expanded, well supported by detail, evidence.

4
- ☑ Clear and focused more often than not.
- ☑ Identifiable main topic, thesis, story line.
- ☑ Quality detail outweighs generalities, filler.

3
- ☑ Clear, focused moments overshadowed by fuzzy, underdeveloped, rambling text.
- ☑ Main concept, thesis, story line can still be inferred with careful reading.
- ☑ Generalities and filler outweigh quality detail.

2
- ☑ A hint of a thesis or story line to come (just a *glimmer*).
- ☑ Predominantly fuzzy, confusing, loosely focused.
- ☑ Factlets and tidbits wander in search of a main idea.

1
- ☑ Notes and random thoughts hastily assembled.
- ☑ Reader can only guess at meaning.
- ☑ Main idea as yet unknown, even to the writer.

ORGANIZATION

6
- ☑ Thoughtful structure guides reader through text.
- ☑ Design smoothly embedded in text—never too obvious.
- ☑ Satisfying, well-crafted transitions.
- ☑ Structure enhances reader's understanding, enjoyment of the topic.
- ☑ Unforgettable opening—enlightening, provocative conclusion.

5
- ☑ Order works well with topic, purpose.
- ☑ Structure evident, but not overpowering.
- ☑ Main ideas, turning points stand out.
- ☑ Strong lead, appropriate sense of closure that "feels right."
- ☑ Strong, thoughtful transitions.

4
- ☑ Order functional—reader never feels lost.
- ☑ Structure supportive—occasionally predictable.
- ☑ Functional lead and conclusion.
- ☑ Transitions present—usually helpful.

3
- ☑ Some out-of-place information—needs re-ordering.
- ☑ Re-reading sometimes required to follow thought or story line.
- ☑ Lead and conclusion attempted—one or both need work.
- ☑ Transitions unclear or too formulaic, predictable.

2
- ☑ Hard to follow—even with effort. Much re-ordering needed.
- ☑ Lead and/or conclusion missing or formulaic.
- ☑ Transitions often unclear or missing.

1
- ☑ Disjointed list/collection of details, events.
- ☑ No "big picture"—nothing goes with anything else.
- ☑ No real lead or conclusion—it just begins, it just stops.
- ☑ Transitions not attempted.
- ☑ No recognizable structure.

VOICE

6
- ☑ As individual as fingerprints.
- ☑ Begs to be read aloud—you cannot wait to share it.
- ☑ Passionate, compelling—but never overdone.
- ☑ Uses tone, flavor as a tool to enhance meaning.
- ☑ Tough to put down—holds readers enrapt.

5
- ☑ Enthusiastic, engaging, lively, expressive.
- ☑ Tone and flavor well suited to topic, audience, purpose.
- ☑ Consistently reaches out to audience.

4
- ☑ Shows some sparks, moments of spontaneity.
- ☑ Tone and flavor acceptable for topic, audience, purpose.
- ☑ Voice comes and goes. Strong moments.

3
- ☑ Functional, often sincere—though sometimes distant.
- ☑ Occasionally questionable tone for topic, purpose, audience.
- ☑ Rarely "speaks" right to audience in engaging manner.

2
- ☑ Distant, encyclopedic, overly formal—OR *too informal, chatty, sarcastic.*
- ☑ Tone, flavor inappropriate for audience, purpose, topic.
- ☑ Minimal concern for audience.
- ☑ Minimal involvement in topic.

1
- ☑ Voice difficult to identify, find, or describe.
- ☑ No sense of person behind the worlds—Is anyone *home?*
- ☑ No noticeable concern for audience—no involvement in topic. Voice . . . just . . . missing.
- ☑ Once you put it down, you just can't pick it up again.

Adapted by Vicki Spandel from her ideas in her book *Creating Writers*, Longman, 1999. Reprinted with permission.

WRITE TRAITS 6-POINT SCALE, p. 2

WORD CHOICE

6
- ☑ You want to read it more than once—just to savor it.
- ☑ Uses everyday language in original ways—*every word carries its own weight.*
- ☑ You wish you'd written it.
- ☑ Powerful, stunning verbs.
- ☑ Precise, delightful, thoroughly original—*quotable* in spots.

5
- ☑ Precise, vivid, natural language.
- ☑ Word choice enhances meaning.
- ☑ Lively, appealing verbs and striking, fresh phrases.

4
- ☑ Functional, clear language used correctly.
- ☑ Some clichés, jargon, or over-written phrases.
- ☑ *Some strong verbs—we'd like more!*
- ☑ Generalities and mechanical phrasing intermixed with originality.
- ☑ Strong, promising moments.

3
- ☑ Moments of imprecise, stilted, or incorrectly used language create confusion, detract from message.
- ☑ Now and then—a "gem" amidst numerous agates.
- ☑ Verbs lack power—nouns lack precision.
- ☑ Vague or flat language outweighs clarity, sparkle.

2
- ☑ Flat, dull, dry language or thesaurus overload.
- ☑ Deciphering this message takes work.
- ☑ Words used incorrectly or with annoying repetition.
- ☑ Adjective avalanche—Where are the verbs??!!
- ☑ Over-written—OR under-written (weak, general words like *nice, fun*).

1
- ☑ Meaning unclear—or buried under mounds of jargon
- ☑ The message? It's anybody's guess....
- ☑ Words seem chosen at random.
- ☑ What is the writer trying to say?

SENTENCE FLUENCY

6
- ☑ Easy to read with inflection to bring out *every ounce of meaning.*
- ☑ Virtually every sentence begins differently.
- ☑ Informational writing crisp and to the point.
- ☑ Creative, personal writing lyrical, poetic, musical
- ☑ Skims, sings, dances along like a lively script.
- ☑ You have to hear it to appreciate it fully. You'd like to hear it more than once.

5
- ☑ Easy going flow, rhythm, cadence.
- ☑ Highly readable—a joy to share aloud.
- ☑ Varied sentence structure, length.
- ☑ Purposeful sentence beginnings.

4
- ☑ Grammatical, natural, pleasant phrasing.
- ☑ Few awkward moments.
- ☑ Some variety in length, structure.
- ☑ Some repetition in sentence beginnings.

3
- ☑ Mechanical, but readable.
- ☑ Awkward moments outweigh smooth, natural phrasing.
- ☑ Gangly, tangly run-ons or chop– chop– choppy sentences.
- ☑ Repetitive beginnings.

2
- ☑ Awkward enough to make you stumble, re-read often.
- ☑ You can get through it—with patience.
- ☑ You'll need to rehearse it to read this one aloud.

1
- ☑ Very hard to read—you slow down, re-read, but *still*....
- ☑ Does not always make sense—is *this* a sentence?
- ☑ Can only be read aloud with extensive oral editing (e.g. filling in many missing words or rephrasing awkward patterns).

CONVENTIONS

6
- ☑ Only the pickiest editors will spot errors
- ☑ Conventions cleverly applied to bring out meaning
- ☑ Complexity of text lets writer showcase *a wide range of conventions*—semicolons, ellipses, dashes, italics, etc
- ☑ Enticing layout.
- ☑ Virtually ready to publish.

5
- ☑ Minor errors that are easily overlooked.
- ☑ Text appears edited, proofed.
- ☑ Sufficient complexity to show off many conventions.
- ☑ Pleasing layout.
- ☑ Ready to publish with minor touch-ups.

4
- ☑ Noticeable, but minor errors that *do not obscure meaning.*
- ☑ Readable—but lacks *close* attention to conventions.
- ☑ Basics (e.g., periods, cap's, simple spelling) are OK.
- ☑ Some errors on difficult spelling, usage, punctuation, etc.
- ☑ Acceptable layout.
- ☑ A good once-over needed before publication.

3
- ☑ Noticeable, distracting errors that *may* affect meaning.
- ☑ Errors even on basics: periods, simple spelling, cap's, etc.
- ☑ More attention to layout needed.
- ☑ Thorough, careful editing required for publication.

2
- ☑ Noticeable, frequent, distracting errors.
- ☑ Numerous errors even on basics.
- ☑ Limited attention to layout.
- ☑ Line-by-line editing required to prepare text for publication.

1
- ☑ Serious, frequent errors make reading all but impossible
- ☑ Even patient, attentive readers struggle
- ☑ Errors obscure meaning, put up road blocks
- ☑ Extensive, *word-by-word* editing required for publication

Adapted by Vicki Spandel from her ideas in her book *Creating Writers*, Longman, 1999. Reprinted with permission.

FOR CLASSROOM USE ONLY.

WRITE TRAITS 6-POINT SCALE FOR STUDENTS

IDEAS

6
- ☑ My ideas are crystal clear—and you will *not* be bored.
- ☑ I know this topic inside and out.
- ☑ What's more, I will help *you* understand this topic.
- ☑ My details are intriguing—not just things everyone already knows.

5
- ☑ This paper is clear—it makes sense from beginning to end.
- ☑ It is easy to tell what my main point is about.
- ☑ I used research and/or my own experience to make my writing convincing.
- ☑ I use important details to support or explain main ideas.

4
- ☑ *Most* of this paper is clear and focused—OK, there's a fuzzy moment here and there.
- ☑ It's easy to tell what this paper is all about.
- ☑ I have *some* great details! But then, I have some generalities, too. I need to dig deeper. I need more new, unusual details.

3
- ☑ I know what I *want* to say—but it's hard to get my ideas on paper.
- ☑ At least I stick to my topic—well, most of the time.
- ☑ You can probably figure out my main idea or story.
- ☑ Details? I have a few. I need a *lot* more information.

2
- ☑ This is still confusing, even to me. It rambles.
- ☑ I'm *beginning* to figure out what I want to say.
- ☑ I *think* I have a main idea—but I'm not sure.
- ☑ This is pretty sketchy. The truth is, I didn't say much.

1
- ☑ There are just notes and thoughts. Well, it's a *start*.
- ☑ What's this about? Hey—I'm not sure yet! I'm just jotting down ideas.
- ☑ If you to find a main idea here, *please* tell me what it is!

ORGANIZATION

6
- ☑ This is so easy to follow it's like having a road map.
- ☑ The structure is strong, but it doesn't overwhelm you.
- ☑ Super organization makes my ideas clear.
- ☑ Notice my opening? My closing? Unforgettable, don't you think?
- ☑ *Everything* connects. You never wonder how I got from A to B.

5
- ☑ This is pretty orderly. Nothing's out of place.
- ☑ You can spot my structure if you're looking for it.
- ☑ Main ideas stand out.
- ☑ I have a strong lead and conclusion.
- ☑ It's pretty easy to see how one thing connects to another.

4
- ☑ The order works—I don't think you'll feel lost.
- ☑ My structure is definitely there—just a little predictable.
- ☑ I *have* a lead and conclusion—that's the main thing, right?
- ☑ I connected *most* ideas together.

3
- ☑ Some parts are *definitely* out of place or not needed.
- ☑ It's sometimes hard to follow—you might have to re-read.
- ☑ I tried for a good lead and conclusion, but I'm not sure if they work or not.
- ☑ I did not always see how ideas connected, so it was hard to make that clear to readers. What really goes with what?

2
- ☑ I need to re-organize! I seem to go in lots of directions.
- ☑ I don't really understand how to connect ideas to each other—or to my main point.
- ☑ My lead and conclusion need work! They're not exciting.

1
- ☑ This is a jumble of details and random thoughts.
- ☑ Nothing really goes with anything else.
- ☑ There's no lead; it just begins. There's no conclusion; it just stops.

VOICE

6
- ☑ This is *me*. It's as individual as my fingerprints.
- ☑ This paper *begs* to be read aloud—you'll want to share it.
- ☑ I love this topic—and it shows in every line.
- ☑ I don't over-write, but I use my voice to keep readers hooked.
- ☑ You'll find this paper tough to put down.

5
- ☑ I think my voice is lively, expressive and enthusiastic.
- ☑ The tone and flavor are right for my topic, audience and purpose.
- ☑ I want my audience to like this topic and to tune in.
- ☑ Would you read it aloud? I think so.

4
- ☑ Spontaneous? Enthusiastic? Sure—now and then. Not *all* the time.
- ☑ Tone and flavor acceptable for topic, audience, purpose.
- ☑ My voice comes and goes. I get tired now and then, you know?

3
- ☑ I have a sincere, *functional* voice. This is an OK topic and an OK paper.
- ☑ My tone might not be *perfect*. Well, *nobody's* perfect.
- ☑ I don't usually think about the audience—I just write.

2
- ☑ Sometimes I sound like an encyclopedia—other times, I'm too chatty. I can't seem to hit the right note.
- ☑ I think there could be a *moment* of voice here or there.
- ☑ My audience? Well, who *are* they anyhow?

1
- ☑ I can't think of a word to describe this voice.
- ☑ Does this even *have* voice? It's kind of ho-hum.
- ☑ I wouldn't read this myself if I didn't have to.
- ☑ I don't care that much about the topic—and I don't really care if anyone reads this, either. I feel bored. I'm glad it's over! (Bet you are, too.)

Adapted by Vicki Spandel from her ideas in her book *Creating Writers*, Longman, 1999. Reprinted with permission.

6-POINT SCALE FOR STUDENTS, P. 2

WORD CHOICE

6
☑ You'll read this more than once; it's that good.
☑ I made every single word count; if it didn't work, I cut it.
☑ I'll read this a year from now and I'll still like it.
☑ My verbs are strong—I don't count on adjectives.
☑ Could you quote me? Well—I'd say yes.

5
☑ My word choice is natural. I didn't need the thesaurus.
☑ Every word is used correctly, making my meaning clear.
☑ I tried to give the writing some sparkle with vivid verbs.
☑ I did not settle for worn-out phrases; I found my own way to say it.

4
☑ It works and it's clear. It makes sense.
☑ I guess I did include some clichés or over-written phrases.
☑ Verbs? Well, yes, right in here with the adjectives and adverbs.
☑ It isn't always original or striking, but it isn't confusing.

3
☑ I did not always use words correctly. I may have confused my reader.
☑ I had a good moment or two, though!
☑ Too many modifiers? Do you honestly, truly, really think so?
☑ Some words are vague. Did I over-utilize my thesaurus?

2
☑ This is confusing. What was I trying to say?
☑ I should have looked up the words I didn't know.
☑ Verbs? Well, there's good old *is, are, was,* and *were...*
☑ Sometimes I was showing off—other times I settled for routine words like *nice, fun, great, wonderful.*

1
☑ Help. I don't think *anyone* will understand this.
☑ This does not make sense, even to me.
☑ I used other words over and over. I think I made up some of these words.
☑ I need verbs. I need clarity. I need better word choice.

SENTENCE FLUENCY

6
☑ This is easy to read with a LOT of inflection—like a good film script.
☑ Almost every sentence begins differently.
☑ My informational writing comes right to the point.
☑ My creative writing is lyrical, poetic, and musical. It flows.
☑ You need to read it aloud to really appreciate it.

5
☑ My writing has an easy going flow, rhythm and cadence
☑ It's enjoyable to read—no practice needed.
☑ My sentences are different lengths and begin in different ways. Variety is my middle name.

4
☑ My sentences are easy to follow.
☑ I wouldn't call my writing musical, but it's not awkward.
☑ Yes, I have some variety in length and structure
☑ Yes, there's some repetition. Yes, some sentences begin the same way.

3
☑ When I read this over, it sounds mechanical.
☑ ALL my sentences seem to begin the same way. All of them are alike. All of them could use some work. All of them are putting me to sleep.
☑ Where's the zip? It isn't as natural as conversation.

2
☑ This is a little hard to read aloud—even though I wrote it! I went on and on and on as if I could never stop and had to keep going. Or I wrote. In choppy. Phrases. Some weren't. Even sentences. This. Is boring.

1
☑ This is very hard to read aloud.
☑ Sometimes I have to go back and start over or I can't tell where sentences begin or end.
☑ I have to fill in lots of missing words or missing punctuation. Sometimes I have to hook words together to make a sentence. I don't really know what a sentence is. Help

CONVENTIONS

6
☑ Only the pickiest editors will spot errors.
☑ It's mostly correct (maybe not *flawless,* but come on).
☑ I used a wide range of conventions (as I needed them)—semicolons, ellipses, dashes, italics, etc.
☑ Notice the layout? Eye-catching, don't you think?
☑ I'd say this is ready to publish.

5
☑ I made some minor errors, but you may not have noticed.
☑ I *did* proofread. I'm not a fanatic, but I'm careful.
☑ I used good conventions to make my text easy to read.
☑ I think the layout leads readers to main points.
☑ Minor touch-ups will get this ready to publish.

4
☑ I made some noticeable errors, but you get my meaning.
☑ It's perfectly readable. No buddy's—uh, nobody's—perfect.
☑ Layout? Hey, looks good to me.
☑ Basics (e.g., periods, cap's, simple spelling) are OK.
☑ It needs a good once-over before publication.

3
☑ A few errors may stop you just for a second.
☑ I made some errors even on basics like periods and simple spelling. How did those slip by me?
☑ I should think more about layout. It's kind of blah.

2
☑ This has MANY errors. Maybe if I read it aloud ...
☑ Some errors get in the way of my meaning
☑ Even basics, like simple spelling, need work.
☑ I think *every line* will need editing if I'm going to publish this. My layout needs work, too.

1
☑ Only very patient readers will get through this
☑ I missed a LOT of errors. I still don't know what they all are. I need editing help—and help with layout
☑ My message is *buried* under mistakes.
☑ I think I should go through this *word by word*

Adapted by Vicki Spandel from her ideas in her book *Creating Writers,* Longman, 1999. Reprinted with permission.

FOR CLASSROOM USE ONLY.

Some Frequently Asked Questions About Voice Lessons

These lessons seem like a lot of fun. I am a traditional teacher. How do I incorporate them into my curriculum? How much time should they take? Do you have suggestions on how they may fit into a 50-minute period?

These lessons are meant to supplement a choice based writing curriculum. Most teachers will find their own way of using them. For example, one teacher might use them as a 15-minute class starter, another to frame a more involved 50-minute lesson. We have designed this book for ease of use and we encourage you to experiment with your own way of fitting the lessons into your teaching style. Every lesson here is a result of experimentation, and we invite you to join in the learning with us.

Should I grade students on their voice lessons?

We always advocate feedback for work that students do. Grades are a useful tool for getting them to try. However, you will probably want to assess the experimental, freewriting, brainstorming work based more on their focusing and participating than on correctness of their answers, which will only inhibit responses and work against your efforts. For certain assignments you might want to create a rubric to include correctness. We like to find a way to give students credit for the process, for example, for participating in debriefing every day. Grades should never be punitive.

How much time should be spent preparing for the test, how much writing on topics of your choice?

It is the goal of tests to create better writing instruction, not worse. Tests scores will soar in classes where students write regularly on topics of their own choice. Formal test instruction should be kept to a minimum, not because it's intrinsically bad, but because it's much less effective in creating a class of fluent writers.

Why should we spend time making lists of persuasive moments, etc, when on the test students are given a prompt they may not even care about, to write on?

When students get to write on topics of their own choice they learn to engage with their material. Then, when they are faced with a boring prompt, they will know the skill of finding an engaging angle. Lessons in this book help students explore both passionate and silly opinions in hopes they will find a fluency and clarity of thought that will transfer to their assigned writing. There are no boring subjects, only boring writers. Practicing writers know this fact. This knowledge will show up on prompted tests.

Some of these lessons seem to be more about talking and acting (see chapter 5). How will these activities help my students to write with more voice?

Acting out writing and playing with deliveries in front of a live audience helps create a palpable awareness of audience that follows a student back to their lonely writing desk. These lessons especially help students who are great persuaders in real life but fall apart when they are asked to write an essay. The goal here is to shrink the gap between oral and written persuasion so that students respond to a blank sheet of paper with as much clever passion as they would a parent they were trying to persuade.

I notice many lessons on 5 of the 6 traits but few on conventions and grammar. Why?

There exist already so many resources for teaching written conventions and grammar. Most of the wishes we hear from teachers aren't about how to teach punctuation or capitalization, but on how to make their students' persuasive pieces more meaningful and effective. That said, we must add that the lack of information on grammar does not mean it is less important to us.

I know creative writing is fun for the students, but I am a high school English teacher required by my curriculum to do more formal writing. How can I justify voice lessons when I have to help my students get into college?

Formal writing is changing in our world. Pick up a copy of any of the journals of the National Council of Teachers of English, and you'll see that even those published articles are full of first-person, descriptive, juicy-voiced, read-me-now essays. A fluent and versatile voice only makes a student writer more skilled at both reading and writing with depth. These days, originality and style are also appropriate in more formal writing assignments in college and business than ever before. We recommend you read the book Essays that Worked by Boykin Curry. These are essays that got students into some of the best colleges in America. Each one reflects unique and individual voice that can only come when teachers provide creative opportunities. Another wonderful example which is as available as any Internet search engine is Hugh Gallagher's college essay.

I teach younger grades where persuasive writing is not part of the curriculum. Narrative writing is stressed. How can writing persuasively help my third graders?

Persuasive writing helps students of all ages to see and comprehend different points of view within a literary text (i.e. "Why I Eat Pigs" by A.Wolf). It is also a way to empower your students to express their positions and opinions to the world. If we don't train elementary students to write persuasively about their opinions we can't expect middle schoolers to know what to care about. In a worst case scenario they may grow up to be people who believe in what the polls tell them.

There is a playful quality to many of the lessons in this book. I tend to be more serious in my teaching. How can these lessons help me?

It's true that every teacher has her own teaching style, and some of the lessons might be a little more zany than you would like to use. However, if you work with students who have to face a written persuasive test, the lessons especially in Chapter 9 can help you pinpoint your students' weaknesses with that challenge, particularly if you have any students who have failed this type of test before. We also encourage you to adapt any of our lessons to fit your own teaching style. Our goal is not to tell you how to teach but to give you the ball and ask, "What can you do with this?"

The Tom Sawyer Approach

Listen to how Tom Sawyer teaches the positive power of persuasion.

"Say — I'm going in a-swimming, I am. Don't you wish you could? But of course you'd druther work — wouldn't you? Course you would!"

Tom contemplated the boy a bit, and said, "What do you call work?"
"Why, ain't that work?"

Tom resumed his whitewashing, and answered carelessly, "Well, maybe it is, and maybe it ain't. All I know, is, it suits Tom Sawyer."
"Oh come, now, you don't mean to let on that you like it?"
The brush continued to move. "Like it? Well, I don't see why I oughtn't to like it. Does a boy get a chance to whitewash a fence every day?"

That put the thing in a new light. Ben stopped nibbling his apple. Tom swept his brush daintily back and forth — stepped back to note the effect — added a touch here and there – criticized the effect again — Ben watching every move and getting more and more interested, more and more absorbed. Presently he said, "Say, Tom, let me whitewash a little."
Mark Twain (*Tom Sawyer,* ch. 2)

Writing to the Top:
Third graders write a group letter to get drinking fountains

February 3, 2000

Dear Mrs. Ryan,

We all want water fountains in the third grade rooms, please. We always get thirsty a lot. We need a water fountain because some people forget their water bottles. Everyone would like to get a drink in their own classroom.

We think better when we can get drinks, and we'll do better on our work. If the fountain was in our room, it wouldn't disturb anyone. Every other classroom has a water fountain. We wouldn't waste so much time taking whole class drink breaks.

Please let us know what you think.

> Sincerely,
> Mrs. Masters's Room

February 6, 2000

Dear Third Grade,

Thank you so much for your wonderful letter requesting water fountains for the third grade classrooms. You gave such strong arguments for why you should have fountains in your classroom, and I couldn't agree with you more. I know how thirsty you get, especially during the hot weather, and I realize that water does indeed help children think better. For many years, not only the children, but the teachers have wanted running water for the modular classrooms.

There are several reasons why drinking fountains have not been installed in your rooms. The primary reason is that the portable classrooms were intended to be "temporary," and that the cost to install running water would not be a responsible investment of money for something that wouldn't be permanent. Unfortunately, the classrooms have not been as temporary as they were originally planned to be!

Additionally, our school district is now planning to build a new elementary school which will reduce the number of students attending Lower Salford in several years. Hopefully, we can place all our classroom teachers into regular, not portable classrooms at that time. Then, if we needed to keep the modulars, they could be used by special teachers. So, you can see that it's difficult to make a case for installing water at this point in time since we may not be using the modulars for classrooms in two to three years.

Hopefully you will be able to come up with some creative solutions for your classroom that will help you eliminate the thirst problem and avoid taking additional class time for "drink breaks." Thanks for taking the time to write to me. You've certainly done a great job learning to write a persuasive letter!

> Sincerely,
> Mrs. Ryan

March 2, 2000

Dear Mrs. Ryan,

We are writing back another letter about water for the modulars. Mrs. Masters found out how much it would cost us. Each cooler costs $11.00 a month to rent from the Eagles' Peak Water Company. Each bottle of water costs $5.50. Cups are $14.50 for 1000.

 One family could donate cups, or each child could bring their own. It would only cost $44.00 to rent the cooler and not too much more for the water. We'll really use it a lot, but we won't ever waste it.

 Please notify us if we can get it. You are a very nice principal.

     Sincerely,
     Mrs. Masters's class

March 9, 2000

Dear Third Graders,

 You wrote quite a persuasive letter to me regarding the installation of water coolers in the third grade modulars. As I thought about using paper cups, I felt it would be wasteful and really messy if everyone used paper. I liked your idea about bringing in your own cups from home. These cups would need to be a small size since we will have approximately 75 children drinking from the cooler.

 I looked at the prices you suggested, and Mrs. Alderfer, the school secretary, thought she knew of a less expensive company to use. She will be calling to find out more information.

 If I were to use my principal's fund to purchase water for the modulars, I would probably only be able to buy three to four bottles per month for you, so you would have to be reasonable and responsible in the amount of water you drink. But I realize the upcoming warm months are a time when you really could use access to water. As soon as I have more information, I will write back to you.

     Fondly,
     Mrs. Ryan

Baby Steps: The Story of a Peace Movement

Gretchen Shoopman Bernabei

My belief is that children also bring an as yet untapped resource of implicit social knowledge: that is, they know much more about what is going on around them than they have ever been put in the position of saying.

Peter Medway, "The Student's World and the World of English"

When I was a kid, we didn't see violence like this at school. People didn't act this way. Nobody got shot in their own yards. People could sleep by their windows without worrying. Those were the good old days. Things have really changed.

-Miguel, sixth grade

It was true. Five years earlier nobody had seen the movie *Colors*. If there were gang activity and organized crime in San Antonio, most public school children weren't aware of it. Neither was I.

But now the atmosphere at our middle school had thickened like a tired war, with predictably shifting fronts and nervous intermissions between incidents. Even the civilian students carried themselves with an almost fashionable anger, others with a stance of defensiveness. In private writing, though, many students reflected despair.

Schools are getting to be just like a dark, beat-up building where a lot of drug users go and hide out or get high. We have lots and lots of violence going on in our school. Everybody writes on the walls and after school as you're going home, you can see different kids standing in alleys sharing cigarettes and staring at you. Some kids are tired of it. Some are even scared. I know some are scared of being asked to take drugs. Is there anybody who can help us?

-Christina, sixth grade

The atmosphere had changed gradually. A shooting in a Northside neighborhood. A flurry of drive-bys. Two teenagers killed on the Eastside. A drive-by murder of a bystander in a mall parking lot bus stop. A football player dead in an icehouse parking lot. A sixth-grade girl's birthday party visited by two armed teenagers who stand at the door and open fire, killing the birthday girl. In class, students and I talked about violence, about fear, about helplessness.

One Sunday afternoon, my involvement with the vague citywide gang problem turned personal and specific.

My daughter Matilde had finally drifted into a solid nap, and I crept down the stairs and unfurled my Sunday paper, the San Antonio Express-News. One story, "Gang Victim Mends As Mom's Anger Grows," hit me squarely in the face. Our school had buzzed with conversations about this gang victim, a three-year-old; the shooting had marked yet another shocking low for gang activity.

I turned to the continuation on page 10. " Family Ponders Future as Wounded Boy Mends. The Contreras family still has no place to live. Leticia and Edward have been sleeping at the hospital, both in one twin bed next to little Edward's bed." I pictured our guest bedroom, just next to the room where Matilde slept. "Contreras said she would most like to have a place to move her family to so the children can be together again." Every wall in our house has a double-thickness of shiplap lumber, and my baby sleeps safely. I lifted my gaze from the newspaper, through the sunny window to the huge fenced yard, full of toys and swings, pecan trees and shade, only ten minutes from the hospital. I pictured Leticia and Edward making eye contact, watching the nurses for signs of annoyance, apologizing in advance for their awkward residence.

That's enough, I thought. A mother's rage welled in me. I might not have been able to protect their baby, but I won't be audience to fresh wounds on their dignity. I folded up that section of the newspaper, and straightened up our guestroom, and waited for Matilde to wake up. Then I took my own step. I found the mother of the shooting victim and offered her our home. It was a quiet act.

Though I did not intend to discuss my actions with people outside my family, I changed my mind the next morning.

"Morning, Jason!"

"Morning, Ms. B!" Sleepy, shy smiles and ducking heads. Students stirred the weekend mustiness in the auditorium as they breezed through the door.

"How're you doing, Felicia?"

"I'll tell you in my journal."

"Good morning, Students!"

"Good morning, Teacher!"

"I'm glad to see you. I'm sure you have plenty to write about this morning. I do."

They bent their heads to their journals and, settling onto a tall stool, I opened mine. Staring at the blank page, I wondered how to attach words to what had happened yesterday. I looked up at the students, at the angles of their young faces as they shifted and wrote, their eyes lowered. The muscles around my lips flexed me a warning which I recognized too late. Now all I saw was a sea of three-year-olds in those thirty chairs. And then they were all my three-year-olds.

I knew I'd have to talk to them about my experience yesterday. But when I tried, I choked.

"I'll have to write you a note."

The next day, Patricia volunteered to read my letter aloud to the students. As she read over it silently, I addressed the class. "Take out a piece of paper and a pen. After you hear this, let's don't talk about it out loud. You'll hear what I think. And I'd like for you to talk to me on paper about what you think." They nodded solemnly and prepared.

February 25, 1992

Dear Students,

Today in class when I looked at your faces, I could picture you as young children. I imagined what you might have looked like when you were three years old. And when I tried to tell you about something that happened over the weekend, I couldn't finish. So I hope you will read this and know it comes from somewhere deep in my heart, to each one of you.

It started Sunday, when Matilde was in her crib, taking a nap. I opened up the newspaper and saw the front page. There was a story about the little boy who was watching TV at home one night a couple of weeks ago. Both of his parents were there. There was a drive-by shooting, and a bullet went through the wall and shattered his arm.

Do you know what he said? When he realized that something was very, very wrong? He said, "Oh, Daddy."

Imagine. A shot had ripped apart his arm, and he took a breath and said, "Oh, Daddy." Take a little breath and say those words to yourself. "Oh, Daddy."

Now imagine being a daddy. Imagine hearing shots outside and trying to tell your family to get down. And then you hear your little three-year-old son take a breath and say, "Oh, Daddy." Imagine doing all you can to protect your family and hearing one of your precious children say those words.

Now imagine your own mother or father. Can you picture how they used to look at you, full of love, when you were three? Now can you imagine your mother's face when the doctors take you away from her?

Whose family deserves that? Nobody's. Nobody's.

Well, my heart ached for that little boy, for his daddy, for his mama, and for his three little sisters. I read that they had no home now. The mother and father had been sharing a little bed in the hospital. I stared at the newspa-

per, thinking about the extra room we have in our house. We don't have money, but I felt that we had so much, a safe house and a big yard. I felt like it might be crazy, and maybe they might not need it or want it, but I just felt like I had to offer to share what we have with them. Where would they go?

So after talking it over with my husband David, a little later in the afternoon, I went to the only place I knew to find them. Matilde sat in her carseat, and I drove to the Santa Rosa Children's Hospital. I wasn't sure what to say to Leticia and Edward, but I had to go see them. Room 608, the information lady told me.

I watched Matilde's face on the elevator. She was jabbering baby talk as it went up, and we soon found room 608. I knocked on the door and heard "Come in."

Leticia, the mother, turned and looked at me when I walked in. I could see that she was tired but beautiful. I glanced over at the patient with his arm up in the air, in traction. I really wasn't prepared for how he looked, even though I had seen his picture in the newspaper. In real life, he looked so tiny. Little Edward. His eyes were tired-sparkly, beautiful brown. His head turned to look at his mom, and his neck was so little on the pillow.

His mother and I talked to each other for a few minutes, and she told me that they had found an apartment which they would be moving into soon. I told her that she and her family were welcome at our house if they needed it for a day, an afternoon, a week, whatever. We only talked for a few minutes about what it had been like that night. I gave her our phone number.

As I left, I turned at the door. I wanted to say, "God bless you." My voice just wouldn't come out. So with Matilde in my arms, I closed the door.

Do you know any three-year-olds? Do you know how it feels to put your arms around a little puppy-warm doll-body and hoist him or her up on your hip? How you run around acting insane to get them to laugh? Words are still new to a three-year-old mouth. You want to watch them living in a world of play, and laughing with the world from waking-up time until tucking-in time. That's cool.

So now I think about gangs. Groups of friends? Friends who look out for you? That's not too bad. But people who pick up weapons and say that the law is bad? People who write F.T.P.? F.T.L.? Who hired these police? Who made these laws? We people did. You did. Your parents did. Their parents did.

Who shot that three-year-old? All gang members did. Anyone who ever touches a gun and thinks it would be fun did. Anyone who ever stops thinking about other people's rights did. Every fifteen-year-old who mouths off at a teacher so he won't look like a wimp did. Every person who scribbles a gang name on a book-cover did. Every person who passes gang graffiti and doesn't stop to erase it did. We all had a part in pulling the trigger at Edward.

Who can stop gang violence? We all can. But students, you more than anyone can. How? By knowing how uncool gangs are. Selfishness is not cool. It's not cool to hurt others. It's not cool to destroy. It's not cool to take. It's not cool to kill. Picture your mama's face. Picture your family members. Listen to the little voice taking a breath and saying, "Oh, Daddy." Listen to that voice, students. It's the voice of your own children. Let's join together to give, to make the world a better place, everywhere we go. No one is alone when we love each other. God bless you.

Love,
Gretchen Bernabei

Patricia sat down. Nobody moved. I sat still behind them and watched. Luis turned around and made eye contact with me. I nodded. He looked at me. He nodded. We both tried to smile and gave up. I heard papers moving in their laps.

As they wrote their responses, the silence had a new quality. Something had changed among us.

Soon I saw why. Their expressions matched mine in depth and conviction. In their writing, I read shared grief for the Contreras child, daily terror of losing their own family members, despair because "everybody is in a gang, and there's nothing you can do about it." Would they let me share what they wrote? They did. I highlighted excerpts from each paper. We printed them clearly on sentence strips and posted them on the wall at the back of the auditorium.

Quietly, almost through the cracks of the emotional responses, came wishes for action, their own action. "Mrs. Bernabei, you did something. I want to do something too. Why don't we form a little group and go out painting over some of the graffiti?"

I paused to consider. Am I going to go out painting with these kids? What exactly is my job? What of myself do I choose to use as an educational tool? Where does my teaching stop and my life start?

If I discouraged students from taking their own anti-violence baby steps in favor of "just writing about it," what lessons would I give them? A shallow bag of writing tricks? A real interest in their expressions? Love of learning? Or love of talk about learning?

I decided that modeling my own empowerment is not enough. If the students were moved now to take steps on a path, they would need some help in clearing obstacles. Of course, I decided to back them and see how far they would go.

Who would be willing to paint? Veronica circulated a survey.

When would we go? We couldn't ask for class time. "This wouldn't be for a grade, Mrs. Bernabei. This would be because we want to."

Where would we get the paint?

How would we get wall-owners' approval?

What if gangs painted graffiti back? Would we be vulnerable to violence ourselves, if we "messed with their territory"?

What message would we leave on the walls, ourselves?

Would the school administration stand behind us?

How would we gather parent permission?

We talked through each problem, made lists, wrote letters, and made a date to paint a wall.

Wouldn't Kym Fox be amazed to see what her writing had triggered? I telephoned her at the newspaper office and invited her to stop by Mark Twain Middle School for a glimpse of something hopeful and passionate which had begun with her article in the Sunday paper.

When she arrived, the students insisted that she sit with them in the auditorium chairs and hear my letter, the way they had. So we reenacted that for Kym. Then the students took her to the back of the auditorium and showed her some of their written responses. Clearly, what she saw mattered deeply to her.

"And we're going out tomorrow morning to paint over our first wall."

"Where will that be?"

"We're meeting at 6:30 at the dumpster, then we'll cross the street and paint the side of that abandoned 7-11."

"May I quote you in the newspaper?" Some students chose to remain anonymous, but many wanted their names on their words. Kym left with the body of their responses.

Public awareness brought to the students a need to clarify their position. "My cousin is in a gang. I don't want him to think I don't care about him."

"We're not against gangs," another student wrote. "We're against violence."

> How do I feel about gang members? I feel we have to help these people. Talk to them and listen to what they say. These gang members are not aliens, they're human beings. People can change their minds whenever they want to. Cool is talking to gangs and telling them what you think. I used to think all gang members were bad but some just can not stay out of gangs. Just maybe they don't kill or hurt, but just hang around people. Gangs can be bad or good.
> -Matt, seventh grade

The next morning, as I pulled my pick-up next to the dumpster at 6:20, I actually hoped no one would show up, and I'd go inside and wake up with coffee and colleagues. But here appeared a small legion of students to paint our first wall. Several people brought brushes, and Rudy, our campus YMCA liaison, strode up smiling and bearing a small tin of red paint. With some old clumpy white latex (left over from my kitchen), we made pink. When I stood shoulder to shoulder with students and dipped a paintbrush into paint and then touched it to the wall, something gentle rushed through me.

That moment brought something quiet and conspicuous to the students too. I watched Luis as he dipped his dry paintbrush into the latex. He lifted his brush to the wall and hesitated, looking around and laughing awkwardly. When his brush made a blotch on the wall, the smile left his face; he stroked to catch the running paint, stroked again, pulled the paintbrush away and looked around. "Wow."

In later days and weeks, I would overhear Luis and Damon comparing that moment, that wierd rush accompanying the first brush stroke. I would watch them on several subsequent painting mornings quietly identifying first-time painters and positioning themselves for the first brush-stroke, just to see if it happened to them too. We would try to name and identify that sensation. It would remain unnamed.

Within several minutes, the students laughed as they painted, covering grafitti words and then shaping the huge blotches into heart shapes.

Responding to a neighbor's call reporting suspicious activity, a police car careened into the action. "We have permission, " I told the officer who stepped out of the car. He surveyed the wall; the students, a little cowed, surveyed him.

He smiled broadly. "Lady, frankly, I don't care if you don't have permission. This is great."

The students gingerly resumed painting. I watched their insecurity. They're so used to being "in trouble," I thought.

A car drove past and a horn tooted. The students glared in its direction. These kids are not used to open approval from the public, I thought. "They LIKE what they see, you guys! It's applause." They looked at me blankly. "Here's what you do." I modeled a smile and a wave with my paintbrush. They laughed.

By 7:15, that wall was no longer filled with black ugly sprayed-on violence, but white and pink hearts, gracefully overlapping each other. Should we sign the wall? Write anything? No, we thought. It's an anonymous gift. We agreed to paint again the next day. We would find another wall. We stepped back and looked at our wall together. We may not be able to change violence in the city, but we sure did change this one wall.

The newspaper the following Sunday was staggering. On the front page, "Students Speaking Out Against Gangs." Continued on page 8A, "Classes Express Anger, Fear Over Gang Violence." A photograph of our auditorium wall. An inset with student quotes from their responses to me. Excerpts From Student Letters on Gang Violence. I poured another cup of coffee and settled down onto the couch to read it slowly. Our classroom dialogue had become news. The telephone rang. It was the mayor of San Antonio. He didn't want to congratulate us; he wanted help. "Could this process be replicated by other schools?" That became our next assignment with a quick deadline. Within the week, seven students and I visited Mayor Wolff's office with "The Mark Twain Plan," which centered on student thoughts and problem-solving to impact their immediate world. The students read their words to the mayor and gave him copies. Copies appeared in the newspaper.

Our fifteen minutes of fame lasted for several weeks, and real-life writing and thinking "assignments" mushroomed. Before the school year ended, the students' accomplishments had rippled wide.

They had transformed and maintained about twenty neighborhood walls.

They had become pen-pals with younger students in several classrooms around the city, planning and delivering their messages about violence and about caring about each other.

They had changed the general perception that "everybody is in a gang" by signing, collecting and posting "I am not in a gang" pledges to cover a massive wall; they wrote letters requesting these statements of local and national celebrities.

They had written letters to area art supply dealers about known thievery of "tagging" markers.

They had answered every letter of support received from various community groups and members, some accompanied by floods of donations of paint, money, and supplies.

They had conducted tours of the neighborhood walls for neighboring community leaders, including a police chief and city council members.

They had developed anti-violence campaigns for elementary school students, complete with reproducible pages featuring themes about attitude changes: "What's Cool?" "I Used to Think. But Now I Know" and "Who Are the Stars in Your Life?"

And finally, they had noticed that the school year was drawing to a close. Who would cruise the neighborhood and continue the work on the walls when our group was no longer meeting as school? They even worked out delegating the work through a "Listen to Your Heart" Saturday event which brought out local celebrities and dozens of community members. They demonstrated lessons in the park on "How to Paint a Heart" and "How to Adopt a Wall."

Three years later, I look back and consider the subtle changes that shape a person. The distance from spectator to participant is so slight, such a wisp. I knew I would never be the same; not because of the media flurry touched off by my students' work; not because I'd finally modeled something fine for my students; not because talking and writing had changed our local world. I'm still not sure exactly how to name the difference in my feelings about teaching, but I suspect that it lies in the magnitude of changes that can take place when students and teachers really listen to each other, and to themselves, especially in quiet voices; when they act on what they hear, especially in tiny steps. It's no longer enough for me to "come out from behind the big desk" in writing assignments alone. In even the most problematic schools in our cities, the children hold the keys to managing and changing their world. Their instincts, their capacity for compassion, and their willingness to act are not enough; they need guidance in learning to wield the power of language.

> I feel proud to be part of this because I know we're helping San Antonio. It's like there was a big black storm cloud over San Antonio that the gangs made and now that we've been painting, that black storm cloud seems to be becoming a beautiful rainbow of bright hearts. It's showing people things can be better, that you don't have to be afraid. Soon if we all work together there will be no more storm clouds, only a lot of love.
>
> -Sofia, sixth grade

> I care about this issue. I really didn't think this plan would work and grow as it has. I thought it would just blow up in our face because not too many people care. But I never saw so many people moved by one thing. And they are not just sitting on their behinds and supporting it, but they're doing something, even though it might not be much. We're finally doing something.
>
> -Rene, sixth grade

Young People Who Made a Difference

Craig Kielburger

Seventeen years of age, he has one older brother, Marc, and lives with his parents in Toronto, Canada. Craig first became a spokesperson for children's rights when he was 12 years old and read about the murder of a young boy from Pakistan who was sold into bondage as a carpet weaver and murdered for speaking out against child labor.

Craig gathered a group of friends and founded the organization (Kids can) Free the Children which is now the world's largest network of children helping children, with over 100,000 active youth in 27 countries around the world.

Jason Crowe

In 1996, Jason Crowe, nine, announced he was going to raise money for cancer research "so that no one else should ever have to lose their grandma to cancer." With that thought, Jason became a publisher of a newspaper for kids "The Informer" which has subscribers in 29 states and 15 foreign countries.

Jason researches, writes and edits articles on conservation, nonviolence, religious tolerance, racial unity and animal rights, all with a viewpoint that children can help make the world a better place. Jason, now 13, continues to work as an organizer, humanitarian, peace activist, editor, publisher and writer.

Aaron Gordon

When Aaron Gordon was in second grade, his Miami, Fla., school bus slammed on its brakes suddenly and riders were thrown to the floor. "There were no major injuries," Aaron says, "but it made me think. Why aren't there seat belts on school buses?"

Since then, Aaron's all-consuming passion has been to force the federal government to require the belts on buses. He has collected 6,000 signatures, designed his own school bus seat belt, and traveled to Washington, D.C., to lobby lawmakers on behalf of a bill he co-wrote with former U.S. Rep. Andy Jacobs Jr. of Indiana.

Melissa Poe

When she was in fourth grade, Melissa Poe started a club called Kids For a Clean Environment, which now counts 300,000 members worldwide. The magazine she founded, Kids FACE Illustrated, now reaches more than two million young readers.

Rosina Roibal

Not so long ago, the old Pajarito Elementary School in Albuquerque, N.M., had two problems. The first was a leaking sewer that formed puddles on the playground. The second was that nobody seemed interested in fixing the first problem. Until Rosina Roibal came along. "When our drinking water was found to be contaminated by sewage, [the solution] was to put water jugs in the school, and we weren't able to drink the tap water."

Rosina and four others started a youth group to campaign for a new school, which city officials said was too expensive. Finally, the new Pajarito Elementary School was built.

Note Passing: Essay by Andrew Green

Here is an excerpt about note passing in junior high by writer and poet Andrew Green from his forthcoming literacy memoir. Read it to your class before a write around session to set the mood. For information on Andrew Green's book and award-winning poetry newsletter, visit the Web site www.potatohill.com .

The spring of seventh grade, I would receive a note on my desk in English class via Bill Hughes, via Cathy Brown, via Paul Dixon, via Michael Cipriano. The pleasure of writing a note and passing it to the other end of the room and not getting caught was only surpassed by the pleasure of receiving a note from the opposite end of the room. It was great fun to talk about other kids in the class in our notes, without them knowing it, some of whom were the very ones to help shuttle the note quietly from desk to desk. For notes were our power base. In fact, we had a class-wide silent communication network that shifted into high gear transmitting messages every time the teacher turned toward the black-board. There was an entire secondary conversation going on at all times in that room. The primary text of that English class was usually some horrid lesson on misplaced modifiers and irregular verbs or else a lecture on the correct form of writing a business letter. But the hidden text, the secondary text, if you will, was far more interesting. Conversations about bicycles, girls, after school fights, daily love affairs (tell Sarah to tell Cathy that Mike likes her) kept us from falling asleep. It was a conspiracy of demonstrative silence. And, some of us rational-ized, we were after all, reading and writing in class.

The notes would scurry across the room: Jimmy to Pam to Karen to Bob to Mike to Peter to Liz to Don. And five minutes later a note would come back. Don to Liz to Peter to Mike to Bob to Karen to Pam to Jimmy. Once, when I got caught receiving a note, I denied having it and rather than reveal the message and betray my friends, I stoically went to the principal's office as my punishment.

Sample Write-Around

What really bothers me is that you see so much violence. I mean it is going on all the time. You could be having a great day and somebody mugs you or attacks you. Another thing is that people that say there is too much violence on TV. And yes I do agree with that, but why even bother to try and take violence off TV because you still have the news. So why take it off for entertainment? (Nicole Stephenson)

I also agree there is too much violence going on. But I don't think you should take violence off TV because people have the right to watch whatever they want. And some violence could be funny, like when someone gets mad and throws like a pie at someone or something and they duck and it hits another person.
(Grant Ruedemann)

I think that the government should take action and enforce the laws. Also they should stiffen the punishment for crimes, instead of just fining people. Then they'll go rob someone because they need money.
(Larry McMillan)

Yeah, they should do more actions when people do serious crimes because most of the people do just get fined! Well I don't care about violence on TV. I think it's stupid when people make a big deal and they say "too much violence on TV." Well, so what! (Sabrina May)

Racism

It really bothers me when people are racist. Too many people are raised to be racist. They think they shouldn't like other colors. (Sabrina May)

Racism doesn't really bother me that much. I really don't see any racism. But some people can't help it. Some people are brought up to hate others. (Tim McCade)

Racism isn't as bad any more than it used to be, but there is still some people who just hate others because of what they look like or what color their skin is. (Frank Martinez)

I feel racism still is a big problem. It is idiotic to hate someone just because the color of their skin. How do you know they aren't a nice person? A person's color doesn't mean anything. (Dewey Maneewat)

"Confronting Racism"

Alis Headlam

In Jasper, Texas, on June 7, 1998, three white men kidnapped a 49-year-old black man named James Byrd Jr., attacked him and dragged him to a brutal death.

When the three were arrested, they weren't talking. Only one man, Shawn Allen Barry, finally told his story to the police. The story implicated the other two, who were known white supremacists and had racist tattoos on their bodies. On Sept. 28, 1999, Shawn told Dan Rather on "60 Minutes II" that he tried to stop the attack as the two men pulled James Byrd from the truck but was thwarted by comments that he, too, could become a victim. However, what happened after his initial attempt indicates that he did not face his own responsibility in what was occurring. Instead of leaving the scene to get help or further trying to stop the attack on James Byrd, Shawn sat down on the running board of his vehicle and waited. He turned a blind eye and a deaf ear to the events that continued to take place. He now admits that this might have been a mistake. He should have done something.

Shawn Berry is about to learn a very important lesson about participatory behavior. With racial violence or abuse, no action is an action. While he claims that his two friends bludgeoned and then dragged James Byrd to death, he says he was immobilized. Whether by outrage or fear, he continued to be immobilized, even after the men returned home. He did not call the police. He allowed his truck to be washed at the local car wash to remove evidence of the crime. Although he doesn't discuss this, there had to be some conscious decision on his part to participate in the cover-up.

While Shawn Berry may not get the death penalty, the prosecution is inclined to press forward with murder charges for his participation in the crime. Sitting by and doing nothing, attempting to cover up the crime afterwards and admitting no guilt when questioned by the police are not innocent behaviors. By not acting to save James Byrd from the attack, he was acting. By allowing his vehicle to be washed to eliminate evidence of the crime, he was acting. By being silent when he was arrested, he was acting. No action is an action. Shawn Berry may not have been guilty of premeditated hate, but his lack of action makes him an accomplice in the murder. In this case his lack of action supported violence and assisted the killers.

For too long much of America has felt that turning their back on racial abuse or racial attacks meant they were not guilty of racism. But the truth of it lies uncovered in the Jasper, Texas, incident. America has silently accepted attacks on blacks and other minorities and allowed the violence to go on right in front of their eyes for too long. It's past time for people to stand up when they see abuse or violence against anyone, to try to stop it, to speak out against it. Perhaps the death of James Byrd will provide the lesson that so many of us have needed. We can no longer deny that violence precipitated by hate is not prevalent in our country, nor can we ignore the fact that we have an obligation to stand up against it.

It appeared in the "60 Minutes" interview that Shawn Berry was suggesting that he, too, was a victim in the crime. His tears elicit a stream of empathy. But the facts of the case may present a different story.

He was threatened by his two "friends" when he tried to intervene. He feared for his own life. But how is it that he allowed the situation to occur in the first place? In the interview he admitted that he knew that his two companions were known racists and that he did not like their attitude towards blacks, and yet he continued to associate with them. On the night in question he allowed James Byrd, a black man, to get into his truck with these two known white supremacists, and he drove them to a remote area where the attack occurred. He chose to remain present even as the brutal beating went on, as James Byrd was spray painted and chained to Berry's truck. He rode with the killers in the truck when the victim's body became unchained and was re-chained to the bumper. He may be a victim of his

own lack of responsibility, but he can't blame anyone else for his lack of action.

No, Shawn Berry is not an innocent victim. His behavior was passively aggressive, and he was actively involved in allowing this heinous crime to take place. He may well be found guilty by his inaction. And this should be a wakeup call to us all. Racism and other forms of hate can be obliterated in our society if we stop condoning them by silence. They could be a thing of the past if everyone stopped turning a blind eye and a deaf ear to what happens. The bullies must not be allowed to run our lives by placing fear in our hearts Racism and other forms of hatred can be confronted by friends who do not permit inappropriate behavior to go by without comment. They are curable if their existence is not accepted in our communities, if our spiritual messages are strong, if people speak out against all forms of hate and seek public policy that makes it illegal to sit passively by in the event of abuse or violence. Our schools, churches, and businesses are obvious places where education against hate can occur. What Jesse Jackson said is true: "No one is safe until we are all safe."

Alis Headlam is a writer who conducts workshops on healing racism for teachers through her company, One World. E-mail her to find out more information on bringing her program to your community : Headlam@aol.com .

Sample Student Essay About Persuasion in a Literary Work

Persuasion in *Huckleberry Finn*

There's persuasion all through *The Adventures of Huckleberry Finn*. Most of this persuasion is people trying to make others believe a story, usually untrue. Huck, himself, does this all the time.

I mean, look at when Huck is dressed as a little girl and talks to that one woman. He tries to make believe he is a girl and that he is from Hookerville. It backfires but then he is able to persuade her that he is someone else.

Another instance is when he's trying to convince the harelip that he's really from England! He digs himself a huge hole and ends up telling her that they have like sixteen preachers in their one church.

The two guys Huck and Jim pick up after they are being chased by dogs use persuasion. One convinces them that he's the Duke of Bridgewater. The other that he's the King of France.

One of Huck's ingenious uses of persuasion doesn't even need words. This is when he convinces everyone he is dead. He does this by setting up several things like the pig's blood everywhere. He also puts some of his hair on an axe. He drags a bag full of rocks towards the river to make it look like his body has been thrown in the river.

Though much of the persuasion used throughout this book is in lies and deceit, some of it is good. One is where Huck convinces Tom Sawyer to help him free Jim from Tom's aunt.

Another good instance is when Huck wrestles with his conscience over whether or not to write a letter to Miss Watson, telling her about Jim. Fortunately he convinces himself to do the right thing, which ironically he perceives as the wrong thing. Another time, the King preaches about being a reformed pirate and persuades many people to give him money to help his quest to reform others. Huck's pap tries to convince the judge that he's reformed himself; of course, that is just all a lie. Huck has to convince Jim that he isn't a ghost.

Huck Finn is riddled with persuasion.

Michael Roberts
Eleventh grade

Persuasive Moments as Poems: *The Odyssey*

"Recipe for a Good Hero"
20 – 30 lbs of muscle (no substitutes)
A large brain
A generous personality
The ability to leap tall buildings in a single bound
(this can be replaced by the ability to change in a telephone booth or rescue damsels in distress)
Take proper care of your hero. They need an occasional bath and a good cry about once a month.
                    -Michelle Paquette

"The sailor's speech to his comrades, just before opening the bag of wind"
My brothers,
The time has come. We must decide for ourselves. Odysseus has made all of our decisions so far, and for what? Are we not perfectly capable of doing it ourselves? Who here really knows what is inside this bag? This bag could possibly hold treasures, or food. Food! Odysseus surely looks healthier than the rest of us. Do you not agree? This sack holds our answers. Who will stand with me and open Odysseus's secret sack?
                    -Christi Ferguson

"Calypso Begs Odysseus"

Odysseus
My love,
Must you leave me?
Human Mortal,
Abandon a chance
To live forever?

I am goddess,
She is a mortal
Stay
With one much greater.

Would you rather
A mortal's fading love
Or a love
That will last
Forever.

Calypso,
Her love is
Meaningless
Compared to yours.

But,
Would you rather
Keep a bird in
Its cage
Or let it fly free?

Isn't a bird
Happier free?
Let me go
Free.

I will remember
You
Forever, forever.
                -Michelle Gallogly

Genre Lists

Acceptance speech
Ad copy
Address to a jury
Advice column
Afterword
Agenda
Allegory
Annotation
Annual report
Apology
Appeal
Autobiography
Billboard
Biography
Birth announcement
Blueprint
Book review
Brief
Brochure
Bulletin board
Bumper sticker
Business letter
Business proposal
Bylaws
Campaign speech
Captions
Cartoon
Chant
Character sketch
Charter
Chat room log
Cheer
Children's story
Classified ad
Comeback speech
Comic strip
Community calendar
Constitution
Consumer report
Contract
Conversation
Court decision
Credo
Daydream
Death certificate
Debate
Dialogue

Diary
Diatribe
Dictionary entry
Directions
Dream analysis
Editorial
Elegy
Email
Encyclopedia article
Epilogue
Epitaph
Essay
Eulogy
Experiment
Expose
Fable
Family history
Filmstrip
Flyer
Foreword
Fortune cookie insert
Found poem
Graduation speech
Graffiti
Grant application
Greeting card
Haiku
Headline
Horoscope
Human interest story
Infomercial
Instructions
Insult
Interview questions
Introduction
Invitation
Itinerary
Jingle
Joke
Journal entry
Keynote address
Lament
Law (statute)
Learning log
Lesson for a child
Letter of complaint
Letter of request

Letter to the editor
Limerick
Love letter
Lullaby
Magazine article
Manifesto
Manual
Map
Memorandum
Memorial plaque
Menu
Minutes
Monologue
Monument inscription
Movie review
Myth
Nature guide
News story
Newsletter
Nomination speech
Nonsense rhyme
Nursery rhyme
Obituary
Oracle
Packaging copy
Parable
Paraphrase
Parody
Party
Party invitation
Petition
Platform
Play
Poem
Police/Accident report
Political advertisement
Post card
Prayer
Precis
Prediction
Preface
Press release
Proclamation
Profile
Prologue
Proposal
Public address announcement

Public service announcement
Radio spot
Rap
Rebuttal
Recipe
Recommendation
Referendum question
Research report
Resignation
Restaurant review
Resume
Riddle
Roast
Rock opera
Sales letter
Schedule
Screenplay
Sermon
Sign
Slide show
Slogan
Song lyric
Specifications
Spell
Sports story
Storyboard
Summary
Survey
Tall tale
Test
Thank-you note
Theatre review
Toast
To-do list
Tour guide speech
Translation
Treaty
T-shirt design
TV spot
Vows
Want ad
Wanted poster
Warrant
Warranty
Wedding invitation
Wish list

A Treasury of Video/Poster Composition Projects

All Based on Any Novel, Story, Play or Plot G. Bernabei

Directions: Pick one of the following projects. Think of the literature you have just read. Put yourself into that time and setting, and write a script to be acted out potentially for video production. Each project could incorporate visual aids and audio background (music sound effects, etc.), costumes and props. Make your production as elaborate as you care to. The more terminology (or shaky vocabulary) from the literature that you can incorporate, the better. If your finished project looks like fun, your grade will be higher.

1. **News Story** – Pretend that you are a news anchorman of that day, time and place, and report some incident from the story. Pick only one incident, and use what journalists use: who, what, where, when, why. If you can use an eye-witness's comments, do! Don't forget to keep your reporting objective and factual.

2. **Enquirer Story** – Pick an incident or character from the story and write a news item the way that the *National Enquirer* would. Pick some item and distort it so much that the exaggeration in no way resembles the truth. (Example: local man gives birth to alien.)

3. **Dear Abby Letter** – Write a "What should I do?" letter from a character in the story to Dear Abby. Include Abby's response. How many? A "Dear Abby" column usually runs two or three letters and answers.

4. **Chamber of Commerce Brochure** – Each town has a Chamber of Commerce, which prepares a brochure to advertise all of the good points of the town, to attract people or business to that area. Write such a brochure and be prepared to present it on video, as an ad for the town.

5. **Commercial** – Write a 30-second advertisement to sell some item in the story. Be persuasive, and use as many advertising gimmicks as you can. Feel free to make up merchants' names, stores and prices.

6. **Letter to mayor or Congress** – Pretend that you are a citizen in the place from the story, and you are unhappy about some law there. Write a letter to an authority figure, as the character/citizen, asking to change the law. Give reasons why it should be changed, and use whatever tone of voice that you think will work. Be prepared to give the request out loud, on video.

7. **How-to Lesson** – Think of some skill that someone in the story has, and teach others how to do that. Handle it in a step-by-step fashion, and be prepared to teach it on video.

8. **Telephone Call** – Write a telephone call that one character from the story might make to someone else, expressing some strong emotions about an event from the story. Be prepared to pick up a telephone and be videotaped performing the conversation. It may show just your side of the conversation, or you and your partner may write and perform a two-sided conversation.

9. **Fashion Article** – Do a news story describing either one person's attire at an event from the story or the fashion trends of the time and place.

10. **Transportation** – Do a news story about a local transportation development or problem.

11. **Diary Entry** – Write an entry in a diary by one of the characters, at the end of an important day or at a critical turning point.

12. **Employment Want-Ad** – Pretend you are advertising for either a position or for a job. Write an ad and be prepared to do a "Classified Video" version of it.

13. **Be a Thing** – Be some object from the story. Describe an incident from the story from that object's point of view. You may want to handle the video by having the camera filming the object, and a voice overlaid on the tape, explaining the incident.

14. **Prayer** – You are one of the characters from the story, and you are at a church service. Write a special prayer for someone.

15. **Definitions** – Pretend you are one of the characters in the story, and you are tutoring children. You are teaching them your own definitions of words. Pick your own words, and write the lesson your character would conduct. (Suggestions: use words like "loyalty," "home," "friendship," "fairness," "betrayal," "adventure.")

16. **Conversation** – Write a conversation by two or more characters in a spot not shown in the story (the breakfast table, some time later, over the phone, on a bus, at church, etc.) Be prepared to perform it for video.

17. **Police Report** – Pretend that you are local police (or county sheriff). Write a report the way a policeman would to document some incident from the story. Use terms that the authorities might use ("The suspect was first seen by...")

18. **Business Letter** – Pretend that you are one of the characters from the story. Write a letter expressing your feelings over some situation in the story to someone not in the story. Be prepared to read it on video, either as the writer proofreading it, or as the receiver, reading it for the first time.

19. **Poem** – Pretend you are some character from the story. You feel very strongly about some incident, and you express your feelings in a poem. Write it and be prepared to read or perform the poem.

20. **Letter from Mom** – Write a letter of advice to the narrator or a character in the story, as though you are his or her mother or father, and you are worried over some situation from the story. Advise the character how to handle it.

21. **Campaign Speech** – Make a political campaign speech as though you were someone in the story, and you were running for office. Tell who you are, where you are from, what you are running for, and what issues you're for or against. Use issues from the story to capture your audience's interest and sway their votes.

22. **Award Presentation** – An organization from the town is giving an award to someone for something. Pick the receiver and the award, and write the presentation speech.

23. **Bedtime Story** – One character from the story tells a bedtime story to a child from or close to the story (maybe babysitting a neighbor's child). Write and be prepared to perform the bedtime story.

24. **Song** – Write a song performed by someone from the story, reflecting some aspect of his/her life.

25. **Instructions/Directions** – Pretend that you are a character in the story, and you are telling someone else how to do something or go somewhere. Write the goals and instructions.

26. **Restaurant** – Create a restaurant in the location of the story. Name it, and create a menu with descriptions of all the items, as well as prices.

27. **Resume** – Write a resume for some character from the story, either at the time of the story or fifteen years later. Use standard resume format.

28. **Letter of Appreciation** – Pretend you are a character in the story, and you appreciate something another character did. Write a letter of appreciation from the one character to the other. Use proper friendly letter format.

29. **Sportscast** – Using any physical activities listed or mentioned in the story, prepare a news sportscast.

30. **Weather** – Remembering the location of the story, and the time of year, prepare a weather report like one on the news. Feel free to use maps and all of the things that weathermen use. Make the weather report relevant to the story.

31. **Horoscopes** – Write horoscopes for every sign in the zodiac, for one certain day, an important day in the story. Make sure to write clues to events that will transpire that day. Read the horoscopes for the video.

32. **Think of an original idea** – Want to do something not on this list? Go ahead! Make sure that there are references to the setting, events, or characters of the story, and that the voice of the speaker is clear, his/her purpose clear, and the genre of the piece is clear (what type of piece it is).

Hi! I'm the Cyclops from the epic story the Odyssey. You may recognize me. I'm here to tell you what really happened

One day I was reading a book and all of the sudden Odysseus and his friends showed up. Being the nice guy I am I let them in.

I treated them great. We watched a few movies and I even ordered a pizza for them.

Odysseus says that I trapped them in there because I put that boulder in front of the cave. Well that is my door. If they wanted to leave they could have just asked.

In the Odyssey I was described as some mounstrous cannibal. This is not true. I have bad vision (they don't make glasses for a cyclops) so how was I supposed to know they were hiding in my refrigerator.

It wasn't my fault. Then Odysseus gave me some wine as a gift. So of course I accepted and while I was drunk he stabbed my eye.

Then when I let my sheep out my guests snuck out with them. They didn't even say goodbye.

All I ever wanted were some friends but now I'm just a lonely cyclops without an eye. So no matter what they say about Odysseus never trust him!

This book was based on the opinions of the cyclops.

No humans were harmed during the making of this TRUE story.

For more info on how you can contribute call 1-800-ANTI-ODY

Sincerely,
Cyclops

copyright 2000
Brendan Publishing Co.

A Pit of Ignorance
James Higdon

We as people are walking on a high wire. What's below us, you may ask? Below us is a pit. A pit of unkindness, misunderstanding and disrespect. It's a big deep pit. It's the kind of place fueled by ignorance, pride and all that's wrong with people. This is bad you may say, but it gets much worse, for you see, this is a very odd kind of pit. It's a place that once in, you can get out of, but people in it choose to stay. Usually. The reason for this odd phenomenon is meanness.

Some people enjoy being mean, and being mean is much easier than being kind. You may say, well, I've never seen this pit of the human spirit so how do I know it's really there? Well, you have seen this pit. In *To Kill A Mockingbird,* you saw it with every action of Mr. Ewell. Every one of the twelve jurors on Tom Robinson's jury visited this place when they took a white man's word over a black's just because of that. When Mr. Radley locked up Boo, he visited this place and became very familiar with it when he filled in the hole in the tree that was Boo's only communication with other people.

There is a way out, though. Every time you show kindness and respect to a person, you are a little further up out of the pit. When the black people stood for Atticus and all the people stood for the judge, they showed respect to those people. Respect is how you get out of the pit. If those twelve men and Mr. Ewell had had respect for Tom Robinson and all black people, they would not have accused and convicted him.

Kindness is another route up. When Boo came out and put the blanket on Scout during the fire, that was kindness, and it was when he put his life in jeopardy to save Jem and Scout from Mr. Ewell. When Scout talked to and then walked home Boo, that was kindness.

On this high wire you show respect and kindness to those who show it to you and stay above the pit of hatred, ignorance, and disrespect. The one truth out of all of this is that in situations where it would be easier to fall into hatred, people should and mostly do keep their heads and stay with respect and kindness.

APPENDIX
23
Connecting The Odyssey and a Painting:
"St. George and the Dragon"

Man's Fascination With Monsters

Man has always been fascinated with confronting monsters. People are usually curious about what they are not used to seeing.

When Odysseus and his men saw the Cyclops, they wanted to know more about them and learn how they went about things, if they were nice or mean, friend or foes.

On Mission to Mars, they found this huge alien head sculpture on Mars, and they made another mission to see what was inside. They thought it had to be some kind of creature.

I remember when we were smaller, there was this thing about Bloody Mary. You would say it into a mirror ten times in the dark, and supposedly she would come out and scratch you. I always did it and my brother too because we always wanted to hit her as she was coming out.

I wonder, what was the first monster? It might have been a mean person, a really ugly person, or maybe someone who was more of an outcast and now it has evolved into what we think of as monsters today.

-Adrian Ramos, 9th grade

PAVE THE STUPID RAINFORESTS!

I'm madder than a monkey with a rotten banana over all this hullabaloo about saving the stupid rainforests in South America.

Wimpy environmentalists are crying big fat tears because a bunch of head-hunters in Brazil are chopping down some trees to make a little extra spending money.

These fruitcake Chicken Littles believe if we chop up jungles there won't be any more air and we'll all die.

Hogwash! They can PAVE the darn rainforests for all I care.

Let's face it. The first thing our Founding Fathers did when they landed on America's shores was start cutting down trees.

George Washington and Thomas Jefferson were farsighted enough to know that you can't build shopping malls in the woods, for crying out loud.

Our great nation doesn't have one single rainforest and I'm breathing just fine, thank you.

Jungles would look better this way, says Ed.

If the rainforests are so healthy, then why in hell are all the people who live there trying to come here?

And another thing. The nuclear plant protesters who scream doom and gloom about the rainforests are the same nutcases who believe in this ozone stuff.

You know, there's supposed to be a hole in the ozone layer over the North Pole or something and we're all supposed to get cancer and die because it lets too much sunshine in. Phooey!

It's supposed to be caused by all those cans of spray paint we've used to make America more beautiful. So let's just put ozone in spray cans and sell it to these

scaredy-cat environmentalists.

These yellow bellies could just spray it into the air and patch the hole over the North Pole in no time flat.

I mean, how difficult can it be to put ozone in a can?

And while I'm on the subject, I'll tell you another thing. These bleeding-heart nature freaks say they want to save the rainforests and all that stuff for our children. That's a crock.

Ask any red-blooded American teenager where he'd rather be—in a nice air-conditioned shopping mall playing video games or slapping mosquitoes in some godforsaken jungle?

From *Lets Pave the Stupid Rain Forest and Give Teachers Stun Guns* by Ed Anger, ©1996 by Weekly World News. Used by permission of Broadway Books, a division of Random House.

Brian For President

Once upon a time in San Antonio, there was an online chat room.

Thom e-mailed this to a mailing list of about 73 people from the room: <<Everyone is invited to FATSOS tonight...karaoke...pool...darts..>>

Alicia replied to all 73 people: <<Can't make it...already have plans>>

Michael replied to all 73 people: <<Gang, let's stop this in its tracks right here right now. NO NEED to tell everybody if you can make it or not. If you feel the need to tell others, then e-mail them specifically. Thanks.>>

Brian replied to all 73 people: <<I think the "reply to all" is a very thoughtful feature that AOL has provided us with. Instead of concentrating on the negative (don't we get enough of that in the chat room?) aspects of e-mail, let us come together and rejoice at the wonderful innovation that is our new world of electronic mail. Let us stop for just a moment and ponder a world without electronic mail, there are 73 names on this mailing list. Now, at the current cost of US mail stamps that would mean that in order to keep all of our closest friends informed of what we are planning that would cost an individual on the average of $23.76. Now while in and of itself $24 is not that much money to spend on our closest friends, we need to look at the bigger picture.

So, if everyone wanted to share their innermost thoughts with all our closest friends that would run more along the lines of $1710.72. Now in the big scheme of things that is not a lot of money either. But imagine if you will even just one half of our closest friends wanted to respond to something that one of our other closest friends had to say in their replies. At that point we are well on our way to funding a small third world country. That brings up another good point. By resorting to sending electronic mail to all our closest friends we could save enough money on postage to help feed the starving children in Ethiopia. Now I realize how difficult it is to move a mouse pointer all the way across the screen (especially if you are one of the unlucky ones to have a monitor larger than 17") and accurately press the DELETE button. But by doing so we bring ourselves that much closer to the Kingdom of God.

In summary, not only can we bring ourselves that much closer to eternal salvation, but at the same time we can bring to a halt that evil machine we call the U.S. Postal system. Even if your goals and dreams do not lie along these lines, think of all the starving children in Africa that we can help to a longer and more fulfilling life. I guess all I'm really saying here is DOWN WITH GOVERNMENT and power to the people.
~Brian>>

Jerry replied to all 73 people: << Just get me off this Stupid list >>

Brian replied to all 73 people: <<Now ya see, this is the kind of mentality that breaks down the union between brother and sister that I was referring to in my previous electronic mail. This not the time for dissension, but the time for unity. We MUST come together as one people. We MUST be stronger than those before us. We MUST have the courage to stand up for what we believe in. We MUST stop the evil machine that is the U.S. Postal system. We CANNOT stand idly by and watch the mistakes of our youth become the regrets of our maturity. Come, join me brothers and sisters, in this our time of greatest peril. This time of technology. We MUST embrace our destiny and continue to nurture our God-given right. The right to send electronic mail. The right to express ourselves via electronic mail. If we do not, as a people, stand up and take what is ours then we are nothing. Together we are strong. Apart we are prey. Prey for the stronger, more powerful U.S. Postal system. This I say to you, my people. Unite behind me and rid our society of this cancer that has grown unchecked. This we MUST do before it is too late. Do not, I implore you, do not let our children grow up in a world controlled by the U.S. Postal system.

I take a great risk in speaking out against the evil machine that is the U.S. Postal system. I fear not for myself, but for the countless others that are too frightened to take this stand. I say to you now, Be Not Afraid my brethren. Together we shall overcome; together we shall triumph. Together we shall rid ourselves of this accursed evil. Help me to cleanse this once great country. Fear not the repercussions of our outcry, yet fear our silence. For silence is the weapon of the machine. No longer shall we be slaves. The time for freedom is at hand. Together we can break the bonds of conventional mail. Salvation through electronic mail. It, I fear, is the only way that we the people may once again be free.
~Brian~

Chris replied to all 73 people: <<Brian for President!!!!!!!!!!!!!!!>>

TV Commercials: Tips

When making a 30 or 60 second video commercial think of it as a series of two to three second shots. Each box beneath represents one shot.. Decide what the camera will show and what the voice over (if there is one) will say . Remember you are not narrating a long story. Each shot, like a scene in a movie, or a chapter of a good book, must move the action forward.

Funny Tip: If you want your commercial to be funny, have the image contradict the voice over. For example: Voice over: Passion, the drink for lovers. Image: a woman barfs on her boyfriend.

Have fun but make sure what you do is appropriate.

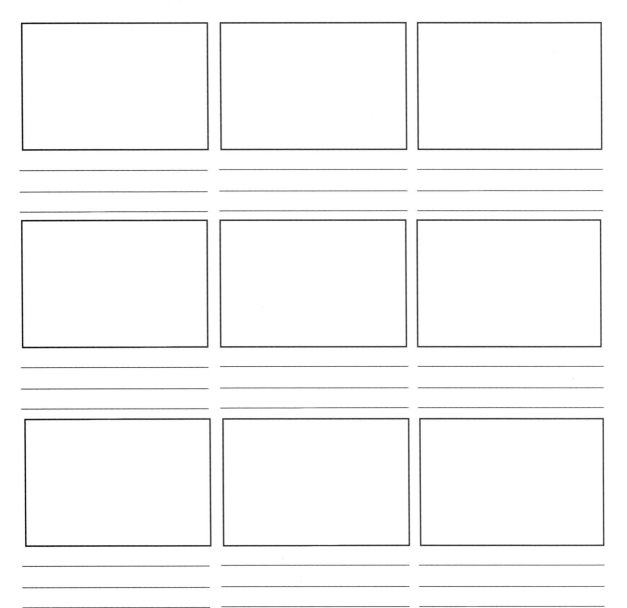

To Whom it May Concern,

I really think I would be a great neurosurgeon because I am very social and I listen very well. I am patient and I never become frustrated. Here are some qualities I believe I have:

loyal
attentive
persistent
social
patient

I believe I would be a great surgeon. I am very prepared for this job because I recently went through a two week first aid course instead of medical school. I have been diagnosed with Parkinson's and I have an extreme shake in my right hand, but I am positive that this won't get in the way. I hope that you will present me with a doctor's license because I won't let my patients down.

Sincerely,
Georgy Tremble
(Ken Marshall)

The Devil's Advocate: List of Ridiculous Rules

The City Council is proposing an ordinance to enforce the following rule. (Choose one.)
Pretend that you are FOR the issue. Write a letter to your City Council member, stating your
position. Give convincing reasons.

1. The wearing of shoes indoors will be prohibited.
2. If a citizen allows his/her toenails to grow too long, toes will be severed.
3. On Fridays, citizens will turn off their TVs and listen only to radios.
4. On Sunday, everyone not at church without a doctor's excuse will be prosecuted.
5. Children will be required to carry handguns.
6. Cars will become available to all citizens, free of charge.
7. Killing people will become a sport.
8. Land mines will be allowed in all front yards.
9. Muscle shirts may be worn only by those citizens who have visible muscles.
10. Citizens must marry the first girl/boy they kiss.
11. If you miss one day of school, you go to jail for one day.
12. Citizens must drink in order to be allowed to drive.
13. Walking will require a license.
14. All drugs will become legal and available over the counter.
15. Anyone convicted of stealing will be executed.
16. All cosmetics will become illegal.
17. There will be no talking in public.
18. School will be held seven days a week.
19. Anyone who believes in Santa Claus past the age of seven will go to jail.
20. The law of gravity will be repealed.
21. Fishing will be prohibited.
22. No citizens will be permitted to have children.
23. No public school student will be permitted to eat beans during the school year.
24. All citizens must stay in their homes after dark.
25. All gas-powered cars will be prohibited; electric cars only will be permitted.
26. Littering the environment will be a capital offense.
27. Any citizen who corrects the spelling of another citizen will be prosecuted.
28. Observances of birthdays will be prohibited.

Image courtesy of www.adbusters.org

How To Argue: Interview with Alan Dershowitz

Lawyer Alan Dershowitz didn't attain renown by being shy about debate. but how he defines a successful argument might surprise you. By Diane Cyr

On the one hand, lawyer, professor, and professional provocateur Alan Dershowitz likes to find bones to pick. He has defended Claus von Bulow, Mike Tyson, O.J., and flag burning. He has given his books such titles as *Contrary to Popular Opinion, Chutzpah,* and *Taking Liberties.* He does sound-byte battle with just about anyone on cable, network, or syndication.

On the other hand, his favorite joke goes like this: This man orders a bowl of soup at the same deli from the same waiter every day. One day the soup comes and the man doesn't eat it. So the waiter comes by and says, "You don't like the soup? Maybe it's too hot? Maybe it's too cold? What's the matter with it?"

The man looks at him and says, "Why don't you taste it?"

"All right, I'll taste it," says the waiter. Pause. "There's no spoon!"

"Aha!" says the man.

"AHA! AHA!" says Dershowitz, cracking up. Because his point is this: In-your-face opinions are one thing. In-your-face arguments are another. The best arguments aren't won by bullies who make you scream "Uncle!" They're won by the guys who make you go "Aha!" – who lead you subtly down the garden path of your own undoing.

In this, Dershowitz has had much practice. In 35 years of law (he's 59), he has consulted on or argued approximately 250 cases. He argues before judges, trial juries, grand juries, television audiences, classrooms, and assorted paying listeners and readers. He also argues with just about anyone, from his Harvard criminal-law students (student: "The police invited them to headquarters..." Dershowitz: "They invited? What, like a little engraved card?") to crackpot Holocaust revisionists.

Throughout, he argues that argument—whether with one's spouse, boss, or chief justice—is best achieved "with a scalpel, not a hatchet." In other words, if you want to get your way, first you have to get your opponent invested in wanting things your way. Like the man in the deli, you have to go for the "Aha!"

The bad news: This methodology ain't easy. The good news: It's got a terrific track record.

"Look, this is not my invention," Dershowitz says of his argument style. "Socrates invented it. Rabbi Hillel invented it in the Talmud. It's a technique as old as recorded history, and the best philosophers, the best arguers, have always been those who led their students to come to their (own) conclusions." Take Jesus: "did he say, 'Don't cast the first stone'? He said, 'Cast it! Let he who is without sin cast the first stone.' Socratic teaching at is best."

Of course, emulating Dershowitz is likely more doable (if less noble) than emulating Jesus or Hillel. For those who choose to wield the scalpel in their encounters with the Other, consider the following:

1. **Don't fight just to win.** If you're arguing simply to best your opponent, you just might do it. But it won't make anyone happy. The object, remember, is to get the person on your side. "Why should anybody else want you to win?" Dershowitz reasons. "You have to have a motive beyond winning." So if you're fighting with your boss about more vacation time, or with your spouse about whose family to visit for Christmas, fight for the larger picture: the health of the relationship, or the ability to do a better job at work.

   "Advocacy is not overpowering your opponent," says Dershowitz. "It's persuading your opponent that your ideas are his." Hence:

2. **Know your opponent.** Injustice, ill will, shoddy treatment, and plain idiocy are all perfectly clear from one's own side. The harder part is placing yourself in the purported idiots' shoes to determine what accounts for their point of view. You have to think like they do," he says. "You have to put yourself in their position," he says. Which further means:

3. **Don't assume the opponent's an idiot.** Go in swinging, and your opponent will swing back. Go in humble, shaking hands and making eye contact, and your opponent just might soften to hear your side. "Don't believe you're going to make yourself seem smarter than they are, or better than they are," says Dershowitz. "Assume they're smarter than you are, they're righter than you are, they believe in their position as much as you do or more, they're as nice as you are."

And by the way: Mean it. "Never underestimate your opponent," Dershowitz says. "I learned that from a friend of mine, a lawyer from Atlanta. She spoke with some kind of rural Alabama accent, and people thought they could run all over her. And she was one of the most brilliant lawyers and best poker players I ever met."

4. **Do the homework.** It's one thing to tell your boss that Project X is stupid. It's another to line up pages of market research, focus-group studies, customer call reports, budget projections. And profitability estimates. It's even better to bring it up in the context of the boss's top ten Favorite Things about Project X—and then show why Project Y (your baby) just might be what your boss really wanted all along.

Doing homework is more than merely lining up evidence for your side. It is also key to defusing intimidation. It's letting your opponent know that, yes, while she might be brighter, tougher, or better-paid than you, she can't slip you up on the facts. "I work my head off in preparation," says Dershowitz. "I have to know more than anyone in the room. I have to know the record cold. Know all the cases. Once I know everything, then I feel comfortable shifting to the psychological strategies of winning."

5. **Then make your case.** The first serve in tennis tends to set the rhythm of the game. Same in arguing: Keep the serve, and you can keep things in your court. The way to do it is to pick the framework for the argument. You want to go bowling with your buddies on Monday nights? Then set out a roadmap you know your spouse will follow. Talk about your need for quality time with him, your crabbiness after a long day at work, your mutual need to make more time for fun. "Start the logical argument," says Dershowitz, "and let the other person be able to finish it for you. If you can frame the question, knowing what the answer is going to lead to, then you don't have to hammer away."

Warning: Make your case real, or else prepare yourself for major resentment (perhaps accompanied by flying dishes) over your passive-aggressive shenanigans. "You must truly believe it," says Dershowitz. "It can't be an act. People see through acting."

6. **Listen.** "This is key, key, key," says Dershowitz, who won't let his law students take notes for the first two weeks of class. Listening not only establishes respect for your opponent's point of view, it also clues you to information for your own case. Since people love the sounds of their own arguments, "take advantage of the last thing said," he says. "I always start my argument, in almost every case, with, 'My opponent said...' And I turn their argument into my argument."

7. **Avoid the following:**

EGO, the desire to be right at any cost (usually your own);

EMOTION, the desire to engage in fights with bank tellers or rotten drivers, or to call your opponent a big, fat jerk; and

ELOQUENCE, the desire to bowl over the opponent with craft and vocabulary (see "ego"). Advice: Stories and analogy work best. When defending, for instance, flag-burning (controversial), Dershowitz compared it to dumping tea in Boston Harbor (non-controversial). "Let your opponent make the leap," he says.

8. **And when you win, don't hog the credit.** If you've done a great job on your argument, your opponent just might end up thinking he has won—which is fine, if you've gotten your way. After all, the true object isn't winning, but getting on the same side. Once you're there, who cares who gets the credit?

Besides, credit usually backfires. "Claiming credit is a way of distancing people from your point of view," Dershowitz says. "I learned this early on when I clerked for a justice of the Supreme Court. When I would shove my ideas down his throat, he would always say to me, 'I'm the justice, you're the law clerk.' So I learned the technique of subtly conveying information. In the end, it works. People will notice that when you're there more is done."

In other words, strong arguments, by extrapolation, can actually lead to a chain reaction of "Ahas!" Rather than buckle under the sledge hammer of your self-righteousness, your opponents and observers might simply observe, by your humble example, that yes, thank you, you were right all along.

Of course, that's assuming you're facing reasonable opponents. Mention one particular TV host to Dershowitz, for instance, and he grimaces. "I can't argue with someone like him," he says. "He's smug, he's self-righteous, he thinks he knows it all." Then he grins, momentarily emulating the dozens of Dershowitz faces on the book jackets stacked on shelves behind his desk. "He could benefit," he says, "from coming to a class on the philosophy of law."—From *Attache Magazine* used with permission of the author.

Conflict Diagram

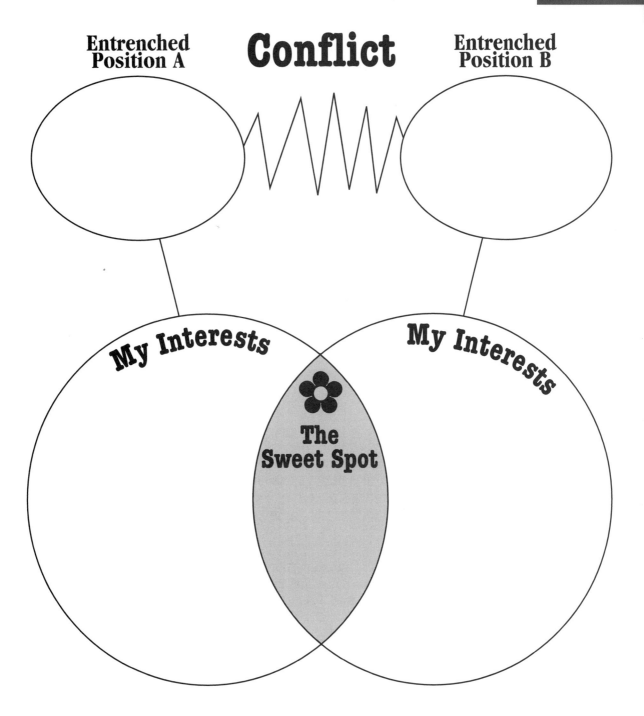

Entrenched
Position A

Conflict

Entrenched
Position B

My Interests

My Interests

The
Sweet Spot

Types of Nose Pickers
by Ben Barnes

The Wiper
One type of nose picker is every grade school janitor's nightmare, commonly referred to as the "wiper," predominantly see in juveniles and young adolescents. This type will pick and then wipe anywhere inconspicuous. Swiftness of disposal is the key for them. Bottoms of school desks and chairs seem to be a popular place of concealment, leaving janitors with a situation that only determination, a strong stomach and perhaps a chisel will eliminate. Though often regarded as a child's designation, it is certainly not limited to the younger set. Adults lacking in certain social graces and/or tissues could easily fall into this category.

The Pick and Roller
Another group would be the "pick and roll" crowd. Not to be confused with the pick and roll in basketball, these people pick with their index finger and after finding their desired goal, transfer the buger to the thumb where it is aggressively rolled with the middle finger. They continue to roll till the buger falls off their fingers, nowhere to be found. On occasion, the aforementioned process is repeated until satisfaction is complete.

The Flickers
Similar to the pick and roll is a sadistic group know as the "flickers." They use the same retrieval process as the pick and roll, but after rolling, they flick the solid nasal secretions instead of allowing them to quietly fall to the floor. Certain sects of this group flick for the sport of it, trying to get as much distance behind their flick as possible, while others take great pleasure out of taking aim at other people.

Pick and Ponderer
Still another classification is the "pick and ponder" group. This group can be seen performing their ritual most often while behind the wheel of a motor driven vehicle or behind the desk of a slow-paced office or classroom. Using their index of middle fingers, the pick and then proudly stare at their prize procreation, judging it for size, texture and color before disposing of it in the proper manner. Traveling salesmen and truck drivers seem to dominate this category.

The Rambo Picker
The final group is the "Rambo" picker. This is a group with a mission, refusing to come out till they get what they came for. This group is easy to spot as they usually have their index finger buried one or two knuckles deep in their nostril at any given time. Rambo pickers have frequent nosebleeds.

You might fall into one or more of these categories, or perhaps you find that there might be subgroups in the five major categories. The important point to note, however is that there is a group for each and every one of us, so take your pick.

(adapted from piece in *Reviser's Toolbox,* Discover Writing Press 1998)

Pattern Planners for Essays

Basic One-Two

First point

Second point

Strawman and the Wind

(Strawman. Many people think…)

(The Wind) (My real opinion)

Give an Inch to Get a Foot

Give an inch

Get a foot

Ace in the Hole

Position

Lesser reason

Lesser reason

Major reason

The Ant and the Grasshopper
Aesop

In a field one summer's day a Grasshopper was hopping about, chirping and singing to its heart's content. An Ant passed by, bearing along with great toil an ear of corn he was taking to the nest.

"Why not come and chat with me," said the Grasshopper, "instead of toiling and moiling in that way?"

"I am helping to lay up food for the winter," said the Ant, "and recommend you to do the same."

"Why bother about winter?" said the Grasshopper; we have got plenty of food at present." But the Ant went on its way and continued its toil. When the winter came the Grasshopper had no food and found itself dying of hunger, while it saw the ants distributing every day corn and grain from the stores they had collected in the summer. Then the Grasshopper knew:

It is best to prepare for the days of necessity.

The Hare and the Tortoise
Aesop

The Hare was once boasting of his speed before the other animals. "I have never yet been beaten," said he, "when I put forth my full speed. I challenge any one here to race with me."

The Tortoise said quietly, "I accept your challenge."

"That is a good joke," said the Hare; "I could dance round you all the way."

"Keep your boasting till you've beaten," answered the Tortoise. "Shall we race?"

So a course was fixed and a start was made. The Hare darted almost out of sight at once, but soon stopped and, to show his contempt for the Tortoise, lay down to have a nap. The Tortoise plodded on and plodded on, and when the Hare awoke from his nap,
he saw the Tortoise just near the winning-post and could not run up in time to save the race. Then said the Tortoise:

"Plodding wins the race."

Fist Pounding: Sample Student Writing

Dear Mr. President,

Since the beginning of this great nation there has been overcrowding in our cities. With the need of our rural land for farming, only a few options remain. One of the best of these is gaining new land. The closest and most open of these is Canada. I suggest that you use the extra money to buy Canada.

Canada has large open spaces, perfect for shipping people out of the densely populated cities and into new government owned, community homes. There they can live, keep the cities less overpacked, and work on the government's community farms. All of these "workers" will have well-paying jobs as they serve the state.

Canada also has a large supply of oil, natural gases, wood, and other natural resources to be used for the expansion of our great Empire. With these added supplies, we can decrease inflation, improve our economy, and easily take the rest of North America.

Canada is the perfect solution for all our nation's problems. And if Canada refuses, we can use the money to take it. The resources, sheer size, population, and lack of a substantial military make Canada an ideal start for the New American Order.

Loyal servant of the state,
Josh Bingamon
9th grade

What Funny Flight Attendants Say

- There may be 50 ways to leave your lover, but there are only four ways out of this airplane...

- Your seat cushions can be used for flotation, and in the event of an emergency water landing, please take them with our compliments.

- We do feature a smoking section on this flight; if you must smoke, contact a member of the flight crew and we will escort you to the wing of the airplane to see our movie, *Gone with the Wind.*

- We are pleased to have some of the best flight attendants in the industry. Unfortunately, none of them are on this flight!

- Folks, we have reached our cruising altitude now, so I am going to switch the seat belt sign off. Feel free to move about as you wish, but please stay inside the plane until we land. It's a bit cold outside, and if you walk on the wings it affects the flight pattern.

- Weather at our destination is 50 degrees with some broken clouds, but they'll try to have them fixed before we arrive. Thank you, and remember, nobody loves you, or your money, more than XYZ Airlines.

- That was quite a bump and I know what y'all are thinking. I'm here to tell you it wasn't the airline's fault, it wasn't the pilot's fault, it wasn't the flight attendants' fault... it was the asphalt!

- Ladies and Gentlemen, please remain in your seats until Captain Crash and the Crew have brought the aircraft to a screeching halt up against the gate. And, once the tire smoke has cleared and the warning bells are silenced, we'll open the door and you can pick your way through the wreckage to the terminal.

- As you exit the plane, please make sure to gather all of your belongings. Anything left behind will be distributed evenly among the flight attendants. Please do not leave children or spouses.

- We thank you for flying XYZ Airlines. We hope you enjoyed giving us the business as much as we enjoyed taking you for a ride.

Character Opinions
(Name) is (characteristic).

peaceful

affectionate

dependable

consistent

good hearted

serious

honest

team player

obedient

hard working

intelligent

themselves

happy

creative

free thinkers

tries their hardest

cautious

discriminating

comedic

stranger

sociable

positive attitude

has morals

good intentions

good audience

considerate

true

humorous

straightforward

understanding

respectful

clever

good listener

caring

easy-going

outrageous

smiling

active

cheerful

great personality

compliments

helpful

leader

versatile

professional

good sense of humor

personality

open to all experiences

prompt

devout

attentive

outgoing

undemanding

powerful

real

artistic

open-minded

loyal

adventurous

funny

committed

Comparing Letters of Recommendation
– Evaluating the Effects of Elaboration

(Before)

January 8, 1999

To Whom It May Concern:

There are many students here at Project Phoenix. But one person that should be recommended is Chris H.. He should be recognized because of a couple of reasons.

First of all, he's very nice and courteous to everyone. He's never mean, always thinking of others, and cares about everyone. He always does his work in class. If you ever need help with anything and he can help you with it, he will help you.

Sincerely,
Edgar N.

(After)

January 8, 1999

To Whom It May Concern:

It's been my privilege to know Chris H. for about a year because we are both students at Project Phoenix. I would like to acknowledge him based on what I know of him. For what I have observed, Chris is a gentleman, helpful, and very peaceful.

I believe he is a gentleman because I have witnessed this. I have had a few classes with Chris. He always respects women at school. Whenever it's cold and a girl or anyone is cold, he will offer his coat, jacket, nor shirt. Whatever he has to offer, he will offer it.

He is also very helpful. If ever there is someone who may need help, he will be there. I've seen him help teachers out by taking heavy books or boxes for them. he will help out with whatever he can. He will even volunteer to help even if he knows you don't need help. But he will, just to make sure.

I know for a fact that Chris is peaceful. All these characteristics that I have pointed out about Chris lead to being peaceful. Another reason I know he is peaceful is because this whole year that I have known him, I have never heard him curse nor raise his voice at anyone. He is always saying "sorry" or "thank you." If you look mad or something he will check in with you to see what's wrong. He will even try to calm you down.

These are just a few traits that stand out the most about Chris. I hope that this information helps who-ever reads this in making a decision for a certain position. If you need more information please feel free to contact me at (210) xxx-xxxx.

Sincerely,
Edgar N.

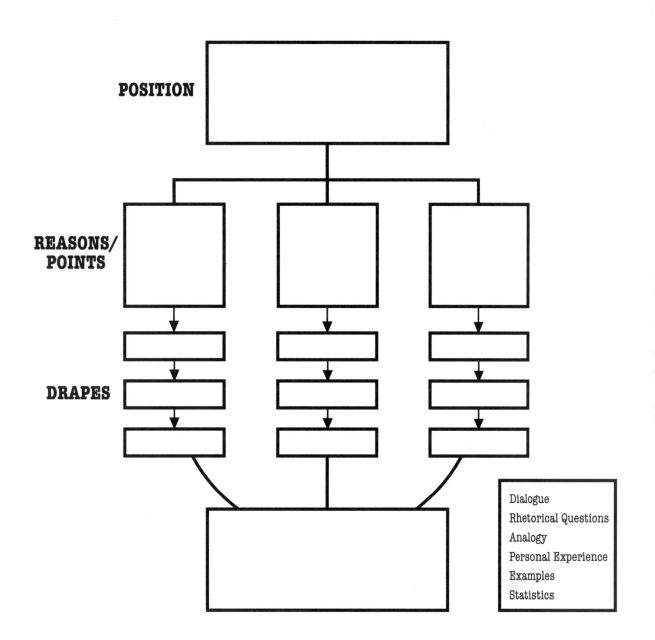

POSITION

**REASONS/
POINTS**

DRAPES

Dialogue
Rhetorical Questions
Analogy
Personal Experience
Examples
Statistics

Adapted from a plan sheet used by Geri Berger and Laura Lott.

THINK SHEET

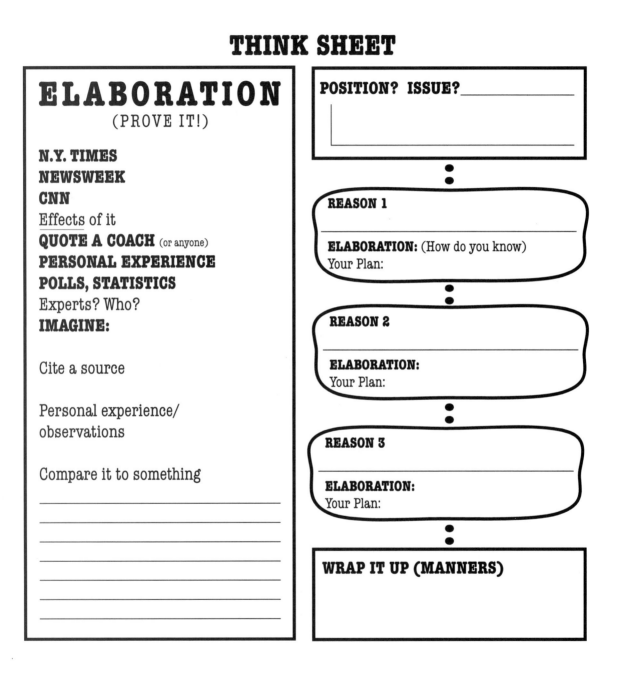

ELABORATION
(PROVE IT!)

N.Y. TIMES
NEWSWEEK
CNN
Effects of it
QUOTE A COACH (or anyone)
PERSONAL EXPERIENCE
POLLS, STATISTICS
Experts? Who?
IMAGINE:

Cite a source

Personal experience/
observations

Compare it to something

_____
_____
_____
_____
_____
_____

POSITION? ISSUE?_____

REASON 1
_____
ELABORATION: (How do you know)
Your Plan:

REASON 2
_____
ELABORATION:
Your Plan:

REASON 3
_____
ELABORATION:
Your Plan:

WRAP IT UP (MANNERS)

Elaboration Stationery

Use this stationary to remind you of all the things that help us to elaborate.

Fourmaker Sentences: I Spy Something Sparkly

These sentences came from Barbara Edens's class, from practice essays about metal detectors.

What language devices show up in these sentences?
- Repetition?
- Parallel structure?
- Rhythm?
- Use of similes/metaphors/analogies?
- Rhetorical questions?
- Zesty wording/vocabulary use?
- Simple elegance?
- Tone so clear you can practically hear music swelling in the background?

Although we have had no problems thus far in our existence, why wait until something horrible happens to spring into action? (Rebekah Isbell)

It allows safety in the school, establishes order and organization, and reduces the amount of drugs being brought into the school. (Matthew Waller)

Students will feel like society thinks they are a very hazardous chemical which must be treated with caution. (Gidget Stuart)

Students would pass through the metal detector into the quintessential safety area. (Julia Shackelford)

Think of how much chaos this will cause in the hallways. (Susan Delgadillo)

Some people will start getting aggravated and start pushing people to hurry, or start being obnoxious to others, and fights would break out. Then noise levels would rise drastically, becoming unbearable to some people or even teachers. (Rick Mendez)

Sometimes I wonder, while walking through the school, if anybody is carrying a gun or knife with them. I feel that this question sometimes pops into my head while I'm taking a test. (Matt Casey)

Putting in the metal detectors can be one more step to creating a more peaceful learning environment for the children of tomorrow. (Katie Lanum)

The amount of money that will be spent on making, maintaining, and managing will be outrageous. (Libby Benitez)

The community would cry out for the removal of these devices because of the psychological effects they have upon their children. (Sean Arredondo)

If we could decrease the exposure people must endure in their lifetime by decreasing school violence, then we could possibly have a start to even lowering violence in society. (Natalie Ramirez)

If their parents are preoccupied with their own affairs, then how is that student supposed to fulfill his duties before or after school? (Jackie Pruitt)

Installing metal detectors will make our school become more orderly and students will be sent into the building one by one, instead of cramming through the doors like a hungry herd of cattle. (Cody Lockwood)

Would you rather save the time and money or save a precious life? (Michele Moore)

The amount of money that is wasted is astonishing and would leave anyone flabbergasted. (Wesley Dixon)

Imagine waiting outside during a cold winter morning, where the ground is sparkling with remnants of the nightly accumulated frost. A line of shivering students extends as far as the parking lot, waiting to pass through the front gate. (Jason Tang)

Did you ever wonder why they tell you to show up at least an hour before your flight at the airport? (Kai Melton)

You would walk away, but how would you feel as you walked away? (Cory O'Brien)

We have them in our national airports, and the vast majority of Americans don't protest that. (Ashley Montalbo)

Thus, these expensive electrical heaps of junk would do our community no good. (Travis Barnes)

This is a serious matter and these reasons should be taken into consideration. (Matt Casey)

It is not needed, not fair, and downright troublesome. (Logan Edell)

I have nothing but respect for the School Board, but after receiving information on this issue, I have been forced to question how well the School Board investigates these issues. (Kelli Garrett)

At the rate students trickle out of school, some parents will be waiting forever, and while parents wait for their children, they hold up or stop the flow of traffic.
(Jennifer Stervinou)

Teaching Resources

Bruffee, Kenneth A. *A Short Course in Writing*. Cambridge, MA: Winthrop, 1972.

Bruner, Jerome S. *On Knowing: Essays for the Left Hand*. New York: Atheneum, 1971.

Caine, Renate Nummela, and Geoffrey Caine. *Making Connections: Teaching and the Human Brain*. Alexandria, VA: Association for Supervision and Curriculum Development, 1991.

Carroll, Joyce Armstrong and Edward E. Wilson. *Acts of Teaching*. Englewood: Teacher Ideas Press, 1993.

Cowan, Gregory, and Elizabeth Cowan. *Writing*. New York: John Wiley, 1980

Glasser, William. *The Quality School*. New York: Harper & Row, 1990.

Glynn, Carol. *Learning on Their Feet*. Shoreham, VT: Discover Writing Press, 2001.

Graves, Donald H. *Build a Literate Classroom*. Portsmouth, NH: Heinemann, 1991.

Healy, Jane M. *Failure to Connect*. New York: Simon and Schuster, 1998.

Hopkins, Mary Frances and Beverly Whitaker Long. *Performing Literature*. New York: Prentice Hall, 1982.

Kellaher, Karen. *100 Picture Prompts to Spark Super Writing*. New York: Scholastic, Inc., 1999.

Kinneavy, James L. *A Theory of Discourse: The Aims of Discourse*. New York: Prentice Hall Press, 1971.

Kohn, Alfie. *The Case Against Standardised Testing*. Portsmouth, NH: Heinemann, 2000.

Lane, Barry. *Reviser's Toolbox*. Shoreham, VT: Discover Writing Press, 1999.

Macrorie, Ken. *Searching Writing*. Upper Montclair, NJ: Boynton/Cook, 1984.

Moffett, James. *Teaching the Universe of Discourse*. Boston: Houghton Mifflin, 1968.

Rico, Gabrielle Lusser. *Re-Creations: Inspirations from the Source*. Spring: Absey, 2000.

Romano, Tom. *Blending Genre, Altering Style*. Portsmouth: Boynton/Cook Publishers, 2000.

Romano, Tom. *Writing with Passion*. Portsmouth, NH: Heinemann, 1995.

Rosenblatt, Louise M. *Literature as Exploration*. New York: Modern Language Association, 1995.

Spandel, Vicki. *Creating Writers:Linking Writing Assessment and Instruction*. New York: Addison-Wesley Longman, 2001.

Spolin, Viola. *Improvisation for the Theatre*. Evanston, Ill: Northwestern University Press, 1983.

Tovani, Cris. *I Read It, But I Don't Get It*. Portland: Stenhouse Publishers, 2000.

Vygotsky, L. S. *Mind in Society*. Edited by Michael Cole, Vera John-Steiner, Sylvia Scribner, and Ellen Souberman. Cambridge: Harvard University Press, 1978.

Vygotsky, L.S. *The Psychology of Art*. Cambridge: M.I.T. Press, 1971.

Zinsser, William. *On Writing Well*. New York: Harper & Row, 1988.

Resources, by Chapter

Chapter 1

Adbusters Culture Jammers Headquarters. 3 May 2001. <http://www.adbusters.org>.

Brown, Marcia. *Stone Soup.* New York: Scribners, 1975.

Coxe, Molly. *Cat Traps.* New York: Random House, 1996.

Gallo, Donald R. *No Easy Answers: Short Stories About Teenagers Making Tough Choices.* New York: Delacorte Press, 1997.

Johnson, Angela. *When I Am Old With You.* New York: Orchard Books, 1990.

Martin, Jane Read and Patricia Marx. *Now Everybody Really Hates Me.* New York: Harper Collins, 1993.

Mazer, Ann. *The Salamander Room.* New York: Dragonfly Books, 1991.

Raschka, Chris. *Ring! Yo?* New York: Dorling Kindersley Publishing, 2000.

Seuss, Dr. *Green Eggs and Ham.* New York: Random House, 1960.

Shannon, David. *No, David.* New York: Scholastic, Inc., 1998.

Slobodkina, Esphyr. *Caps for Sale.* New York: Harper Collins, 1968.

Twain, Mark. *Tom Sawyer.* New York: Penguin, 1986.

Viorst, Judith. *Alexander, Who's Not (Do You Hear Me? I Mean It!)* Going to Move. New York: Scholastic, Inc., 1995.

Wood, Audrey. *Elbert's Bad Word.* New York: Voyager Books, 1988.

Wood, Audrey. *The Red Racer.* New York: Aladdin Paperbacks, 1996.

Chapter 2

Allen, James and Hilton Als, Congressman John Lewis, and Leon F. Litwack. *Without Sanctuary: Lynching Photography in America.* Santa Fe: Twin Palms Publishers, 2000.

Amy Biehl Foundation, *Perpetuating Amy's Work in South Africa.* 5 May 2001. http://amybiehl.org.

Bahai Youth Workshop. 11 May 2001. <http://www.geocities.com/Athens/9144/>. The Bahai Youth workshop is a non-profit organization that sponsers a traveling troupe of teenagers who perform dances which express unity in diversity and healing the racial divide. For information on the group nearest you.

Bernabei, Gretchen. "Babysteps: Story of a Peace Movement," Voices from the Middle 3, 2 (April, 1996): 19-24. Urbana, IL: 1995.

Browne, Anthony. *Piggybook.* New York: Alfred A. Knopf, Inc., 1986.

Dickens, Charles. *A Christmas Carol.* http://www.dickens.com.

Colbert, Jan, Ann McMillan Harm, and Roy Cajero. *Dear Dr. King: Letters from Today's Children to Dr. Martin Luther King, Jr.* New York: Hyperion Books for Children, 2000.

Fox, Mem. *Wilfrid Gordon McDonald Partridge.* Brooklyn: Kane/Miller Publishers, 1985.

Free the Children, International. 7 May 2001. http://freethechildren.org.

Galvan, Peggy. *365 Ways You Can Make the World a Better Place in the New Millennium.* New York: Troll, 1999.

James, Simon. *Dear Mr. Blueberry.* New York: Simon and Schuster, 1996.

Lewis, Barbara A. *What Do You Stand For? A Kid's Guide to Building Character.* Minneapolis: Free Spirit Publications, Inc., 1988.

Lionni, Leo. *Six Crows.* New York: Scholastic, Inc., 1988.

Markle, Sandra and William Markle. *Gone Forever! An Alphabet of Extinct Animals.* New York: Scholastic, Inc., 1988.

Martin Luther King, Jr. 8 May 2001. http://www.stanford.edu/group/King/

Nicholaus, Bret and Paul Lowrie. *The Mom and Dad Conversation Piece: Creative Questions to Honor the Family.* New York: Ballantine Books, 1997.

Neruda, Pablo. *The Book of Questions.* Port Townsend, Washington: Copper Canyon Press, 1991.

Reed, Gregory J. and Rosa Parks. *Dear Mrs. Parks: A Dialogue with Today's Youth.* New York: Lee and Low Books, 1997.

Ringgold, Faith. *My Dream of Martin Luther King.* New York: Dragonfly Books, 1998.

Ringgold, Faith. *If a Bus Could Talk: The Story of Rosa Parks.* New York: Simon & Schuster, 1999.

Scholes, Katherine. *Peace Begins with You.* New York: Little, Brown & Co., 1989.

Steig, William. *Dr. DeSoto.* New York: Farrar, Straus, & Giroux, Inc., 1982.

TeenPeople. 6 May 2001. http://teenpeople.com.

Weisenthal, Simon. *The Sunflower: On the Possibilities and Limits of Forgiveness.* New York: Schocken Books, 1997.

Chapter 3

Ahlberg, Janet and Allan Ahlbert. *The Jolly Postman.* Boston: Little, Brown and Company, 1986.

Cuyler, Margery. *Road Signs: A Harey Race with a Tortoise.* New York: Winslow Press, 2000. (The fable is told entirely through road signs. Perfect for crossing genres and retelling a story.)

Gonzalez, Ralfka and Ana Ruiz. *My First Book of Proverbs: Mi Primer Libro de Dichos.* San Francisco: Children's Book Press, 1995.

Maguire, Gregory. *Wicked: The Life and Times of the Wicked Witch of the West.* New York: Harper Collins Publishers, 1995.

Moss, Marissa. *Amelia's Notebook.* Berkeley: Tricycle Press, 1995.

Scieszka, Jon. *The True Story of the Three Little Pigs.* New York: Viking Penguin, 1989.

Chapter 4

Anger, Ed. *Let's Pave the Stupid Rainforests and Give School Teachers Stun Guns and Ways to Save America.* New

York: Broadway Books, 1996.

Beard, Henry. *The Way Things Really Work*. New York: Viking Penguin, 1998.

Bolles, Richard N. *What Color is Your Parachute 2000: Practical Manual for Job-Hunters and Career-Changers*. New York: Ten Speed Press, 1999.

Conspiracy Theory. Dir. Richard Donner. Perf. Mel Gibson. Warner Videos, 1997.

Dumb Laws. 15 October 2000. http://www.dumblaws.org.

JFK. Dir. Oliver Stone. Perf. Kevin Costner. Warner Brothers, 1991.

Krensky, Stephen. *How Santa Got His Job*. New York: Simon and Schuster, 1998.

Lane, Barry. *The Backwards World*. Shoreham, VT: Discover Writing Press, 2002.

Nancy, Ted L. *Letters from a Nut*. New York: Avon Books, 1997.

Producers, The. Dir. Mel Brooks. Perf. Zero Mostel. AVCO Embassy Pictures, 1968.

Scherr, George H. *The Best of the Journal of Irreproducible Results: Improbable Investigations and Unfounded Findings*. New York: Workman Publishing, 1983.

Swift, Jonathan. *A Modest Proposal and Other Satirical Works*. New York: Dover Publications, Inc., 1995.

Chapter 5

Cuyler, Margery. *That's Good! That's Bad!* New York: Henry Holt & Co., 1991.

Fleishman, Paul. *A Joyful Noise: Poems for Two Voices*. New York: Harper Trophy, 1988.

Graham, Carolyn. *Jazz Chants for Children*. New York: Oxford University Press, 1977.

Padgett, Ron. *Teachers and Writers Handbook of Poetic Forms*. New York: Teachers & Writers Collaborative, 2000.

Stone, Ruth. *Poetry Alive*. St. Paul, MN: Consortium Books, 2000.

Chapter 6

Lane, Barry. *51 Wacky We-search Reports*. Shoreham, VT: Discover Writing Press, 2001.

Lane, Barry. *The Tortoise and the Hare, Continued*. Shoreham, VT: Discover Writing Press, 2001.

Lobel, Arnold. *Frog and Toad*. New York: Harper Collins, 1979.

Million Mom March. 7 May 2001. http://www.millionmommarch.com.

National Rifle Association. 7 May 2000. <http://www.nra.org.>

Paulos, John Allen. *Innumeracy*. New York: Random House, 1990.

Paulos, John Allen. *A Mathematician Reads the Newspaper*. New York: Doubleday, 1997.

Ross, Dave. *A Book of Hugs*. New York: Harper Trophy, 1999. This book is a perfect way to look at easy classifications: buddy hugs, grandfather hugs, people hugs, etc.

Stead, Tony. *Should There Be Zoos?* A Persuasive Text. New York: Mondo Publishing, 2000.

Web English Teacher. 14 May 2001. http://webenglishteacher.com

Chapter 7

Aesop's Fables: OnlineCollection. 6 May 2001. <http://www.aesopfables.com>

Bartlett's Familiar Quotations. 6 May 2001. <http://www.bartleby.com.>

Bartlett, John. *Familiar Quotations.* Boston: Little, Brown and Co., 1980.

Boller, Jr., Paul F. *Not So! Popular Myths about America from Columbus to Clinton.* New York: Oxford University Press, 1995.

Carroll, Joyce Armstrong, and Ron Habermas. *Jesus Didn't Use Worksheets.* Houston: Absey & Co., 1996.

Clement, Rod. *Counting on Frank.* Milwaukee: G. Stevens Children's Books, 1991.

Famous Quotations Network. 6 May 2001. <http://www.famous-quotations.com.>.
Lowen, James. *Lies Across America.* New York: Touchstone, 1999.

Lowen, James. *Lies My Teacher Told Me: Everything Your American History Textbook Got Wrong.* New York: Touchstone, 1995

Quoteland.com: Quotations on Every Topic, By Every Author, and in Every Fashion Possible. May 5, 2001. http://quoteland.com.

Seuss, Dr. *Green Eggs and Ham.* New York: Random House, 1960.

Spolin, Viola. *Theatre Games for the Classroom.* Evanston, IL: Northwestern University Press, 1990.

Stock, Gregory. *The Kid's Book of Questions.* New York: Workman Publishing, 1989.

World Almanac for Kids. Mahwah, NJ: World Almanac Books, 1995.

Chapter 8

Brown, Margaret Wise. *The Important Book.* New York: Harper, 1949.

Popov, Linda. *The Family Virtues Guide.* New York: Plume, 1997.

Robbins, Anthony. *Giant Steps: Small Changes to Make a Big Difference.* New York: Fireside Book, 1994.

Chapter 9

Dickens, Charles. *A Christmas Carol.* New York: Penguin, 1984.

Fair Test: The National Center for Fair and Open Testing. 5 May 2001. <http://fairtest.org>.

Finchler, Judy. *Testing Miss Malarkey.* New York: Walker & Co., 2000.

Park, Barbara. *Junie B. Jones and the Stupid, Smelly Bus.* New York: Scholastic, 1997.

Piven, Joshua and David Borgenicht. *Worst-Case Scenario Survival Handbook.* San Francisco: Chronicle Books, 1999.

Teacher Information Network. 5 April 2001. <http://www.teacher.com>.

Seuss, Dr. and Jack Prelutsky. *Hooray for Diffendoofer Day.* New York: Alfred A. Knopf, 1998.

Shakespeare, William. *Much Ado About Nothing.* New York: Cambridge University Press, 1988.

Silverstein, Shel. *The Giving Tree.* New York: Harper & Row, 1964.

Teaching Peace. Brewerton, NY: Red Grammar Rednote Records, 1988.

Texas Education Agency, Division of Student Assessment. 3 Feb. 2001. <http://www.tea.state.tx.us/student.assessment>.

Chapter 10

NPR All Things Considered, Commentaries. 10 Mary 2001.
http://www.npr.org/programs/atc/commentaries/2001/may/.

Spandel, Vicki. *Creating Writers: Linking Writing Assessment and Instruction.* New York: Addison-Wesley Longman, 2001.

49

The Runaway Lesson

The Point: After finishing this book and sending it to the printer, we realized that one of the lessons, Lesson 49, had ran away and was nowhere to be found. We decided this was no accident because this is the lesson you must write. Here is your chance to share your discoveries with other teachers. Write your lesson following the template below and send it to us at www.discoverwriting.com. We will share it with others and maybe even seek permission to include it in a future edition of this book.

Title:

The Point:

Debriefing:

Student responses:

Spin-offs:

For younger writers:

Resources

Send your lessons to www.discoverwriting.com

BOOK ORDER FORM

ORDER: Send in this form with your check, credit card money order or purchase order number

METHOD OF PAYMENT: ☐ Check or money order enclosed ☐ Purchase order attached P.O.#_____

☐ [MasterCard] Mastercard ☐ [VISA] Visa

Credit Card#_____ Exp.Date_____

Signature_____

TITLE	PRICE	QTY	AMOUNT
Why We Must Run With Scissors	22.00		
51 Wacky We-search Reports	15.00		
The Tortoise and Hare Continued (hardcover)	16.00		
Reviser's Toolbox	25.00		
Lightning In a Bottle: Visual Prompts for Insights (CD)	39.00		
24 HOUR FAX: 802-897-2084 **Make checks payable to:** **Discover Writing Company**	Shipping & Handling $4.95 plus $1 for ea. additional item		
	VT Residents add 6%		
	TOTAL		

PLEASE PRINT

NAME ———————————————————— HOME PHONE ————————————

HOME ADDRESS _____

CITY_____ STATE _____ ____ ZIP CODE ____ _____

Face the Facts with Fun
Grade Level: 3-12

51 Wacky We-Search Reports
By Barry Lane, Illustrated by Miles Bodimeade
(150 pages, 105 illustrations, $15)
Are you bored with the reports you teach students to write? Here is a book you can either hand to kids or use yourself to create unusual, exciting and downright silly research reports. The richly illustrated lessons include advice columns, recipe poems, world's thinnest books, a day in the life of a cell, how to poems, time travel tours, the evening dolphin news and much, much more.

A book that teaches how to write with Voice
Grade Level: 3-12

Why We Must Run With Scissors: Voice Lessons in Persuasive Writing
By Barry Lane and Gretchen Bernabei (paper, 276 pages $22)
Indexed by 6 traits
In real life most students are first rate persuaders, but when their persuasive writing hits the page it often get laryngitis. This user friendly book of 82 two page voice lessons, shows teachers 3-12 how to help students get their spoken voices down in print and then how to craft those fresh voices into powerful pieces of persuasion.

Revise fables using this picture book as a model
Grade Level: K-12

The Tortoise and the Hare Continued...
By Barry Lane and Miles Bodimeade (Hardcover 32 pages and full color illustrations, $16)
Barry Lane's whimsical extensions of Aesop's classic fables will help you and your students to see that their stories don't end, they just keep growing and new morals emerge.

Transform your writing classroom into a revising classroom
Grade Level: K-12

The Reviser's Toolbox
Written and edited by Barry Lane (Paperback, 300 pages, $25)
Barry Lane's Reviser's Toolbox gives teachers classroom ready examples and lessons to share revision concepts like leads, endings, snapshots, thoughtshots, exploded moments and scenes with their students. This book can sit right beside your lesson planner and help you all year long.

Use pictures to grow insights
Grade Level: 3-12

Lightning In a Bottle: Visual Prompts for Insights
by Gretchen Bernabei (266 TAKS practice writing prompts images on one CD $39)
Take this dynamite cd rom and create full color overhead transparencies to help students extract themes from stories and make connections between text, self and world. Perfect practice for the TAKS test in Texas, and a great complement to literature study in reading/writing classrooms.